Narratives of Mexican American Women

Narratives of Mexican American Women

Emergent Identities of the Second Generation

Alma M. García

ALTAMIRA
PRESS

A Division of
ROWMAN & LITTLEFIELD PUBLISHERS, INC.
Walnut Creek • Lanham • New York • Toronto • Oxford

ALTAMIRA PRESS
A division of Rowman & Littlefield Publishers, Inc.
1630 North Main Street, #367
Walnut Creek, CA 94596
www.altamirapress.com

Rowman & Littlefield Publishers, Inc.
A wholly owned subsidiary of The Rowman & Littlefield Publishing Group, Inc.
4501 Forbes Boulevard, Suite 200
Lanham, MD 20706

PO Box 317
Oxford
OX2 9RU, UK
Copyright © 2004 by AltaMira Press

British Library Cataloguing in Publication Information Available

Library of Congress Cataloging-in-Publication Data

García, Alma M.
    Narratives of Mexican American women : emergent identities of the second generation / Alma M. García.
        p.   cm.
    Includes bibliographical references and index.
    ISBN 0-7591-0181-7 (hardcover : alk. paper)—ISBN 0-7591-0182-5 (pbk. : alk. paper)
        1. Mexican American women—Interviews.   2. Children of immigrants—United States—Interviews.   3. Women college students—United States—Interviews.   4. Mexican American women—Social conditions.   5. Children of immigrants—United States—Social conditions.   6. Women college students—United States—Social conditions.   7. Intergenerational relations—United States.   8. Mexican Americans—Ethnic identity.   9. United States—Ethnic relations—Case studies.   I. Title.
    E184.M5G344 2003
    305.48'86872073—dc21   2003012016

Printed in the United States of America

♾ ™ The paper used in this publication meets the minimum requirements of American National Standard for Information Sciences—Permanence of Paper for Printed Library Materials, ANSI/NISO Z39.48–1992.

To my nieces and nephews, the future generation:
Nick, Kris, Giuliana, Carlo, Jenni, Michael

And, as always, to ZZ

CONTENTS

PREFACE

Throughout my academic career I have never lost sight of the need to reform higher education in the United States, to open its doors more widely not only to Mexican American students but to students, from all underrepresented groups, making the educational system truly reflective of the racial and ethnic diversity that has formed the core of American society. I have always maintained a passionate concern for the increased recruitment and retention of Mexican American women college students. Over the past twenty years, I have had the privilege of teaching many Mexican American women, many of whom have gone on to become lawyers, doctors, business owners, social workers, elementary and secondary school teachers, and, to my special delight, university professors. Unfortunately, many left college for a variety of reasons and found themselves in more precarious economic situations than their peers who graduated.

I remember many of them, even those who were my students in the early 1980s. As one of the very few Mexican American women faculty, many came to me seeking academic and personal advice. I saw them at their best and their worst, sharing with them their successes and disappointments as undergraduates, particularly those who were daughters of Mexican immigrants. I watched them mature both academically and politically. I observed their struggles to come to terms with themselves, their ethnicity, gender, and social class. I also witnessed their interactions with members of other groups at the university, whose lives were worlds apart from these women and their immigrant parents. Indeed, I witnessed the collision of these worlds, attempts to reconcile them, and their effects on these second-generation women. In addition, I had the opportunity to meet their parents, many of whom were Mexican immigrants who shared their family stories with me. Their life histories echoed those of other immigrants who came to the United States in search of better lives for themselves and, above all, for their second-generation children. These Mexican immigrant parents recalled the struggles they encountered as

ix

they left Mexico behind geographically but kept their homeland with them in their hearts and minds as they settled in the United States, raising their American-born children: the second generation. Their memories of Mexico, most of them nostalgic yet tempered by distance, never clouded their vision for their children. Theirs was the age-old immigrant dream: the American dream. Education represented a pathway to this dream, one to which they dedicated their entire lives. Along the way, Mexican immigrant parents faced persistent social structural obstacles that worked against them, raising doubts that they would be able to secure a better life for their children. Against all odds, the Mexican American women in this study passed through the university gates with dreams of successfully completing their college education and joining that very small percentage of college-educated Mexican American women. Although their parents had very little formal education and worked in low-paying service and semiskilled occupations with little chance for upward mobility, they provided their daughters with steadfast support and encouragement. These second-generation Mexican American women attempted to navigate between the worlds of their Mexican parents and the larger American society, specifically the world of higher education.

Like other second-generation individuals, these women found themselves surrounded by questions of ethnic identity, questions that form the core of this study. I set out to explore the ways in which Mexican American women recreate, reinvent, and reimagine themselves as they look back to the world of their parents and forward to their lives as college-educated Mexican American women. Their ethnic narratives capture their journeys of self-discovery and self-reflection, a process filled with tensions, contradictions, and ambiguities. My aim is to capture the spirit of their struggles: to understand their sense of self, culture, and society. I was honored that the women in this study allowed me into their worlds. My hope is that even though they represent such a small sector within the Mexican American population, their stories will provide us with an understanding of the struggles and triumphs facing second-generation individuals, one of the fastest growing groups in the United States. Looking exclusively at the Mexican immigrant sector, their second-generation children outnumber third or later generations of Mexican Americans living in the United States. In the Southwest, specifically California, Mexican immigrants and their American-born children have now become the largest ethnic group, and it is estimated that first- and second-generation Mexicans will be the largest group in general, surpassing the white population. To understand the world of the second generation is to understand the very fabric of society in the United States.

Following in the tradition of the research literature on the second generation, I pose a series of questions to explore the social construction of ethnic identity among my respondents.

- How is the ethnic identity of second-generation Mexican American women shaped by the experiences of their Mexican immigrant parents?

- How does the second generation navigate through the worlds of its immigrant parents, the university setting, and the larger American society?

- What meanings do the second generation attach to their ethnicity, and what kinds of ethnic group boundaries do they renegotiate?

- How does ethnic identity emerge over time for second-generation individuals?

- How do gender and social class shape these emergent identities?

- In general, how does this second generation recreate and reinvent their ethnic identities?

As a university professor, daughter of a Mexican immigrant father, and a second-generation Mexican American mother, I have informally considered these questions, looking for answers as I experienced the world of higher education. Listening to the women I interviewed over three years, I saw my own life reflected in their stories. I recognized their struggles to navigate their way through a university setting, a world that came to represent one of constant turmoil. Our similarities are deeply rooted, but my own life as a researcher provides me with the tools to capture their second-generation lives in hopes of improving the educational experiences of those like us who will embark on such an educational journey.

This monograph is based on in-depth oral interviews with undergraduate second-generation Mexican American women. Although many Mexican American women who attend colleges and universities are third, fourth, or later generations, my study focuses exclusively on the "new" second generation whose parents came to the United States after the immigration reform legislation of the mid-1960s. Prior to the mid-1980s, immigration research looked at the first generation's immigration and settlement in the United States. The literature on the second generation now dominates the research agenda as the numbers of second-generation immigrants continue to grow. Following in the tradition of other scholars who have contributed to studies on children of immigrants, my objective in focusing exclusively on the lives of immigrants and their children is to provide a deeper understanding of one of the fastest-growing sectors in American society.

This project concentrates exclusively on the emergent, gendered, ethnic identities of American-born daughters of Mexican immigrant parents. While other research projects have included an examination of the effects of gender, my work focuses directly on the everyday experiences of women. Their identities are examined through the prism of ethnicity, gender, and social class, integrating various theories to conceptualize both the second generation and their immigrant parents. Any study of university women students who are Mexican Americans raises several research issues. Perhaps the most basic question is this: Why study a section of the Mexican American population that represents a small percentage of the total population of Mexican Americans? The women in this study have already surpassed many obstacles in reaching the university, yet an understanding of the dynamically complex development of their ethnic identities in a world so far removed from those of their families and communities will contribute a specific dimension to the understanding of an increasingly diverse U.S. society, one with embedded obstacles for groups such as Mexican Americans. For example, Mexican American women and men are still less likely than non-Hispanic whites to have completed high school. Moreover, Hispanic girls are leaving school at higher rates than both African American and European American girls. They also leave school at an earlier age than all groups of males or females and are the least likely to return to school. Not surprisingly, a dramatic and historically long-standing educational gap exists between Mexican Americans and other groups in the United States.

Nevertheless, this study represents an important area of research at many levels. Although it is predicted that the numbers of such women who enroll in and graduate from college will continue to be small in comparison to other groups in the United States, any study of their educational experiences, such as this monograph on the formation of their ethnic identity, will shed light on what factors contribute to or constrain their path to institutions of higher education. In addition, this study examines their experiences in a university environment and in their gendered family lives and their interaction between the private worlds of their immigrant parents and the larger American society. I hope that this study will contribute to the development of future educational policies aimed at creating a better, more welcoming educational environment for Mexican American women and students from other underrepresented groups. An examination of second-generation Mexican American women will assist educational administrators in formulating policies that will, I hope, increase the recruitment and retention rates of Mexican American women. An understanding of the development of their emergent ethnic identity will uncover the power dynamics within institutions of higher education. The life stories of the women in this study capture, on the one hand, the constraints that they encounter as Mexican American women in a predominantly white institution. On the other hand, their narratives reveal the survival strategies they developed to cope with these difficulties. Both forces shape their emergent ethnic identities. In this way, my study will provide the basis for comparison and will contrast not only with studies on second-generation individuals but also with studies on the college experiences of other women, such as African American and Asian American women. Furthermore, it will establish a framework with which to compare and contrast the development of ethnic identity with Mexican American men. My expectation is that this monograph will establish a strong foundation upon which administrators, faculty, and staff can design and implement university policies and curriculum changes that will improve the situation for Mexican American women students. Above all, I would like an analysis of their gender ethnic narratives to provide role models for incoming Mexican American women as they embark on their own journeys into higher education.

Many people gave me their support and encouragement without which I could not have completed this book. Each in their own way helped me through the entire project, and I offer my heartfelt thanks and appreciation to:

The second-generation Mexican American women who shared their struggles and triumphs with me—their stories are the heart and soul of this book;

Richard A. García, my brother, colleague, and best friend, and Francisco Jiménez, colleague and very special friend, for providing me with intellectual guidance and, above all, their friendship;

Santa Clara University, for awarding me a grant to conduct this project;

Perlita Dicochea and Alicia Hernández, for their research assistance;

Vicki L. Ruiz, for her insightful comments on an early draft of this manuscript;

Rosalie M. Roberston at Altamira Press, for her patience and understanding during the preparation of this book; and

Phil Erskine and Sandee Chiaramonte, for their amazing patience in teaching me computer skills, and Joanne Cornbleet, for her generous technical assistance.

During the completion of this manuscript, I faced a serious illness, and I would like to thank all those who offered their prayers and support to me during this most difficult time in my life. My mother, Alma A. García, remained a rock of support and optimism, and without her I would never have been able to keep a spirit of optimism. All my brothers—Richard, Edward, Mario, and Leonard—and their families pulled together to show me what I have always known: their unconditional love. I want to express my special thanks to my nephews, Nick and Kris, for always making me smile and teaching me the wonders of being an aunt.

This book is about the development of ethnic identity, and, over the course of researching and writing, I added a new layer to my own social identity. My conversion to Judaism, under the mentorship of my teachers Rabbi Daniel Pressman and Hazan Melanie Fine of Congregation Beth

David, Saratoga, California, brought out a spiritual side that, I now realize, had always existed within me. They have instilled in me the beauty of Judaism as a religion and a way of life, one with an unwavering commitment to social justice. Without their spiritual guidance and the acts of lovingkindness extended to me by the entire Beth David congregation, I could not have survived this ordeal.

NARRATIVES OF SECOND-GENERATION MEXICAN AMERICAN WOMEN

Three Stories

María's Story

María's parents left their home in Guadalajara to join their relatives, neighbors, and many others who had already made the journey to *El Norte*: the United States. Although her parents did not have any immigration documents, they knew that they would be able to cross La Frontera at Tijuana, Mexico, with the help of their cousins who would be waiting for them, ready to take them to their home in east Los Angeles. Her parents eventually settled into a daily routine, one followed by thousands of immigrants who leave Mexico for a life in the United States in search of the often elusive American Dream. Her father had very little formal education and had worked as part of construction crew in Mexico, which required him to leave his home to travel to various nearby towns where buildings and roads were being built. Once in the United States, he joined his cousin on a crew that worked for a more established Mexican immigrant who, after about ten years, had started his own gardening business. The two cousins found themselves working side by side, leaving east Los Angeles every morning to tend the yards in the surrounding Los Angeles neighborhoods. María's mother had even less formal education than her husband. She had never worked in the paid labor force in Mexico, and now, in the United States, she continued her traditional role of wife and mother, eventually raising her three American-born daughters.

María says that she remembers her parents telling their story. Even now, at family gatherings, some eighteen years since her parents left Mexico, María tells of how proudly her father recounts their family story, a story that he says is a testimony to what he set out to accomplish the day that he and María's mother left Mexico, crossed the border, and started what they dreamed would be a new life in the United States. After only a year working as a gardener's assistant, María's father and his cousin decided to combine their efforts, save whatever money they could, and go into business for themselves. "My father used to say something like 'I didn't come here [the United States] to work and work and have someone else get most of the money. I wanted more for my children.'" María recounts her father's story of working extra hours, saving as much money as possible, and continuing to live in a crowded, rented house with his cousin's family. Then, a few years later and after he had become an American citizen, his boss told him that he was retiring and wanted to sell the business. He was willing to sell it to him for a small down payment with the balance to be paid over time. This is how María's father became a co-owner of a small gardening business with a long-standing clientele. María says that during her childhood she did not see much of her father; he left early in the morning and took on extra jobs such as painting houses or putting in floors several evenings a week. "I felt like I had only one parent and I felt bad. My mother would tell me that my father had to do this because he wanted more for us. She quickly added that she wanted more for us too." María admits that she sometimes did get tired of hearing the same story over and over again, especially when she was in junior high school:

> But you know, one day we had to do a project for our English class. We were supposed to write a family history. I just wrote down what my father always used to tell us. The day we had to read our stories I felt proud of what my parents had done. I was a little embarrassed at all those times I just didn't want to hear it again.

María soon became interested in her family's history and, given her father's long hours away from home, she began to ask her mother for more information. Her mother's stories paralleled those of her father but eventually took on new dimensions. Her mother spoke of her worries about coming to the United States and raising a family in a place so far from Mexico. Even though she wanted to make a better life for her children, she still worried:

> My mom would tell us that she had heard that "Mexicanos" had problems in the United States. One of her cousins had returned from the

United States with a lot of money but had told her that her that life was hard and some people didn't like Mexicans. Her cousin came back home to Mexico. But my mom said that she knew she didn't want to go back. She wanted us to have more things. I guess she meant a better chance to live better. So my mom would say that she put these things, well, behind her and decided to "hacerle la lucha" [take on the struggle] in the United States.

María's mother knew that she and her husband would never go back to Mexico; they were here to stay but they were "Mexicanos." María relates that her family life was indeed a "Mexican" one with all the visible sources of material Mexican culture. Although her parents were able to speak English, they always preferred Spanish. The neighborhood store, El Mercado Mexicano (The Mexican Market) supplied the family kitchen with all the essential ingredients for her mother to maintain "un cocina Mexicana" (a Mexican kitchen). Although María never really liked this Mexican music, her parents, during those rare moments when they were together and able to relax, listened to their favorite Mexican radio station that played "corridos" (Mexican ballads): "They would look sad and I would think that they were really wishing they were back in their home town in Mexico." María remembers that her mother never forgot that she was an immigrant, but she always stressed the importance of her children being American citizens. For María's mother, the family's cultural heritage would always remain Mexican, but her children would move beyond this experience. The life of her second-generation daughter would be different, but her Mexican heritage would shape her ethnic identity. María recalls pensively:

It took me a long time to figure it out. Now that I am in college and taken some sociology and history classes, I am seeing that my parents wanted us to move beyond them like upward to achieve more. I left home to come here [to college], and I keep hearing my family's story in my head. Sometimes it's hard here, so alone, but then it helps to remember how my parents wanted so much for me.

When asked what her parents would want her to remember as long as she lived, María did not hesitate. She said that they would want her to "hacerle la lucha" (take on the struggle) and be proud of her family's story—one of hardship, endurance, and perseverance.

Sonia's Story

Like María, Sonia's parents left Mexico soon after they were married to follow a long line of family members who had also uprooted themselves from a small town outside of Guadalajara. Their relatives, mostly single, male cousins, told them that although life was very difficult in the United States, Mexicanos could find work and eventually save enough money to improve their living conditions once they returned to Mexico. They said that even when they were the most discouraged and homesick they tried to remember that their stay in the United States was only temporary. Sonia's mother told her that many of her relatives stayed for several months or even a year, then returned to Mexico. However, once they realized that the money they had earned in the United States did not last very long and, more importantly, that conditions in their small Mexican town showed very little economic improvement for them, they returned to work in places like San Jose or Los Angeles. But they continued to hope that conditions in Mexico would eventually improve:

> My mom said that she didn't want this kind of a life. She wanted to come to the United States and maybe go back for a visit, especially to see her mom. But she always would tell me that for her leaving Mexico was the only choice she and my dad had to get better things.

Like María's immigrant parents, Sonia's parents had relatives living in Los Angeles. One of these had married a few years after making the solo trip to the United States and now, some seven years later, had been employed as an unskilled construction worker, one of many Mexican immigrant men, a combination of documented and undocumented workers, who supplied an ample and regular workforce for American companies. According to Sonia, her parents never really talked about the details of their trip to Los Angeles, and they were even more vague about how they had obtained legal immigration documents. Like María's father, Sonia's father, once in Los Angeles, started to work alongside his cousin. Her mother, also like María's, continued in her role as homemaker. Her parents lived in a small apartment in east Los Angeles among other recently arrived immigrant families with both Mexican- and American-born children. Sonia was born one year after her parents left Mexico, and her brother was born two years later. Her father worked long hours and, like many other Mexican immigrants, took on odd jobs on the weekends to make ends meet. During these early years, they did not return to Mexico for visits as they had originally intended, but they did help two nephews come to the United States, one of whom lived with them, worked in a nearby car wash, and slept on their small, living-room couch.

Sonia also describes her family environment as a "sort of Mexican one." She spoke only Spanish at first but eventually began to speak both Spanish and English. Again, like other Mexican immigrants, her parents spoke to each other in Spanish and preferred that their children speak to them in Spanish even though, as Sonia recalls,

> they did understand a little bit when me and my brother talked in English, but they didn't admit it. I never thought much about it, my brother and I would just switch back from one to the other, and I guess the reason this didn't seem weird was that all my friends at school did the same. We just did this.

Interestingly, Sonia remembers her parents, but particularly her mother, telling her that she needed to study hard: "she would tell me and my brother to 'aprender el ingles' [learn English]." Sonia became defensive as she recalled that some of her cousins, who had just arrived from Mexico, would make fun of her Spanish and call her "Pocha," a term, not necessarily derogatory, used by Mexicans in referring to American-born children of Mexican immigrants or Mexican Americans.

When Sonia was twelve, her father injured his back at a construction site and eventually had to go on full medical disability, making it necessary for her mother to look for employment. With her daughter and son, ages twelve and nine, she decided that she had no real choice but to make the transition and enter the paid labor force. A few years earlier, her sister and her husband had followed them to Los Angeles, starting their own family, and living only a few blocks away from their apartment. Sonia remembers that her mother asked her aunt to watch them every day after school, even though their father was home. Sonia expressed a sense of sadness and isolation as she spoke about her father:

He just wasn't the same after the accident and my parents started to argue more. My mom found a job at a cannery, but she worked from 3 P.M. to midnight. I liked my aunt but missed my mom and how we had been when she didn't have to go out and work.

Sonia remembers that it was about this time when her mother started to confide in her about the difficulties of being an immigrant. She would tell her that she never thought life would be so hard in the United States; she believed that she and her husband could make a better living than in Mexico and give their children more opportunities. Her mother's reliance on a husband's income as an unskilled worker ended with his accident. She now found herself with no alternative but to begin working outside of her home, a job she took reluctantly because she still believed that she should be a homemaker, taking care of her husband and children. The traditional gender roles had reversed themselves. Sonia says that at first she began to notice only little differences in her mother's attitude and behavior. Although her mother worked alongside other Mexican immigrant women and could spend her entire workday speaking only in Spanish, she began to take an interest in learning more English. She still listened to the Mexican radio stations but, according to Sonia, started to ask for the English translation of everyday words. Her mother had relied on Sonia and her brother to serve as intermediaries when she had to deal with people who were not bilingual, such as the workers at the social security office or the bank.

> But then my mom wanted to do it herself. She would get all frustrated when she messed up trying to learn more English. But she was sort of stubborn and I could see that something was going on. My dad would get mad and tell her to forget it and let us kids help. It was really funny, you know, one day she tells me that she doesn't want to hear my dad get so upset, so she says, "Let's practice English when he is out or asleep or something."

Sonia recalls that her mother always encouraged her to get a good education. When her mother found herself the primary wage earner, she changed her opinion of conventional gender roles, as Sonia explains:

> My mom started telling me, more than my brother, that she wanted us to study hard and try to be the best students. She didn't want me to take

even little jobs like babysitting for extra money. She wanted me to work on my classes. I sort of knew that my mom didn't really know what stuff we did in school, she couldn't help me with my homework or anything. But what I remember is her always telling me that school is important, and then she would say that it was really important for me.

Sonia's mother did not want her to become a factory or domestic worker. She told her daughter she wanted more for her. Sonia's parents had always stressed the importance of an education; they believed that their children were getting a far better education in the United States than in Mexico. This value on education became a constant theme woven into Sonia's family story. Sonia, however, explained that her mother began to stress education even more after she started working in the cannery. Sonia says that when her mother would talk to her she would somehow always manage to say how much she wanted Sonia to get as much education as possible. Sonia recalled her mother's advice:

> I would be complaining about all the homework I had and my mom would just start up the "education" story. She would say that she didn't care where or what I would rather be doing, I had to do all of my home-work. My mom said cannery work helped us survive, but she didn't want me to end up there. She wanted more for me, to get what she called a "profesión" [career].

Sonia believes that her mother did not resent giving up her traditional role as wife and mother; she had no choice but to do so. Sonia, however, associates her mother's job as a cannery worker with the beginning of a real change in how she looked at herself and the world around her. Her mother did not set out to change her family, but, as time went on, she knew that relations within her family would never be the same. So, according to Sonia, her mother changed, adapting, not always smoothly, to her new world, one in which she was now wife, wage earner, decision maker, and mother. Sonia admitted that she compared her mother to her girlfriend's mother—a single parent, working in a clothes factory, and raising three children. As Sonia's father retreated to the background of the family, Sonia witnessed her mother undergoing a dramatic transfor-mation. Sonia believes that her mother's new story, a Mexican immigrant woman who experienced a dramatic reversal of gender roles, provided her with an example of what both her parents had always wanted for their children: to always "hacerle la lucha" (take on the struggle).

Carmen's Story

Although María's, Sonia's, and Carmen's parents all left Mexico at about the same time, Carmen's family's immigrant experiences were shaped by their different social class background and, perhaps more importantly, the social class experiences of their relatives who had been living in the United States for almost fifteen years. Carmen's parents lived in the same town as Sonia's parents, but their daily lives were very far removed from the majority of Mexicans who eventually made the trip to the United States. Her parents experienced the same deteriorating economic circumstances that plagued Mexico, but their social class status provided them with some cushion from Mexico's poor economy and, eventually, a distinct context for their immigrant experiences. Carmen's father came from a family of small business owners in their hometown in Michoacán. As owners of a small restaurant and a Mom-and-Pop neighborhood store, Carmen's paternal grandparents had been able to protect themselves from Mexico's economic problems. As entrepreneurs, Carmen's grandparents had secured sufficient capital to purchase a small parcel of land on which they built a modest house, the home in which Carmen's father spent his childhood with his brothers and sisters. Their economic circumstances not only allowed them to weather Mexico's fluctuating economy but also provided them with the financial resources to send their children to a private school. Carmen's father, the eldest child, completed his primary and secondary education and, after his first year in a nearby business school, decided to visit his paternal uncle in the United States.

His uncle had been living in the San Francisco Bay area for over ten years, during which time he started a small, neighborhood Mexican grocery store, established with the savings he brought with him from Mexico. His customers were primarily Mexican immigrants and Mexican Americans living in the surrounding neighborhood. He carried the local Spanish-language newspapers, sold some grocery staples (such as large bags of rice, beans, and flour), and, as a favor to many of his regular customers, allowed them to take incoming calls from Mexico. Carmen's father had intended to visit for only one month, returning to Mexico to finish business school, and then, upon his graduation, marry his longtime hometown girlfriend. This family story took a dramatically different, but not altogether unwelcome, turn. According to Carmen:

> My dad tells it like this. He liked his life in Mexico. I guess he thought he would take over his dad's business and raise a family like that. But he says he liked what he saw here. His uncle's store was really popular and he started telling my dad that he wanted to start another one, but sort of closer to downtown. I guess they just started talking and anyway my dad tells us that's how he decided to come over here after he got married to my mom. He worked and got the other place ready and then was in charge.

Carmen's family joined a community of Mexicans living in the United States whose lives would be affected collectively by immigration experiences of the mid-twentieth century but whose particular, and mostly uncommon, relative social class advantages differentiated them from the majority of Mexican families trying to "hacerle la lucha" in the United States.

Carmen says that her father and uncle became quite successful over the years. She was born two years after her parents settled in San Jose, California, and her brother was born three years later. Her mother, who had graduated from secondary school in Mexico, stayed home and raised the children, but once they started elementary school, she began to work in the family store. She remembers the day that they moved into a small house close to the downtown area, near Japan Town, where she and her family continue to live. Although Carmen's father had attended a private school in Mexico, he enrolled his children in the local public school until a dramatic turn of events unfolded. As their grocery store continued to flourish, Carmen's parents hired regular wageworkers; her mother spent less and less time at the store and, instead, became active in her children's school activities:

> My mom started going to the school meetings, and, when I started playing volleyball, she even helped at some fundraising things, and she brought food from our restaurant. It sold out. I guess I never really thought about it back then. She didn't speak too much English but nei-

ther did my friends' moms. They all got along. My brother and I used both English and Spanish, but all day we talked in English and with our friends, too.

Carmen does not remember the exact circumstances herself but recalls her mother's version of the event that would alter Carmen's early educational experience. Her mother told her that some of the parents heard that a certain teacher had been making remarks about "all those illegals" living in San Jose. Some children had also told their parents that some of the Anglo American children had called them names. The parents never heard the teacher make these remarks but relied on the words of other teachers and some students. Although many complained and asked for some kind of explanation, many eventually forgot the issue, but not, as it turns out, Carmen's parents.

> My dad was really upset. He kept saying that he worked just as hard as anybody. He was legal; his kids were born here. I guess he started look-ing around, and he told me that some of his regular customers told him that our school was getting a bad reputation and that he should look around and maybe put us in a Catholic school. He says that they told him their kids were there and they could tell right away that everything was better there.

Carmen's parents had the financial ability to move their daughters to a private Catholic school, an option limited to only very few Mexican immigrants. In order to meet these new expenses, Carmen's mother took on a job working at a day care center. She also did a little private catering for weddings and baptisms.

> My mom was always figuring out some new ways to make extra money. Once she even went to work at the cannery for about a month in the night shift. But she hated it and quit. My dad was working long hours at the grocery store, but she always tried to be around when we got home from school.

For Carmen's parents, life in the United States represented a dramatic change. Although they had worked hard to make their grocery store a success, the work responsibilities fell primarily on Carmen's father. Small business ownership brought a certain degree of economic stability. Their decision to open a restaurant in the downtown area provided them with an even deeper economic cushion; they gained a steady clientele of professionals and office workers, most of whom were not Mexican. Still, the high costs of tuition pushed Carmen's parents to work harder at the family businesses. Perhaps more importantly, Carmen's mother quickly diverted her energies as a school volunteer and designed several business enterprises of her own.

> My mom was so hyper all the time. She would be finishing one catering job and then be on the phone making other contacts. Once she wanted to go back to Mexico for a visit and bring back all sorts of things to sell to people, you know like party favors for Quinceañeras. But my dad said she could get in trouble sneaking them over here. Then she started to work on her English. She would try to read the paper and then give up and ask me to help. One summer she took a night class at the community center.

Carmen's parents settled into their world of work and family in the United States with a trip back to Mexico every two years or so, more often if one of their parents became ill. For them, life was hard in the United States, but, as Carmen remembers, the prize was "una vida mejor para nuestras hijas" (a better life for our daughters). Their dreams were the dreams of other immigrant parents who hoped that their children—the second generation—would move closer to the American Dream. María, Sonia, Carmen, and all the other Mexican American women in this study are daughters of Mexican immigrants living in the United States. As second-generation children, these women have lived in the cultural worlds of their parents and that of the larger American society, a multicultural society whose increased diversity stands as a challenge to these and other children of immigrants. The most recent scholarship on the second generation, however, has challenged the traditional assimilationist model of immigrant adaptation, replacing it with alternative perspectives that can be used to explain various dimensions of both the immigrant and the second generations, including the social construction of their ethnic identities.

Studying the New Second Generation:
Daughters of Mexican Immigrants

The term *second generation* refers to the American-born children of immigrants. Some researchers have expanded this definition by including children with at least one parent who is an immigrant. Others include foreign-born children who came to the United States with their immigrant parents when they were less than four years old. My study uses the first definition. I selected women who were the American-born children of Mexican immigrant parents. My intent is to draw as sharp a line as possible between the two generations, although I recognize that it would have been possible to chose Mexican-born children who came to the United States when they were younger than age four or five: the "one-and-a-half" generation. Research on the "new" second generation focuses on these children of immigrants whose parents came to the United States after the 1965 immigration reform period.[1] The first and second generation face specific socioeconomic and political conditions in the United States that differ from those experienced by immigrant groups and their American-born children from previous periods, particularly Western European immigrants from the turn of the twentieth century. Min Zhou provides an overview of several key characteristics of this "new" second generation. First, Zhou points out that the new second-generation individuals are children of immigrants from countries outside Europe and represent a major contributing factor in shaping the multicultural fabric of American society. Second, contemporary immigrants continue to come from diverse economic backgrounds, directly shaping the life circumstances of their American-born children. While their earlier immigrant counterparts shared a low socioeconomic status upon entering the United States, the contemporary influx of immigrants reveals a continuum of economic backgrounds. Mexican immigrants, in contrast to most Indian immigrants, enter the United States with little economic resources, low levels of education, and very limited occupational skills. Zhou cites one additional factor that differentiates the new second generation: geographic concentration on the West as opposed to the East Coast. This factor is of specific importance to my study of second-generation Mexican American women students.[2] With the Mexican immigrant population representing the fastest growing one in California, studies on second-generation Mexican Americans represent an important area of scholarly concern. Moreover, research on the new second generation has largely concentrated on Asian Americans with few studies on second-generation Mexican Americans.[3]

Research on the new second generation has challenged the assimilation theory representing the model developed to explain the process through which immigrants adjust to life in the United States. Alejandro Portes and Rubén G. Rumbaut refer to assimilation theory as "the master concept in both social theory and public discourse to designate the expected path to be followed by foreign groups in America."[4] Spearheaded by the Chicago school in the period between 1910 and 1930, the works of Robert E. Park and Ernest W. Burgess, W. I. Thomas and Florian Znaniecki, and Louis Wirth shaped decades of research on the lives and adjustment patterns of immigrants.[5] The assimilationist framework argues that immigrant groups arrive in the United States with a set of "traditional" cultural baggage. Although immigrants may retain traits of their traditional culture, W. Lloyd Warner and Leo Srole characterize the process of adjustment as one in which immigrants discard their cultural baggage of values, beliefs, language, and, in general, their ethnic identity.[6] Immigrants move toward an acceptance of an American culture, a way of life in which immigrant ethnic loyalties and attachments are replaced with a belief in and a commitment to a common American culture. From an assimilationist view, immigrants experience a movement away from their specific national identification as immigrants—German, Irish, Italian—and make a transition to collective identity becoming "new" Americans. Successive waves of immigrants coming to the United States became a crucible for *et pluribus unum*—the desired social outcome for "the first new nation."[7]

The fabric of American society was shaped by progressive and successful integration of immigrant groups, specifically with the decline in ethnic allegiances. The assimilationist perspective allowed for differences in levels of assimilation by specific immigrant groups. Most theorists, like Milton Gordon, outline different stages and eventual outcomes in the assimilation process, but, as Zhou points out, this perspective sees cultural assimilation as a universal first stage.[8] Nevertheless, this paradigm acknowledged the existence of sociocultural and structural barriers that act as a brake on the assimilation process for certain immigrant groups who experienced, in specific times and places, significant levels of prejudice and discrimination. Such struggles are most likely to occur during the initial contact between immigrants and the larger American society. Warner and Srole argue that although such impediments represented severe constraints on the integration of immigrant groups and their second-generation children, such obstacles were not permanent but rather an initial stage, one which was understandable in terms of intergroup conflict.[9] In general, studies of specific immigrant groups grounded in the assimilationist tradition traced their integration and eventual upward mobility. A common theme running through these studies is that successful assimilation rests on the decline of an immigrant group's "old world" weltanschauung and behavior patterns. Studies show that intermarriage increases the decline of what Stephen Cornell and Douglas Hartmann call the "thick identity" of ethnicity providing an acceleration of successful assimilation. Second-generation children are therefore less likely to see their immigrant parents' ethnicity as salient in their own lives, ones characterized by "thin identities" of ethnicity.[10]

Critics of the assimilation paradigm do not discount the findings of such studies but rather build their most powerful criticism by drawing a distinction between research on Western European immigrants and later waves of immigrants. Mia Tuan begins a critique of the assimilation paradigm by addressing this issue:

> The point to emphasize here is that assimilation is seen as a linear and racially blind process whereby, as each generation becomes further removed from the original immigrants, the salience of ethnicity and its meaning in their lives weakens . . . . These predictions and the [assimilation] model that they are based on are derived from the experiences of white ethnics, the descendants of earlier European immigrants.[11]

Similarly, Zhou points out that such studies were based primarily on Western European immigrants who came to the United States between 1920 and 1950.[12] Researchers studying the second generation are also critical of the assimilationist framework for making generalizations about immigrant groups based on studies of Western European immigrants to the United States at the turn of the twentieth century. Critics argue that an understanding of the specific geopolitical and socioeconomic context of both the home and host country of any given immigrant group is needed to analyze the process of assimilation. Moreover, without an understanding of such a context, systematic comparisons and contrasts among immigrants will be problematic at best. For example, some studies that adopted an assimilationist perspective concluded that Mexican immigrants were culturally deficient because they had not assimilated, unlike Western European immigrants who had experienced successful integration either in their own generation or in their children's. Such research ignores the persistence of race as a marker in American society, one which plays a critical role in determining the nature and degree of structural assimilation.[13]

Recent developments in the study of the new second generation have furthered critiques of assimilation theory. Challenges to classic models have led to a theoretical reconceptualization of assimilation and the process of cultural change from the first generation to the second generation. Scholars now view cultural and structural assimilation as a variable rather than an end product. Immigration studies operationalize assimilation as a process through which immigrant groups experience varying degrees and kinds of integration into American society.

Studies suggest that immigrants' adjustment to their new society does not necessarily erase all of their culture. Traditional culture can, in fact, survive within the context of an unfolding "new" American one capable of persisting into the second generation. Assimilation theory did not foresee the persistence of ethnicity nor its reappearance after a period of decline. The lives of second-generation individuals are ones characterized by tensions, conflicts, and negotiations between themselves and their immigrant parents and between themselves and the larger society. The process is neither a smooth one nor one capable of reaching some endpoint along an assimilation continuum. Studies continue to show both decreased ethnicity and the continuation of specific forms of ethnic allegiances, although assimilation theory predicted that the immigrant and the second generation's ethnic identity and attachment to their home country would decline with their evolving assimilation into their host country.[14] Critics also add that assimilation theory cannot explain the decline of ethnicity and its later reappearance within communities of immigrants and later generations. For example, some Mexican and Mexican American communities have experienced a revival of ethnicity under

15

conditions of anti-immigrant sentiments.[15] Research on Mexican American communities and other Latino communities reveals the persistence of ethnic identification and ties.[16] The decline or resurgence of ethnic attachments varies across studies, with some suggesting that second-generation individuals show progressively decreasing identification with their racial ethnic heritage.[17] Other studies find that second-generation individuals often construct their sense of ethnic self, which may indeed differ from their parents in both degree and kind.[18] These studies trace the complex process through which the second generation's ethnic identity emerges with some aspects of their immigrant parents' identity combined with their own experiences as American-born children of immigrants. Yen Le Espiritu reviews several studies of second-generation Asian Americans and concludes that children of immigrants do not lose their ethnicity but, instead, find themselves experiencing an emergent ethnicity that blends the old and the new, merging their parents' sense of ethnicity and their own, but still constructing ethnic identities that are similar but not the same as those of their immigrant parents.[19] Jean Bacon's work on Asian Indians explores this new basis for ethnic identification, focusing on both the micro level and macro level factors:

> The evidence presented here suggest that the "'best of both worlds'" solutions to the "'two worlds'" problems has not followed parents' own feelings of an "American" outside self, and an "Indian" true self. Instead the best of both worlds for the second generation, at least at the level of collective ethnic identity, is a synthesis of Indian and American ideas and values into a generational identity.[20]

Current studies on the second generation ground themselves in a theoretical framework that focuses on differential outcomes of assimilation experienced by distinct immigrant groups and their children—ones not accounted for in the dominant assimilationist framework. Research questions examine two major processes: 1) constraints on and levels of structural assimilation, and 2) saliency of ethnicity in lives of the second generation. The conceptualization of "second-generation decline" and "segmented assimilation" represent key issues in such studies of the new second generation. Following in the tradition of Herbert Gans, research on "second-generation decline" focuses on their downward social mobility

due to the social structural constraints experienced by the second generation in areas such as the labor market and the educational system in order to
explain persistent poverty, crime, and unemployment of second-generation
populations.[21] Children of immigrant parents from low socioeconomic
backgrounds, particularly those "marked" with dark skin color, find themselves facing severe blockages to upward mobility, a trend that further
challenges straight-line assimilation. Joel Perlmann and Roger Waldinger
conclude that problematic pathways for the upward mobility of the children of post-1965 immigrants produce conditions for "second-generation
revolts" that intensify as the second generation experiences unfulfilled rising expectations. Children of Mexican immigrants are most at risk given
the persistent economic disadvantages of their parents. Moreover, Mexican, Latin American, Caribbean, and Asian immigrants "will not be able
to separate themselves from caste-like treatment, unlike the immigrants
from the past."[22] Interestingly, Gans had predicted that children of immigrant groups who arrived in the United States with economic advantages
(such as high education levels, professional occupations, and access to other
financial resources) may actually retain ties to their parents' ethnic attachments in their attempts to disassociate themselves from other immigrants
and second-generation individuals who find themselves in disadvantaged
sociocultural positions. Thus, Gans's thesis of second-generation decline
is complemented by its polar opposite: the possibility that the second generation will maintain ties to their immigrant parents' ethnic communities
and allegiances. In an ironic twist to the classic assimilation model, Gans
predicts that some second-generation individuals who achieve "viable ethnic niches" within American society, with the help of their immigrant
parents' economic and social capital, will not manifest the decline of ethnicity but rather will assume stronger ethnic attachments. They will
"become Americans" while retaining ethnic allegiances.[23]

Research on segmented assimilation continues to explore present circumstances and future possibilities for the new second generation. Portes
and Rumbaut conceptualize segmented assimilation as a framework for
studying the contingencies of the assimilation process. Segmented assimilation accounts for divergent paths leading to various outcomes. Some
groups will indeed follow a unilinear assimilation path with a decline of
ethnicity. Others will move into the American mainstream with an
accompanying foundation of ethnic ties. Yet, others, whose race and eth-

resent social markers associated with cultural and structural con-
o their upward mobility, will have an ethnicity that "will neither
be a matter of choice nor a source of progress but a mark of subordination."[24] Portes and Rumbaut outline major factors related to such cases of
segmented assimilation:

> 1) the history of the immigrant first generation; 2) the pace of accultura-
> tion among parents and children and its bearing on normative integra-
> tion; 3) the barriers, cultural and economic, confronted by second-
> generation youth in their quest for successful adaptation; and 4) the
> family and community resources for confronting these barriers.[25]

For Portes and Rumbaut and other scholars, including myself, the
second generation finds itself "making it in America" in ways that are
fluid, changing, emergent, and always "segmented." Assimilation is neither smooth nor unilinear; it is characterized by divergent paths, full of
twists and turns and varying outcomes. Studies by Zhou, Portes and
Zhou, Zhou and Carl L. Bankston, and Rumbaut have all addressed the
question of segmented assimilation among various children of immigrants. Their research emphasizes the importance of the first generation's
incorporation into American society as a critical factor in the process
through which their children integrate into American society. Segmented
assimilation refers to a continuum of opportunity structures and possibilities experienced by the second generation.[26] A running theme in research
on segmented assimilation is the interrelationships between the material
and ideational capital inherited by children of immigrants, their location
in this assimilation continuum, and the ethnic identity of the second generation. For example, Zhou and Bankston argue that the value system of
Vietnamese immigrants with strong work ethics provides their children
with the social capital to adapt to American society. Continued attachment to their immigrant parents' worldview serves as a cultural map to
navigate successfully without cultural assimilation.[27] Similarly, Waters
finds that West Indians may indeed "become American" by not "becoming" American blacks, given the barriers resulting from persistent racial
discrimination. West Indians distance themselves from African Americans by staying ethnic and, as Waters concludes, "groups reflecting linear
ethnicity resist acculturation to the United States and ultimately provide

better opportunities for the second generation."[28] In sum, Rumbaut stresses that assimilation and ethnic identity formation follow a segmented path and therefore,

> becoming American . . . takes different forms, has different meanings and is reached by different paths. But the process is one in which all children of immigrants are engaged—defining an identity for themselves. . . . To be sure, this process is complex, conflictual and stressful, and profoundly affects the consciousness of immigrant parents and children alike.[29]

Mexican American Studies scholars, such as George J. Sánchez and Vicki L. Ruiz, have also challenged the assimilationist perspective. Mexican immigrant and second-generation Mexican American culture has historically been seen by groups of social scientists as atavistic, representing a major block to the group's assimilation. Studies of Mexican immigrants and the second generation have questioned this assimilationist perspective's assertion in one of two ways. First, studies have stressed the role of structural barriers facing Mexicans.[30] Second, and more importantly for this study, studies such as those by Sánchez and Ruiz suggest that immigrants do not merely retain cultural forms but experience dynamic changes discernible from the early stages of the immigration process. Sánchez concludes that

> [Any] notion that individuals [immigrants and second generationers] have occupied one undifferentiated cultural position, such as "Mexican," "American" or "Chicano" [Mexican American], has been abandoned in favor of the possibility of multiple identities and contradictory positions. . . . Ethnicity [is] not a fixed set of customs surviving from life in Mexico, but rather a collective identity that emerged from daily experience in the United States. As such, ethnicity arose not only from interaction with fellow Mexicans and Mexican Americans but also through dialogue and debate with the larger cultural world.[31]

Ruiz's description of a second-generation daughter of Mexican immigrant parents captures this same process in which the second generation (re)define themselves and (re)construct boundaries around themselves, between themselves, and between others, such as their immigrant parents:

[A] young Mexican woman may have looked like a flapper as she boarded a streetcar on her way to work at a cannery; yet she went to work (at least in part) to help support her family as part of her obligation as a daughter. The adoption of new cultural forms certainly frightened parents, but it did not of itself undermine Mexican identity. The experiences of Mexican American women coming of age between 1920 and 1950 reveal the blending of the old and the new, fashioning new expectations, making choices, and learning to live with those choices.[32]

Revisionist works on Mexican immigrants reveal this straddling of cultures by integrating a transnational and transcultural framework to explain adjustment patterns among Mexican immigrants who often, but not always, travel back and forth from the United States to Mexico. Such border crossings contribute to a dynamic unfolding of identity, one far removed from that theorized by classic assimilation literature. Transnational immigration research findings illustrate the development of new immigrant communities that construct ethnic identities as a direct response to conditions of migration, settlement, and remigration. Recent studies reveal several ongoing processes. First, "tradition and modernity" can indeed coexist within first-generation and second-generation worlds. Second, this process unfolds within a postmodern process of ethnic identity formation. This transnational migration and subsequent patterns of emergent identities take place within a postmodern context as Roger Rouse describes:

> We live in a confusing world, a world of crisscrossed economies intersecting systems of meaning, and fragmented identities. Suddenly, the comforting modern imagery of nation states and national languages, of coherent communities and consistent subjectivities, of dominant centers and distant margins no longer seem adequate.[33]

The second generation does not merely inherit cultural identity forms from its immigrant parents but, on the contrary, its identity emerges through a multifaceted and multidimensional process. While Sánchez's analysis refers to ethnic identity construction among Mexican immigrants, it is equally applicable to the second generation:

> Whether accommodation, resistance, or indifference marked an individual's stance toward American culture, everyone reacted to living in the

United States. For those who chose to stay, their cultural adaptations would have lifelong implications. For over time, as Mexicans acclimated themselves to life north of the border, they did not remain Mexicans simply living in the United States, they became Mexican Americans. They assumed a new ethnic identity, a cultural orientation which accepted the possibilities of a future in a new land.[34]

Current research on the new second generation and ethnic identity continues to challenge assimilationist perspectives for downplaying the role of race as a barrier to immigrant assimilation both at the individual and community level. Researchers argue that classic assimilation theory is limited to white European Americans because race has always mattered in American society, specifically as a factor in defining immigrants as "others." It is not that structural assimilation, as defined by Gordon, is impossible as evidence in the growing professional class among some Asian American groups such as Japanese Americans. Various immigrant groups and their children, those who are not European American, must contend with externally imposed definitions of themselves. As Tuan concludes, second-generation Europeans such as Irish can opt to be ethnic, but Asians are "forever foreign."[35] Indeed, even though some groups, such as Japanese American professionals, believe that their racial and ethnic identity has limited saliency in their everyday lives, their experiences with racial hostility may lead to increased levels of ethnic solidarity.[36] Japanese Americans find themselves in a society in which their racial and ethnic identity is not optional but rather a social construct that they as individuals must deal with when defined by the larger society. Asian Americans, "despite being longtime Americans, lack the option to cast aside their racial and ethnic affinities as European ethnics, who by birthright are part of the American mainstream."[37] Nevertheless, other studies of second-generation individuals also show that upwardly mobile, middle-class individuals may live in private worlds in which being ethnic has little impact on their sense of identity. In fact, even though Tuan's respondents talk about being Japanese in terms that can be characterized as optional or symbolic, it is not uncommon for second and later generations of Japanese Americans to embrace their cultural heritage as a response to their experiences with racial hostility, prejudice, discrimination, and racism. Tuan explains the apparent decline of ethnic identity among her Japanese

American respondents as not so much a rejection of Japanese culture, but rather a result of the nature of an emerging culture that adjusts itself to changed environments.[38] David J. O'Brien and Stephen Fugita also agree, pointing out that Japanese immigrant parents may socialize their second-generation children to retain parts of their culture and, at the same time, adopt certain characteristics of the larger society within which they will be spending most of their lives.[39] Immigrant culture was not merely transplanted by the first generation of immigrants and then passed on to their American-born children. Culture and ethnic identity is fluid, dynamic, and, above all, an emerging social phenomenon. Thus, it is not so much that second, third, fourth, and later generations do not identify with Japanese culture but rather that they have been raised into a changing, emerging culture. The second generation experiences a process involving a selection of the two, a blending of cultures.

Research on ethnic identity formation among first- and second-generation women has further documented the process of "becoming American" as one that challenges the assimilationist perspective. These studies have focused on the historical and contemporary experiences of immigrant women and their daughters as they navigate and negotiate their way in American society. Nazli Kibria's research on Vietnamese immigrant women illustrates the immigrant and gender conflicts that these women confront and eventually contest. Kibria's women are neither Vietnamese nor American; they struggle to retain their Vietnamese "culture" and adapt to American society. They find themselves caught between the two cultures, developing identities that show vestiges of the past and imprints of their present.[40] Studies on Mexican and Mexican American women also suggest that the second generation does not become American by eliminating immigrant traces.[41]

Reconceptualizing Ethnic Identity: Bridging Social Constructionism and Postmodernism

Building on her analysis of these two perspectives, Karen A. Cerulo provides an excellent review of the strengths and weaknesses of social constructionism and postmodernism. I suggest a reconceptualization of ethnic identity, specifically for the study of the new second generation by proposing a theoretical bridge between a social constructionist framework and a postmodern one.[42] My study adopts a social constructionist perceptive on ethnic identity viewed through a postmodern lens. Although scholars have engaged in debates that juxtapose social constructionist and postmodernist frameworks, I argue that a theoretical bridge is possible between the two for the analysis of ethnic identity construction. Fredrik Barth's introductory essay to his anthology, *Ethnic Groups and Boundaries*, firmly establishes a social constructionist framework for the study of ethnicity. He explains the development of ethnicity as a process by studying interactions between groups and their attempts to establish group boundaries. Barth argues that ethnicity is created through the boundaries used to define a group both by its members and outsiders. A group's cultural features may change, but the lines demarcating the group's boundary may remain the same. For Barth, it is "the ethnic boundary that defines the group, not the cultural stuff that it encloses."[43] The ethnic group selects the nature of such boundaries through a process of self-definition and a response to external structural factors, specifically the group's interaction with other groups who are similarly creating their own ethnic boundaries. Barth proposes that the study of ethnic groups focus strongly on the emergence, maintenance, and (re)negotiation of the existing boundaries of groups who find themselves in sustained interaction with each other.

Moving away from the traditional assimilationist view of ethnicity as an ascriptive cultural heritage transplanted from immigrants to their children, William Yancey, Eugene Ericksen, and Richard Juliani build on Barth's analysis of ethnic boundaries by reconceptualizing ethnicity as a social phenomenon constructed out of and contingent upon the structural conditions under which groups exist within American society. They raise two basic questions that inform this study on second-generation daughters of Mexican immigrants: "[U]nder what conditions does ethnic culture emerge? Specifically, what social forces promote the crystallization and development of ethnic solidarity and identification?"[44] Arguing that ethnicity is an emergent rather than an ascribed phenomenon, Yancey, Ericksen, and Juliani conclude that

> ethnicity is a variable. . . . Rather than a constant ascribed trait that is inherited from the past, ethnicity is the result of a process which continues to unfold. It is basically a manifestation of the way populations are

organized in terms of interaction patterns, institutions, personal values, attitudes, life styles and presumed consciousness of kind. The assumptions of a common heritage as the essential aspect of ethnicity is erroneous. Ethnicity may have relatively little to do with Europe, Asia, or Africa, but much more to do with the exigencies of survival and the structure of opportunity of this country.[45]

My study of the emergence and development of ethnic identity among second-generation Mexican American women thus focuses on the process through which their identities emerge and unfold as they struggle to (re)construct and (re)negotiate their ethnic group boundaries while navigating their way between and within the worlds of their parents' and their own, creating, indeed "imagining," their second-generation identities. Social constructionism places power relationships at the center of the ongoing formation and (re)formation of identity. Cerulo summarizes this perspective, stating that "every collective becomes a social artifact—an entity molded, refabricated, and mobilized in accord with reigning cultural scripts and centers of power."[46] Social constructionism emphasizes the changing nature of identities, entities that are molded by and responsive to external situational changes, networks of social relationships, and structures of power.

Ethnic identity is fluid, malleable, contested, negotiated, and contingent. Social identity is, as Joane Nagel argues, emergent, capable of changing, adapting, and always a product of internal and external forces that confront individuals. Ethnicity is constructed through individual selection and reaction to external factors. For Nagel and others, agency and structure combine together in the process of ethnic identity formation. An analysis of this contingency of ethnicity focuses on the "the ways in which ethnic boundaries, identities and cultures are negotiated, defined and produced through social interaction inside and outside ethnic communities."[47] Social constructionism emphasizes the confrontation of ethnic groups in delineating such boundaries. These confrontations take place, according to Lisa Lowe, "in the travel between cultural sites and in the multi-vocality of heterogeneous and conflicting positions."[48] Both Elaine Kim and R. Radhakrishnan add to Lowe's perspective, each viewing identity as changeable and contingent, able to, in Kim's term, "migrate" between cultural sites.[49] I suggest further that these cultural sites are ideational in nature and metaphorically geographical in space for the second generation in their negotiation of identity.

My research on the social construction of ethnic identity among Mexican American women bridges a postmodern lens and a social constructionist perspective. In the same way that social constructionists criticized essentialist frameworks in the study of identity formation, postmodern theorists have been critical of social constructionists for lacking a thorough analysis of variations within categories of identity such as race, class, and gender.[50] Although postmodernism is not a monolithic theoretical framework, a general postmodern critique of social constructionism argues that it does not adequately address the dynamics of differences, or what Maxine Baca Zinn and Bonnie Thornton Dill call a "matrix of domination" to explain the structural and ideological conditions that play a contributing role in ethnic identity construction.[51] Patricia Hill Collins, Gloria Anzaldúa, Bonnie Thornton Dill, Judith Butler, and Jane Flax have criticized social constructionism for overlooking the role of power relations and hierarchies within identity categories.[52] In addition, these scholars argue that social constructionism may lead to a variation of essentialism even though it emphasizes social interaction as a defining element in identity construction because it understates the impact of multiple identities.[53] Although Collins outlines core themes in black feminist thought, she is careful to point out that "diversity among Black women produces different concrete experiences that in turn shape various reactions to the core themes."[54] Not only is there no universal category of "women," but there is no universal category of "black women," rather, as Hill Collins argues, a multiplicity of categories within categories—a postmodern condition of multiple identities, contradictions, and ambiguities.

My study examines the social construction of ethnic identity of second-generation Mexican American women with an understanding that categories of identity are not fixed within this group but, on the contrary, are in and of themselves capable of emerging as fluid and changing, never essentialist in nature. To analyze the process of ethnic identity formation and construction, I propose the use of the concept "palimpsest of identity" in viewing a social constructionist perspective through a postmodern lens.[55] I depart from studies of ethnic identity that conceptualize it as a layering of multiple sources of identities. I suggest that "layering" does not completely capture the dynamic and fluid nature of identity construction, focusing more on differences in types of identities that are superimposed on each other and not on movement between layers or the blending of layers. Similarly, identity has been conceptualized in terms of multiple positionalities, whereby an individual "occupies" different, multiple identities within specific contexts of interrelationships. Such identities reflect the changing and evolving dimensions of an individual's identity, but such conceptualization lacks a focus on the relationship between multiple selves and the possibility that some of these may become more salient under specific circumstances of a person's lifetime. In addition, I suggest that various dimensions of ethnic identity can disappear and reappear at the same time and under specific circumstances. I consider ethnic identity construction as best captured by the use of the term *palimpsest of identity* based on two definitions of the word *palimpsest*. First, a palimpsest refers to a text, usually written on parchment, on which more than one text has been inscribed with previous texts incompletely erased and some parts still visible. Second, a palimpsest may refer to a place or setting or even object that reflects its history. Using both definitions, ethnic identity formation can be conceptualized metaphorically as the process through which a palimpsest is constructed. Identity emerges as writings on an individual's "manuscript," in which layers of texts can appear, reappear, and disappear only to appear once again. Moreover, ethnic identify reflects an individual's history and, in the case of second-generation Mexican Americans, both the (re)imaginings of Mexico "translated" for them by their immigrant parents and, just as importantly, (re)imaginings of the United States "translated" by their parents and by themselves. Ethnic identity has historical dimensions constructed by both individual and collective sociohistorical experiences. At one level, an individual's palimpsest of identity contains traces from her immigrant parents' palimpsests—ones that are fluid, never fixed in what an assimilationist framework calls "traditional culture and identity." At another level, the second-generation individual constructs and (re)constructs her identity on this metaphorical palimpsest in which traces of past and present identities have been inscribed. I see ethnic identity among the second generation emerging as a fluid, malleable, and contingent social construct formed as an individual negotiates through a maze of highly nuanced, ambiguous, contested, and often irreconcilable power and social relationships within both historical and contemporary contexts.

The Mexican American women in this study are engaged in a process of self-invention and (re)invention, of (re)imagined selves and (re)imagined communities. Their emergent ethnic identities evolve from their private and public historical moments. They emerge as active agents responding to the interplay of their experiences as daughters of Mexican immigrants living in American society. Ethnic identity emerges as a negotiated discourse between an individual, her personal and public network of social relationships, and the patterns of interactions within which individuals construct, invent, and (re)invent their ethnic identities and group boundaries. I am also suggesting that second-generation Mexican American women's identities are neither similar nor completely different from that of their immigrant parents. Second-generation individuals contest and (re)negotiate their relationships with their parents whose traditions, values, and behavioral patterns may produce both continuity and change within their American-born children. For the daughters of Mexican immigrant parents, like other second-generation individuals, the past shapes the present, the present (re)imagines the past, and the present reflects on the future—all producing palimpsests of identities in which traces of each are present although not always visible.

Using a social constructionist and postmodern theoretical perspective to explore the emergent identities of second-generation Mexican American women, this study raises a series of questions:

- How is ethnic identity of second-generation Mexican American women shaped by the experiences of their Mexican immigrant parents?

- How does the second generation navigate through the worlds of its immigrant parents, the university setting, and the larger American society?

- What socially constructed group boundaries and meanings emerge among second-generation Mexican American women?

- What meanings do the second generation attach to their ethnicity and what kinds of ethnic group boundaries do they (re)negotiate?

- How does ethnic identity emerge over time for a second-generation individual?

- How do gender and social class shape the emergent identities of second-generation Mexican American women?

Studying Mexican American Women in Higher Education

This study follows in the tradition of other studies that have examined the lives of college women, specifically women of color. These studies on college-educated women have spanned nearly a century, focusing on a variety of critical issues facing women during their undergraduate years and their later lives as career women. Using both quantitative and qualitative research designs, studies have analyzed the educational, family, and career aspirations of more than fifteen age cohorts of women. Beginning with studies conducted as early as the 1900s, researchers have shared a common perspective of examining "women's lives through time" within the historical context of their era and the changing gender roles they experienced.[56] Although a large volume of research on women's experiences in higher education exists, there is a serious paucity of social science literature regarding the lives and educational experiences of women from diverse racial, ethnic, and social class backgrounds. In their introduction to their anthology *Women's Lives Through Time: Educated Women of the Twentieth Century*, Kathleen Day Hulbert and Dianne Tickton Schuster indicate one of the major limitations of studies on undergraduate women:

> [These studies] present primarily the lives of white, middle-class women who have lived relatively advantaged lives and whose experience may have limited relevance to women from other backgrounds. This limitation reflects the realities that American higher education has been relatively inaccessible to women of color and that longitudinal research has failed to address the experiences of marginalized groups.[57]

Current research on women of color in higher education has emerged to fill this gap.[58] Research on Mexican American women in higher education has focused on a variety of questions related to their academic successes and failures. The majority of studies point out that a multiplicity of interrelated factors contribute to specific college experiences. These include such family factors as: 1) parental support; 2) parents' immigrant status; and 3) parents' level of education, occupation, and income. A student's experiences in high school are also closely related to college participation and eventual graduation. Specifically, studies highlight the critical role played by high-school counselors and teachers in supporting Mexican American students, particularly women, in selecting courses geared toward college admissions. Moreover, their support was also identified as a key factor related to increased numbers of their students applying for college admissions.[59] Studies also identify the supporting role of mothers in encouraging their daughters to attend college. Conversely, such factors as tracking, inadequate support systems, and overt and covert racism and sexism all formed an interlocking system of power relations—a matrix of domination that operates against Mexican Americans in their pursuit of a higher education. Denise Segura's study of the educational system highlights several factors associated with negative outcomes for Chicanas in high schools: deficient teacher instruction, problematic counseling, and an exclusionary curriculum. These factors create major roadblocks that Mexican American women face in pursing post-secondary education. Interestingly, parents provided support for their daughters' education although they did not participate actively in school activities. Segura concludes that the educational system created and perpetuated structural barriers specifically for the women in her study.[60]

Research studies have identified a combination of sociohistorical and economic factors to explain the persistent underrepresentation of Mexican Americans in higher education. Using an approach that emphasizes the historical and contemporary institutionalized structural barriers to the participation of Mexican Americans in higher education, researchers have examined, using a variety of methodologies, such barriers as segregation, tracking, cultural biases in administrative and curricular organizations within schools, inadequate funding and financial support needed to attract the best teachers and administrators in predominantly Mexican American communities. The constant influx of Mexican immigrants, the majority of whom arrive with very limited education, presents another problem, but not a "cultural value" one (to use the language of the cultural deficiency model). Studies have shown that Mexican immigrants inculcate very specific values related to educational achievement in their children.

Survey research documents that Mexican immigrants and Mexican American parents place a very high emphasis on education, stress the importance of mastering the English language, and believe in the importance of graduating from school.[61] Nevertheless, a family's persistently high levels of poverty, unemployment, and blue-collar career opportunities represent underlying social structural barriers for Mexican American students.[62]

Research also continues to focus on the gender-specific effects of education on Mexican American women in high schools and colleges. An early study concluded that structural barriers, not Mexican cultural values, worked against Mexican American women achieving success within the educational system.[63] Other studies identify inadequate university support services and faculty mentoring as major factors in high-school drop-out rates among Mexican American women. Studies on these women continue to analyze the persistence of educational barriers accounting for their underrepresentation in institutions of higher education. Scholars view embedded discrimination, racism, and prejudice as significant barriers to higher rates of college attainment levels. Current studies are now integrating feminist theoretical frameworks to analyze the experiences of Mexican American women students who have "slipped through the cracks" of the American educational system.[64] Harriet D. Romo and Toni Falbo examined the institutional structures of Texas high schools by using an analysis that combined the factors of ethnicity, social class, and gender to explain the high levels of high-school dropouts among Mexican American youth.[65] Their work includes an analysis of those educational policies designed specifically along gender lines, such as the treatment of girls who become pregnant. In addition to the social structural factors, Mexican American women are often confronted with traditional gender specific ideologies and roles that function as constraints. The most recent and innovative work on Mexican American women's experiences in higher education adds a new dimension to the traditional social structural approach. Scholars have integrated a systematic analysis of the constraints of patriarchal ideology and contestations. Studies suggest that a Mexican immigrant and Mexican American families use their own specific types of "ideational capital" as a support system for their children, particularly for those who are first-generation college students.[66] Nevertheless, although Mexican American women students may have access to such ideational capital, it is often gender specific, with sons of Mexican American families receiving more direct and indirect encouragement to remain and succeed in both high school and college.

Demographic data illustrate the persistently low levels of education among Mexican Americans. Although population differences related to such factors as immigrant status and geographical distribution produce marked diversities within their communities, Mexican Americans have historically lacked access to higher education. Major gaps exist between the Mexican American population and the white population. In 1970, 11 percent of whites were college graduates in comparison to 2 percent of Mexican Americans. By 1990, 22 percent of the white population had completed four years of college or more in comparison to only 5 percent for Mexican Americans. Data for 2000 show little improvement, with 26 percent of the white population completing four years of college or more in comparison to only 7 percent of Mexican Americans. This census material on educational attainment compares Mexican Americans with other groups. In 2000, for example, 23 percent of all Cuban Americans had completed four years of college or more, in comparison to only 13 percent of Puerto Ricans and 16 percent of African Americans. Asian and Pacific Islanders have the highest percentage (44 percent) of individuals with four years of college or more.[67]

Census data, specifically on Mexican American women, continue to be difficult to obtain since many census tables that include data on the Mexican American population (or the category "Hispanic") do not disaggregate by gender. Similarly, when data is presented using the umbrella term "Hispanic," information on specific groups, such as Mexican Americans, is not provided. Longitudinal data from 1970 to 2000 for Hispanic women, including Mexican American women, reveals the drastically low numbers of students completing four years of college or more. In 1970, 4.3 percent of all Hispanic women had completed four years of college or more. This percentage increases to only 6 percent in 1980, 7.3 percent in 1985, 8.7 percent in 1990, 8.4 percent in 1995, and stands at 10.6 percent in 2000.[68]

Although research findings suggest that Mexican American women will continue to have limited access to higher education, studies on those women who, against all odds, do attend and complete a college education will contribute a new dimension to the understanding of the changing dynamics and complexities unfolding within Mexican American communities in the United States. The ongoing research studies on Mexican American women in higher education reflect scholars' efforts to integrate a gender analysis within the discipline of Mexican American and ethnic studies. Just as the study of college-educated women has focused almost exclusively on white, middle-class women, research on Mexican Americans in higher education has only integrated a systematic gender analysis of the educational experiences of Mexican American women within the last ten years.

The Study

This study follows Portes and Rumbaut's conceptual framework for examining the new second generation. My work contributes to the literature on second-generation individuals for several reasons. First, although research on the second generation continues to proliferate in the social sciences, only a few studies have focused on Mexican Americans. In addition, although several studies on ethnicity have included both second and later generations, my work focuses on the development and ethnic formation of American-born children of Mexican immigrants. Another feature of my work is that it places women at the center of the study, especially the experiences of American-born daughters of Mexican immigrant parents. Although my research follows traditional monographs and articles on the first and second generation, it departs from these by using a systematic gender analysis in order to bring women's experiences from the margins to the center of the investigation. This study is grounded in a long-standing tradition of feminist scholarship that has introduced a wide range of theoretical frameworks and concepts with which to analyze women's experiences and, in this case, those of second-generation Mexican American women. As such, this work weaves the various dimensions of patriarchy, hierarchy, power, ideology, and structural constraints into its analytical fabric.

This book is based on twenty-five interviews with Mexican American women undergraduates enrolled in a small, private university in northern California and was conducted between 1997 and the winter of 1999. (With only two exceptions, respondents requested that the name of the university remain anonymous. They believed that their privacy would be jeopardized. I made the methodological decision to respect their request.)

Due to the small number of second-generation daughters attending this university, I conducted several waves of interviews over three years in order to draw a sample of twenty-five women who were daughters of Mexican immigrants. My respondents were all born in the United States and were the first members of their families to attend college. Respondents had gained admission to the university with the direct assistance of their scholastic record of achievement. All of the respondents described the importance of two types of recruitment efforts. All but four of the women had attended public high schools. The entire sample identified a high-school teacher or counselor as fundamental to their pursuit of higher education. They described how these individuals, all women, had gone out of their way to mentor them. In addition, all of the women had been contacted by a university recruiter who explained the excellent financial-aid package they would be eligible for if admitted to the university. Although a few had friends who were currently in other colleges, none of them had any direct contact to currently enrolled students

Using information provided by the university student records office, my respondents were selected using a nonrandom sampling technique. At the beginning of the study, all self-identified Mexican American women students received a letter from me describing the study and asking for volunteers. I limited the sample to juniors and seniors in order to ensure that the respondents had several years of college experience. The criteria for final selection from those who agreed to be interviewed was that both parents were born in Mexico and had immigrated to the United States as adults (eighteen years of age) after 1965. The initial group of students provided me with names of other students whom they believed would fit the criteria for participation in the study. Although my respondents represent a small sector of the Mexican American population, this study focuses on their lives in order to shed light on all Mexican American women whose ethnic identity development and college lives are only now beginning to be examined, not because of lack of interest but because of the stark reality that less than 10 percent of all Mexican American women have a college education.

Semi-structured interviews were tape-recorded, and all quotes are verbatim selections from the transcripts with names changed to protect the privacy of the respondents. This study provides "thick descriptions" of the construction of social identity among this sample of second-generation daughters.[69] Through their reflections on their world and that of their immigrant parents, this study explores the process through which respondents (re)create and (re)invent the meanings they attach to their ethnic, gender, and social class identities. Their narratives uncover what Clifford Geertz calls "webs of significance" and "meaningful structures of interpretation"—both of which provide a map for understanding the various dimensions of social identity.[70]

These women's life stories do not paint a broad landscape. On the contrary, their histories provide us with in-depth portraits that may provide insights into larger studies, both qualitative and quantitative. Moreover, I selected a sample of university students because I believe that all individuals from this age group experience major changes, and, therefore, those who are second generation will have additional and specific types of changes in their lives. Gender and social class also play into this scenario, making undergraduate, second-generation Mexican American women an intriguing group for the study of ethnic identity construction. In fact, Kibria begins her study of second-generation Korean and Chinese American university students with a quote from Ruth Sidel's book on identity issues among undergraduates:

> The traditional college years, the late teens through the mid twenties, are years of extraordinary maturation and growth. These are years when many young people leave home and meet very different kinds of people often for the first time, come upon previously unheard of ideas, and have the opportunity, and indeed, the task, of defining for themselves and for others who they are—what they think, the values they hold, and their place in a world beyond the one in which they grow up.[71]

Constructing a demographic profile of the total number of second-generation undergraduate Mexican American women attending a university poses several problems. First, the category used to describe these women is the umbrella term "Hispanic" making it difficult to disaggregate them into the specific category of "Mexican American." In addition, and most critical for this study, records do not allow students to identify their generation status (such as second-generation children of immigrants). Nevertheless, a demographic profile of the entire student population by race and ethnicity (during the years I conducted this study—1997 to 1999) provides a context for this research. A demographic profile of the "Hispanic" population by sex will provide a more specific context for the

university environment (table 1.1). Hispanic women outnumbered Hispanic males in every year between 1995 and 1999. In general, there are
about 10 percent more undergraduate women than men. The implications
for such a difference will be discussed in more detail in chapter 5, but it is
important to note here that university records do not include information
on parents' nationality, and, therefore, these numbers represent all self-
identified "Hispanics," including foreign-born, first, second, and later
generations.

Although European Americans represent more than fifty percent of
the undergraduate population, a pattern of decline is apparent. Asian
American/Pacific Islanders are the second largest group on campus, maintaining an average of about 19 percent, with only a small decline in 1999.
Hispanic Americans represent about 14 percent of the total undergraduate population. The profile for African American undergraduates is strik-
ingly low, never rising above 3 percent (table 1.2).

It is important to remember that the Mexican American women in
this sample are not representative of the Mexican American population.
Despite some narrowing of the educational gap, stark differences exist in
the educational attainment levels of Mexican Americans in general compared with the rest of the population. Nevertheless, a study of this small
sector of the Mexican American population will allow for a sharp focus
on the process of emergent identity and will provide a foundation for
future research on identity formation among other new second-generation
Mexican Americans in higher education, including studies that compare

Table 1.1   Total Hispanic Undergraduates by Sex, 1995–1999

	Hispanic Men	Hispanic Women	Total Hispanic
1995	46%	54%	100%
	(268)	(316)	(584)
1996	45%	55%	100%
	(258)	(311)	(569)
1997	44%	56%	100%
	(248)	(313)	(561)
1998	44%	56%	100%
	(256)	(327)	(583)
1999	41%	59%	100%
	(231)	(338)	(569)

Source: University Office of Institutional Research

Table 1.2   Total Undergraduates at the University by Race/Ethnicity

	1995	1996	1997	1998	1999
Hispanic	14.3	14.2	13.1	13.5	13.1
	(584)	(569)	(561)	(583)	(569)
African American	3.0	2.7	2.7	2.6	2.3
	(123)	(115)	(116)	(113)	(103)
Asian/Pacific	18.3	19.7	19.9	19.5	18.8
Islander American	(750)	(834)	(852)	(845)	(842)
European American	54.8	53.8	53.8	53.8	54.2
	(2,247)	(2,276)	(2,304)	(2,331)	(2,428)
Total	4,100	4,230	4,282	4,332	4,479

Note: Percentages do not equal 100 because some students failed to report their ethnicity or marked the category listed as "other." Source: "Student Profiles, 2000," California Postsecondary Education Commission.

and contrast the experiences of men and women even though their numbers probably will not increase significantly. It is my hope that even though the total number of Mexican American women in higher education will continue to lag behind those of the total population, given all the socioeconomic indicators, this study will provide rich insight into the experiences of a group of Mexican American women who, against all odds, overcame historically persistent structural and cultural barriers to enter higher education institutions.

The use of in-depth interviews enabled these university students to tell their stories "in their own words."[72] I share the ethical concerns, raised most strongly by feminist researchers, that scholars using in-depth interviews maintain the integrity of their respondents.[73] I have attempted to use this study's qualitative data in ways that will, as Susan Matoba Adler stresses, allow respondents to construct "who they are . . . from their own historical perspectives, told in their own voices with their own interpretations."[74] From a feminist methodological perspective, in-depth interviews provide a rich source of information that is a powerful methodological tool for best capturing the nuanced lives of women such as these. Moreover, scholars have identified in-depth life interviews of women of color as a powerful methodological tool capable of bringing into focus the complex interrelationship between race, gender, and social class. Gloria Hull, Patricia Bell Scott, and Barbara Smith believe that this methodology, more than any other, is capable of uncovering the "multilayered texture of black women's lives."[75] Similarly, Gwendolyn Etter-Lewis emphasizes that:

> Oral narrative offers a unique and provocative means of gathering information central to understanding women's lives and viewpoints. When applied to women of color, it assumes added significance as a powerful instrument for the rediscovery of womanhood so often overlooked and/or neglected. . . . Specifically, articulation of black women's [and Mexican American women's] experiences in America is a complex task characterized by the intersection of race, gender, and social class with language, history and culture.[76]

Understanding the strength of in-depth interviews while studying the lives of women must, however, recognize some of the inherent limitations of this type of qualitative research technique. I encountered several of these methodological problems in conducting this research project. As a Mexican American professor, I share a similar cultural background with my respondents, although I was a generation older than all of the students in this sample. My own family background and educational experiences provided me with a direct and empathetic tie to their worlds, and, therefore, I had "insider" access to my respondents. According to several leading specialists in qualitative research methods, an "insider" status can reduce the level of social distance between researcher and informant, and, because of this, it is possible to reach a deeper level of shared meanings between the two. As Baca Zinn concludes, "the lenses through which they see social reality may allow minority scholars to ask questions and gather information others could not."[77] Nevertheless, researchers of women of color who conduct oral history interviews with respondents who share their own cultural background will continue to face the methodological problem inherent in their status as "insiders."

Sherna Berger Gluck and Daphne Patai point out that women researchers conducting oral history research must address the methodological problem of shared intimacy between themselves and their respondents.[78] In her study based on oral interviews with Puerto Rican women, Rima Benmayor concludes that the social distance between researcher and respondent gradually diminishes over time.[79] My experiences in these interviews lead me to believe that both scenarios coexist. An "inside" researcher, like myself, continues to rely on a shared set of meanings and symbols with her respondents. As the respondent reveals more of herself and her life story, the researcher's shared intimacy can, in fact, recede into the background as the respondent's story comes into focus. Another methodological problem in this type of research may develop, further complicating the relationship between researcher and respondent. The researcher may find that her respondents are beginning to see her as more than an interviewer conducting a research study. Respondents may begin to view the "inside" researcher as a source of support or even a confidante. Julia Curry-Rodriguez describes her experience with the Mexican immigrant women in her study who turned to her for support in times of domestic and economic difficulties, thereby narrowing the distance between herself as the researcher and her respondents.[80] My own work on Mexican American women entrepreneurs supports the need to address this methodological problem. Many of my respondents asked my advice on their personal problems with their husbands and their children.[81] These methodological issues related to the "insider/outsider" status between researcher and subjects are inevitable as more studies are conducted on populations that have not been the object of sustained investigation by researchers who share a cultural background with their participants.

From the earliest stages of this project, I recognized the likelihood that the undergraduate women whom I was interviewing might turn to me in time of personal need. A few of the students who eventually became part of this project had already come to see me about some of their academic and personal problems. Interestingly, only two of the twenty-five women came to see me regarding an academic problem during the interview process; however, later I recorded visits from eight women who were having personal problems either at school or at home or both. I chose to talk to them in general terms about their problems, and in all but one of these cases I had concluded my interviews with the students. I asked my student assistant to conclude the interview with the other student. I encouraged all of the students who came to see me about personal problems to seek the help of another, more appropriate, university staff member. Only six of the respondents had already been enrolled in one of my classes. Their interviews were coded like the others, but I did not have access to the page with the corresponding names, and additional attention assured that these students would remain anonymous.

In sum, this study of second-generation Mexican American women follows the tradition of feminist methodology by relying on the respondents' "own words" to uncover the complex process through which these women attach meanings to their ethnic identity. Brief sketches of María, Sonia, and Carmen at the beginning of this chapter serve as an introduction to this monograph, exploring the postmodern worlds of second-generation Mexican American women who find themselves navigating through geographies of culture, space, place, home, and self.

CHAPTER TWO
(RE)CREATING MEXICO

The study of immigration—specifically Mexican immigration—to the United States has undergone major revisions over the past fifteen years. Scholars have developed a variety of critiques of this research literature in order to understand the dual process of immigration and settlement, both of which provide a context for studies of the second generation. First, immigration scholars have challenged the classic assimilationist school by adopting postmodern frameworks to study immigrants. Instead of the traditional framework of immigrant assimilation and acculturation, new immigration scholarship maintains that immigrants "become Americans" through diverse paths, some of which may indeed be linear, but most of which are full of bends and detours suggesting that immigrants do not meld uniformly into American society. Immigrants leave their homelands behind in the geographic sense, but, as they settle in the United States, they keep their ethnicity alive through memories of their native countries. Their ethnic identity and attachments to their culture—to being Mexican, their "Mexicanidad"—do not fade with their permanent settlement in the United States. According to interviews with second-generation daughters, their parents engaged in a process of "becoming American" as they created and (re)created "Mexico" in their memories, families, and communities. Such a community, in Benedict Anderson's sense, is an imagined one where "in the minds of each [Mexican immigrant] lives the image of their communion."[1] For Anderson, immigrants (re)invent themselves through this process of becoming which they share with their American-born children. This process, in turn, contributes to the development of their children's second-generation ethnic identity. Anderson argues that nations—or in the case of this study, immigrant communities—emerge out of a bond of "horizontal comradeship."[2] Building on Hugh Seton-Watson's notion that a nation is formed when people consider themselves one or behave as if they had created one, Anderson underscores the word *imagined* to refer to a sense of becoming

41

by a group, such as my study's Mexican immigrants and the second generation.[3] Another revision of immigration studies involves integrating a systematic analysis of gender dynamics and patriarchy. The growing research
on gendered patterns within immigrant families and communities shows
that immigration affects women and men differently. Women have a specific impact on the formation and development of their immigrant communities within the United States, and the process of immigration may
lead to a decline in patriarchal constraints within families. Immigration is
a gendered process, but one that reveals divergent dimensions based on a
heterogeneity of immigrant experiences. These two revisions within
immigration studies provide a critical context for this study's examination
of ethnic identity construction among second-generation Mexican American women. This chapter focuses on two general processes: 1) the process
through which the immigrant generation creates a (re)imagined relationship with Mexico and its effect on their second-generation children, and
2) the process through which immigrant mothers confront and contest
patriarchal constraints and how this affects the gendered ethnic identity
of their daughters.

Setting the Stage for Immigration

The Mexican Revolution of 1910 resulted in a massive influx of Mexicans
who fled the social, political, and economic upheavals of this turbulent
period in Mexican history. Immigrant communities flourished in such
cities as El Paso, San Antonio, San Diego, and Los Angeles where Mexicans lived in close proximity, (re)creating the country they left behind and
to which many, if not most, had dreams of returning. Historical records
document that only a small percentage of these immigrants actually
returned to Mexico, settling instead into communities within *El Norte*,
the common name for the United States. Studies of this period in Mexican and Mexican American history have analyzed the dynamic processes
played by the sociohistorical and political factors that set in motion this
mass migration—the actual process of immigration, the patterns of settlement and community formation, political leadership and activism, and
working-class struggles in particular.[4]

The post-1965 immigration reform period represents the context for
this study. All respondents' parents came to the United States after 1965,

mostly as young married couples, with only two parents, both men, making the trip alone (although they married soon after their arrival). Several key factors provide a context for the passage of the Hart-Cellar Immigration Act of 1965, legislation that marked a significant development in U.S. immigration policy. During World War II, the Bracero Program was developed to bring Mexican workers to the United States, primarily to work in the agricultural fields of California. This period in immigration history witnessed a massive influx of both documented and undocumented Mexicans who strengthened existing U.S. Mexican immigrant communities, many of which became magnets for the parents of the daughters in my study. In addition, studies show a marked transition from agricultural to urban employment among Mexican workers. The immigrant parents in this study, with three exceptions, did not have any experience as agricultural workers. Although the Bracero Program ended in 1964, immigration rates did not decrease. The passage of the 1965 Hart-Cellar Immigration Act represented a major reform in immigration legislation that led to the increase of immigrants from Latin America and Asia. The Immigration Act of 1965 limited the number of immigrants from the Western Hemisphere and ended the existing quota system, considered by many to favor Western European countries. Its family reunification clause provided for unlimited numbers of spouses and unmarried children to enter the United States.

At the same time that U.S. immigration laws were being reformed, economic conditions developed in Mexico that contributed to increased immigration during this period. Pierrette Hondagneu-Sotelo provides an excellent summary of major structural transformations in Mexico that led to increases in Mexican immigration.[5] Although Mexico was experiencing political stability and economic growth between 1940 and 1965, the Mexican "miracle" of economic development, an economic policy of import substitution adopted to transform Mexico into a competing actor on the international economic stage, experienced severe bottlenecks. Import substitution led to specific agricultural policies aimed at bolstering production for national consumption in an attempt to cut back on Mexico's imports. In turn, government subsidies to large-scale agricultural firms led to encroachments of peasant landholdings, contributing directly to marked increases in rural to urban migration. Other import substitution policies undermined employment options in the urban areas, drastically limiting the options for the newly displaced rural population. Still other programs, such as the Border Industrialization Program, were implemented to reduce unemployment but created more economic difficulties. For example, the discovery of vast oil fields in the state of Veracruz in 1972 led to Mexico's petrolization program that relied on extensive international loans to subsidize the infrastructure needed to develop the oil industry. The collapse of the oil market left Mexico economically stranded, with only limited hopes of future returns from oil revenues with which to repay its astronomical foreign debt. Ultimately, Mexico was forced to devalue the peso in 1976 and, at the insistence of the World Bank and the International Monetary Fund, adopt severe austerity measures. This general economic decline also exacerbated the economic difficulties for the urban working class and the middle class. Mexico's international debt crisis signaled the end of the always dubious "Mexican miracle."[6] Taken together, immigration reforms and Mexico's declining economy set the stage for the influx of post-1965 Mexican immigration.

The twenty-first century will continue to witness growing immigration, particularly from Latin America. Rubén G. Rumbaut and Alejandro Portes identify this mass immigration as one of the "most profound demographic transformations in a century."[7] The majority (52 percent) of the influx of post-1960 immigrants came from Latin America and the Caribbean. Approximately one third left Asia and the Middle East. The historic trend of immigrants from host countries clustering in specific geographic regions within the United States continues with the majority of Mexican immigrants taking up residence in the Southwest, specifically California and Texas.[8] A new second generation of children of Mexican immigrants represents one of the major factors contributing to the growing complexities and tensions of American society. Further studies on the relationships between Mexican immigrants and their American-born children will provide a framework for better understanding the evolving questions of ethnic attachments, loyalties, emergent identities, and interethnic relations—questions at the core of national identity.

Memorias de Mexico

Interviews with second-generation daughters reveal that their parents' stories of immigration—their *memorias* of Mexico—left their imprint on the second generations' palimpsests of identity: layers of (re)memberings of Mexico, both real and imagined. All of the second-generation respondents were born in the United States and had only visited Mexico for brief periods, ranging from one week to three months. Only a few made regular trips to Mexico, or, as they called Mexico, "over there," or "back there," or "where they're from," or "where my parents lived before." Nevertheless, their parents' memories of Mexico and their border crossings unfolded as a recurring trope in their narratives. Sonia recalls one such story:

> My dad would start out his usual story by saying something like he knew that once he crossed that line that was it, he would never be the same. But then later in his story he would say something different, kind of confusing, he would say he tried to keep something from Mexico for us. When I was little I would ask him where is it. You know, like if it was a present or something. But now that I have read about immigrants in my classes here [the university], I know that he meant he tried to give us a part of Mexico he carried with him, inside him.

Their family's memories of Mexico became a family heirloom, an intangible treasure, but one valued perhaps even more than some actual material keepsake brought by their parents to the United States. For many, the most dramatic image of Mexico came from their parents' recollections but was not limited to this. Transnational immigration patterns result in the creation of popular cultural images and symbols of Mexico that surround second-generation Mexican Americans. Music, movies, soap operas, Spanish-language newspapers, and television networks all blend together contributing to the formation of what I call a second-generation "Mexicanidad" (an imagined Mexican self shaped by immigrant stories, memories, and popular cultural motifs that surround the second generation, particularly those living in communities with large numbers of Mexican immigrants such as those in east Los Angeles and east San Jose). When asked to tell about their family backgrounds, these women often exceeded a basic narrative of their family's immigrant saga. It was very common for these narratives to include some kind of self-reflection. Indeed, the retelling of such family immigration stories represents a direct insight into the dynamic process of ethnic identity construction. For example, many respondents shifted back and forth from their recollections of how their mothers felt about leaving Mexico to how they themselves reacted to their stories. In the following passage, Julia expresses sentiments similar to many of the other respondents when she reveals ambivalent feelings toward Mexico:

> My mom liked to tell us about how she grew up in a small town near Guadalajara and married her neighbor's cousin. She said she had heard about what it was like here and wanted to leave and try to do better here. My mom's parents—my grandparents—. . . didn't want her to leave because they wanted to see their grandkids grow up. My mom says she told her mom not to worry, that they would come back and maybe stay if things didn't work out here. Well, they [her parents] are still here and I don't think I could ever go live in Mexico. Even when I visited there one Christmas break, I didn't like the way my cousins and some neighbors made fun, you know, calling us names because of how we spoke Spanish. I told my Mom, forget it, I know we are Mexican, but I don't think about Mexico like you and Dad. I'll always be sort of a tourist there. When I said this she sort of looked at me like I said something wrong. Maybe I hurt her feelings but, I don't know, Mexico is sort of part of me, I know that, but it's still not like what it is for them.

Julia, like many others, acknowledges that Mexico was "sort of a part of" her, yet she also recognizes that she is different from her Mexican "born and raised" cousins who called her "la Americana" (the American). Visits to Mexico did not represent a strengthening of a Mexican-based identity for the second generation. Unlike the generation of Cuban Americans whose parents left Castro's Cuba in the early 1960s and who saw themselves as Cuban political refugees anticipating, if not actively working for, Castro's overthrow, second-generation Mexicans had no visions of returning to Mexico.[9] Interestingly, Caroline Bettinger-López's study of exiled Cuban Jews living in Miami found a generalized sentiment to return to Cuba among the first and second generations.[10] It should be pointed out, of course, that the Cuban post-Castro immigration case is completely separate from Mexican immigration, given the sociopolitical context of the Cold War and the relationship between the United States government and Cuban exiles. Unlike Cubans, Mexican immigrants and their children could make trips, however frequent, to Mexico. Their daughters crossed the border into Mexico with their parents whose stories had provided them with a basis for ethnic self-reflection particularly at this stage in their lives. These women experienced the physical and social geography of a Mexico that had been (re)created for them by their immigrant parents. Erica describes her experience in a way that reveals her emergent second-generation identity:

> We had visited Mexico a couple of times when I was still in grade school, but it was the summer of my freshman year [in college] that I really began to look at things. You know, I had been there and seen all the places where my parents had lived, and then we even went to new places like tourist places. I guess this last time I wanted to really see how Mexico made me me, well actually part of me since I'm not Mexican Mexican but born here. I usually say Mexican American.

This passage captures a recurring trope in the lives of the respondents. Erica demonstrates a highly nuanced view of her ethnic identity. She defines herself by who she is not: a "Mexican Mexican." She sees herself as being a "Mexican American." Erica's quote illustrates Fredrik Barth's theory of ethnic group boundary formations.[11] Erica discusses her experience with Mexico by constructing group boundaries between herself and Mexico. Like the other second-generation respondents, Erica's boundaries are not rigid but fluid; she acknowledges that her identity is indeed shaped, at least partially, by the geography of her parents' selves. Erica looks toward Mexico to "see how Mexico made me me, well actually part of me."

Women who had visited Mexico within the last five years prior to their interviews with me made references to these trips by using phrases such as "look at Mexico," "see Mexico," "check it out," "figure it out for myself," and "see for myself what my parents had been talking about." Mexico became myth and reality, memory and experience for them. For other second-generation children, such as the Vietnamese Americans who came after the fall of Saigon in 1974, their parents' memories of Vietnam shaped their goal of establishing a new family home in the United States. Nevertheless, many second-generation Vietnamese Americans did make a return journey to explore their parents' homelands. Like second-generation Mexican Americans, they encountered unsettling challenges to their identity based on their own self definitions and the reactions of Vietnamese who saw them as outsiders.[12]

My respondents describe their reactions to Mexico during these family visits with mixed emotions. They define themselves as second-generation daughters of Mexican immigrant parents, yet their narratives describe incidents in which they were reminded of the differences between themselves and their relatives, friends, and Mexican society in general. One of the most common themes revealed in their memories of these visits is the response by Mexicans to their "Americanized" Spanish. Even those who said they spoke Spanish at home, with their parents and, in some cases, with their grandparents, recalled that they experienced different levels of criticism for their accents. Some remembered these incidents in a joking spirit, but others expressed both sadness that they did not have better Spanish language skills and anger that they were being treated harshly. Elena illustrates her understanding that ethnicity is not a fixed category constructed with rigid lines when she says, "You know, it's sort of funny at first, but then it starts to get on my nerves. I am proud to be Mexican, but I just can't be expected to talk the same way that Mexicans over there speak Spanish." Elena draws a symbolic map, a geography that locates Mexico "over there." Echoing these sentiments, María recalls an argument that she had with her cousin when she visited her parents' hometown of Morelia one summer:

> We went to this club to dance and some guys she knew came over and started talking to her and then to me. I really only said a few things, and then she said, "Hey, can you understand her Spanish? It's American Spanish." I got so mad I started yelling at her in English, and I felt better, you know, yelling at her in English. I don't think I could have said all the things I wanted to say to her in Spanish.

When second-generation Mexican American women travel to Mexico, they encounter basic cultural and identity problems based on their "Americanness" most often defined in terms of language differences. Their reactions to these encounters reveal that they do identify in some general, symbolic way with Mexico and, even when confronted with problems, continue to refer to themselves as "Mexican" or "sort of Mexican" or "part Mexican." Clearly, family trips to Mexico at this critical time in their ethnic identity construction served as a bridge between these "*memorias* de Mexico" and their own "imagined Mexico." I see both as key inscriptions in their identity palimpsests. They are both Mexicans and Mexican Americans whose ethnic boundaries are constantly in a state of flux, collision, and emergence.

At the same time that the Mexican American women recalled stories of cultural rifts between themselves and their Mexican relatives and friends, all of them expressed wonder and appreciation at having the opportunity to "see" Mexico during these trips, however infrequent they were. Visiting Mexico allowed them to watch their parents in a different environment. Many of their parents continued to have difficulties speaking English, but in Mexico their American-born daughters witnessed their parents in a context in which they felt at ease. Moreover, respondents referred to their trips to Mexico as ones of discovery. They can now add their own experiences with Mexico to their parents' stories and memories—both combined into a new kind of memory, geography, and space for the second generation. Before their visits to Mexico, their parents provided them with an immigrant revisiting of Mexico, and now, after visiting Mexico, their own vision of Mexico has become part of their lived experience and their identity. For many of these second-generation women, their first impressions of Mexico were visceral ones in which the country's sights and sounds became inscribed in their lives, as Sylvia points out: "I didn't really like Mexico, but I can't really forget it. Now when my parents tell me about where they grew up, I don't have to imagine it, I was there but I didn't want to stay there." Sylvia's statement underscores the process of ethnic group boundary formation. She constructs her identity by redefining her parents' memories of Mexico with her own experiences in Mexico and acknowledges her own world in the United States by affirming that she "didn't want to stay there." Other respondents talked about their memories of Mexico in similar ways, emphasizing how different Mexico was from California, even though all but two lived in predominantly Mexican immigrant and Mexican American communities. Yvonne captured a frequently expressed feeling regarding the second generation's reaction to Mexico:

> I wasn't expecting things to be so different. I had a hard time understanding people, even my relatives at times. Their Spanish is different. Just so many things were different. The way people dress and cook and just going to a regular grocery store. I went to the vegetable section and

they had lots and lots of kinds of chiles. It was really great to go to the marketplace—it was like the flea market but not exactly.

In her family epic, *Caramelo*, Sandra Cisneros captures similar sights and sounds of Mexico as she describes crossing the border into Mexico during her family's annual summer trip to Mexico.

> As soon as we cross the bridge everything switches to another language. *Toc*, says the light switch in this country, at home it says *click*. *Honk*, say the cars at home, here they say *tan-tan-tan*. . . . Sweets sweeter, colors brighter, the bitter more bitter. . . . Churches the color of *flan*, vendors selling slices of *jicama* with chile, lime juice, and salt. . . . Breakfast: a basket of *pan dulce*, Mexican sweet bread. . . . Every year I cross the border, it's the same—my mind forgets. But my body always remembers.[13]

The second generation carries its own memories of Mexico and these unfold in their lives in unexpected ways as cultural nationalism (as will be shown in chapter 5).

Second-generation individuals confront a basic question: What is their relationship to their parents' ethnicity and the meanings that they attach to their own ethnic identity? Respondents attempt to reconcile the world of their parents with their world in the United States. On the one hand, they live in the United States with Mexican immigrant parents whose rememberings of Mexico continue to serve as a basis for their own sense of self. Yet, on the other hand, second-generation individuals "read" these stories through a special lens. They understand and, indeed, share a sense of "Mexicanidad" with their parents, a sense of ethnic self-definition reinforced by their parents' immigration memories. Still, they question the role that this "Mexicanidad" actually plays in their own lives. Their narratives reveal a process of (re)negotiation between their parents' ethnic identity and their own. Such a distinction does not take the form predicted by an assimilationist perspective. It does not establish a linear transformation from Mexican to American. Some scholars explain this nonlinear path of assimilation by drawing a distinction between two types of ethnicity. A primordialist ethnicity maintains individual and community ethnic solidarity based on a collective weltanschauung: a "community of culture." Instrumental ethnicity maintains a group's ethnic solidarity on the basis of shared interests rather that a shared worldview: a "community of interest." Recent scholarship on the new second generation blurs the distinction between the two, finding both types of ethnicity playing key roles in the lives of immigrants and their American-born children.[14] My respondents' reflections on the relationship between their parents' memories of Mexico and their own American realities remain blurred, usually tenuous, and frequently ambiguous. Their narratives capture their challenges to the meanings that their parents attach to Mexican ethnic identity. They question preexisting ethnic boundaries as they attempt to create new ones.

Many Mexican immigrant communities in the United States are both integrated into the everyday fabric of their surrounding larger communities, but they still maintain visible manifestations of "little Mexicos" in places such as east Los Angeles, south El Paso, and east San Jose. Interestingly, all but two interviewees lived in predominantly Mexican and Mexican American neighborhoods, but the common sentiment was to see Mexico as a family symbol recreated by their parents, a part of their family lore. These second-generation women, nevertheless, recognize that their parents share their "*memorias* de Mexico" with other Mexican immigrants, both family and nonfamily members. In addition, they heard similar stories from recently arrived Mexican immigrants now living in their neighborhoods. Mexico surrounded them in a transnational and postmodern geography, yet their own narratives reveal tensions and ambiguities regarding the place Mexico occupies in their emerging identities. Carmen describes how she found herself surrounded by Mexico:

Even when my parents aren't actually telling us about how they lived in Mexico, Mexico is all around my neighborhood. I hear Spanish everywhere, somebody is always just getting here from Mexico, and you can go to this kind of mall near my house where you can buy all kinds of Mexican stuff like for baptisms and weddings. There's even this drugstore where I go with my grandmother, and she buys her regular medicine for her blood pressure, I think, and then we go to this other store that sell all kinds of herbal stuff made in Mexico. It's actually pretty interesting. All of the Mexicans who are new to the U.S. shop there. I try to imagine my mom and dad when they first arrived here from Mexico. I guess it was really hard for them. They like to tell us kids about how they used to miss Mexico, and then once I said, "But how can you miss poverty and all the other problems?" My mom said it wasn't the problems she missed, it was her family and just Mexico in spirit. I guess it would be like if I left here to go to some foreign country like Mexico and start a life there. I guess I would always be American but just living someplace else.

Carmen, like other respondents, tries to understand her immigrant mother's longing for Mexico by imagining how she would feel if she moved to another country where she would "always be American." The second generation attempt to understand their immigrant parents and their "Mexican memories" by switching roles and imagining themselves as American immigrants to another country, such as Mexico. Some even refer to their friends, who are also either sons or daughters of immigrants from other countries such as Vietnam and El Salvador, and try to make a connection with them at a generational level. Elena compared herself to her best friend:

One of my high-school friends had parents who were raised in El Salvador and came here. She says they are always telling stories about life there. It's just like with my family. She even said the same thing I did—that she wouldn't want to go live there, it's not her country and it's not her parents' anymore either. It's the same with my parents. Yeah, they are Mexicans, but they've been here so long, they're different too.

Elena's remark underscores the findings from Mexican immigrant studies, which show that immigrant identities eventually change in American society. Similarly, Yen Le Espiritu and Diane L. Wolf found that the formation of ethnic identity for both first- and second-generation Filipinos is not one of straight-line assimilation. Filipino Americans maintain an attachment to the world of their immigrant parents while at the same time experiencing a transformation of their own ethnic identities.[15]

These second-generation Mexican American women, all of whom were interviewed when they were nineteen to twenty-one years of age, were experiencing a period of concerted self-reflection. As university undergraduate students at a predominantly white, middle-class university, they found themselves at a critical juncture in their lives, a time of remembering the past and anticipating the future. Several of the Mexican American women referred to their own lives in terms of a new life, a new start resulting in a better life. In fact, many drew a direct connection between their "entering" the university and their immigrant parents' "entrance" into the United States. As they recalled their parents' stories, this group of second-generation women recast their own lives as newcomers crossing into a new world. Perhaps this is why their narratives stress the stories their parents told them about their own crossing, from Mexico to the United States.

Immigrant Fronteras and Second-Generation Borderlands

The ambivalent reactions by the daughters of Mexican immigrants to their parents' memories of their border crossings unfold as a theme throughout the interviews. An analysis of the border represents one of the most significant areas of scholarly concern within the field of Mexican immigration, one critical for understanding the dynamics between immigrant parents and their American-born children. The border—*la frontera*—represents a complex, highly nuanced reality and metaphor in the lives of Mexican immigrants and their children. Stretching across approximately 2,000 miles between the United States and Mexico, this national boundary is like no other border separating two countries, two peoples. Unlike their European counterparts, Mexicans do not cross the Atlantic, the long-time symbol of U.S. immigration. Nor do Mexicans cross over from " a different shore," as Asian immigrants do.[16] Mexican immigrants cross the Rio Grande, a river that is, for the most part, neither formidable nor large but one that nevertheless defines the physical and metaphorical boundary between the two countries. Mexican "desert immigrants" have always confronted the dangers of this physical and national boundary separating the two countries.[17] Tragically, many have died attempting to cross the border at various isolated desert crossing points or have suffered deaths at the hands of smugglers—coyotes—who crowd them into poorly ventilated trucks, often leaving them in isolated parts of the border where many have died. Anti-Mexican attitudes have always had the potential for escalating into violence, contributing to the dangers along the border. Still, the *frontera* has long been a sign and symbol for Mexican immigrants, a fluid, unfolding metaphor, one adding a specific layer to the identity palimpsests of immigrants and their second-generation children.

Mexican immigrants look back toward the border and their border crossing as metaphors for their changing identity, from "Mexicanos de adentro" (Mexicans from the inside) to "Mexicanos de afuera" (Mexicans from the outside).[18] Immigration scholars have examined the problematic nature of this border in the lives of Mexican immigrants, in their identity and their children's identity:

> [The border] is both symbol and reality in the Mexican American experience and has confronted each generation with questions: What does it mean to be a Mexican in the United States? How should Mexican Americans relate to the continual influx of Mexican immigrants? How much of Mexican culture and identity should one retain? How should Mexican Americans relate to Mexico? These and other questions assume relevance because of the propinquity of Mexico and the heavy concentration of Mexican Americans in the Southwest and along the U.S.–Mexican border. How each generation has responded has determined particular political strategies for coping with the ethnic, race, class and cultural positions Mexican Americans have occupied in different historical periods.[19]

Each historical period in Mexican immigration history provides a context for an immigrant's (re)visioning of *la frontera*, some of which are specific to a given period, while others provide a common immigrant weltanschauung. For example, Mexican immigrants, unlike other immigrant groups who do not share a common border with the United States, express a seemingly contradictory mindset. On the one hand, they express their longing to achieve the American Dream if not for themselves then for their children. Yet, on the other hand, they retain, if only in a far corner of their minds, the possibility of returning to Mexico, a possibility with a greater potential for realization given the proximity and fluidity of the border. Nevertheless, studies show that Mexican immigrants, particularly in the early twentieth century (1900–1930), expressed strong sentiments for retaining their "Mexicanidad"—their cultural ties and identity with Mexico although they had indeed crossed the *frontera* into the United States. Mexicans believe that they carry their Mexican culture and identity with them across the border. Immigrant newspapers reflect these sentiments, describing Mexicans living in the United States as an extension of their Mexican homeland.[20] Sonia tells of her mother's and grandmother's attempts to "keep Mexico alive" in the United States through the practice of religion and the maintenance of religious rituals and symbols. Alicia describes her family's home altar:

> My mom and grandmother [both born in a small village in Mexico] kept all sorts of religious stuff in the living room and their bedrooms. There was this small plastic statute of the Virgin de Guadalupe that my mom said she brought with her when she came to the United States. She used to say that the Virgin was an immigrant too. She laughs when she says this. But she would get serious, sometimes, I think, sort of sad too, I guess. Well, it turned into a family joke. Hey, does the Virgin have immigration papers? My mom would get sort of mad when she heard us say this. She likes to retell the story of how she crossed over from Mexico with her Virgin.

Yolanda tells a similar story, but her father's *memorias* of crossing Mexico did not use religious symbols:

> My dad makes it a habit. I don't know if that's the right word. We always have to watch at least one old Mexican movie, and then while we're watching it, he's always telling me this is what's going on during that time, these actors were in this other movie or whatever. So we always watch at least one. The music is always rancheras and traditional, typical Mexican music. I don't know. We do a lot of stuff. I don't really realize that it's actually tradition since we're so used to it. My dad's stories are just so real and we hear them all the time. His ranchero music, well, he loves it. He even cries sometimes when he hears it. Once I asked him why and he said he always remembers that he heard that song on the radio even though he had already crossed into the U.S.

Respondents describe how their Mexican immigrant parents expressed their "Mexicanidad" in other, more direct, ways. Although I did not interview these immigrant parents, I asked my respondents to tell me how their parents identified themselves. Without exception, their parents call themselves Mexicans and usually use the Spanish word "Mexicanos." Although most have lived in the United States over twenty years, their daughters point out that they continue to refer to themselves as "Mexi-canos" even if they became American citizens. In addition, their parents identify themselves as Mexicans, but as Mexicans "who were here now but from Mexico." Julia's parents call themselves "Mexicanos" but use various terms to refer to their American-born children:

> My parents always say that they are Mexican, but they did become American citizens, but, come to think about it, I really don't remember them calling themselves anything but Mexicans. They would say to me stuff like "don't ever forget: we are Mexicans but now you are Americans and Mexicans through us."

Some of the respondents talked about how their parents wanted them to identify with their Mexican heritage, stressing their "Americanness" as a citizenship status rather than a form of ethnic or cultural allegiance. Isela remembered one specific family episode:

> I remember this time that my aunt [paternal] from Mexico came for a visit. Before she got here, I heard my mom talking to my dad and sort of complaining. She was saying that his sister was always on her case because she had been changed because of living here. My mom said that my aunt just didn't get it. Her kids were—I'll tell you in Spanish—son nacidos aquí pero son como Mexicanos. [They are born here but are like Mexicans]. I guess she wanted to make sure my aunt knew we knew our family background. She said to always remember that we are Mexicans but also Americans.

These passages from Julia and Isela dramatically illustrate how their immigrant parents constructed boundaries around themselves as immigrants and their children as Americans. At the same time, however, they remembered that their parents described them as "also Americans" but "Mexican through us." Interestingly, when Mexican immigrant mothers defend their American-born children from those who question their sense of ethnic roots, they use these incidents to reinforce their own "Mexicanidad." María Castañeda's interviews of Mexican immigrant cannery workers further suggests that even those women who have lived in the United States over twenty-five years maintain strong ideological and cultural roots in Mexico.[21] In addition, like some of the Mexican immigrant mothers in my study, several of the cannery women in Castañeda's study had legal status in the United States, and some were in the process of applying for U.S. citizenship. Yet, the words of one Mexican woman echo the sentiments of the mothers of the second-generation Mexican American women: "I am Mexicana. I think I am Mexicana because I was born in Mexico. On papers I am a U.S. citizen but, in my blood I am Mexican. My roots are in Mexico."[22]

Memories of Mexico remain with immigrants as they recount their journeys to their American-born children. Cultural practices animate these memories by visibly recreating Mexico through religious symbols and popular cultures in their homes and communities. Although Mexican immigrants could, and many did, return to Mexico and then reenter the United States, studies show that from the early 1900s to the present, the majority of Mexican immigrants settled in the United States, seeing themselves as the generation that would produce a second generation of American-born children.[23] Yet, even though these immigrants may not actually return to Mexico by physically crossing the border, Mexico always remains in their memory, forming part of their identity. With the constant influx of Mexican immigrants living in close proximity, the border and Mexico "come" to the Mexican immigrant who, like those in my study, has lived many years in the United States. At the same time, varying degrees of circular migration allow Mexicans to renew their ties with Mexico, if not by actually returning to Mexico, then through their interactions with the constant arrival of immigrants. An emergent view of the border takes place at an ideological level among Mexican immigrants as they carry with them some level of "Mexicanidad" even after years of settlement in the United States. Autobiographies by Latina authors emphasize the process of cultural renewal and the (re)emergence of ethnicity produced by ongoing patterns of immigration.[24]

The border represents many things for Mexican immigrants and the second generation: a physical boundary, a geographic space, a source of cultural continuity, a source of cultural change, a path away from Mexico's sociopolitical and economic troubles, a path toward the American Dream, and a detour to the harsh realities of "otherness." The border is a social construct whose meaning changes over time, yet, at the same time, it remains the same and one in which multidimensional identities unfold. The process of transnational migration has led to a redefinition of "community of origin." Migrants not only experience the possibility of circular migration, but they continue to live in a social landscape that includes their community of origin in Mexico and their community of settlement in the United States. Such an understanding of the lived experiences of immigrants diverges from binary concepts of tradition and modernity, of Mexico and the United States. Recent immigration studies attempt to explain the sentiments of Mexican immigrant parents by analyzing the effects of transnational capitalism and its role in the "the details of people's daily lives within this new border landscape: 'the social space of postmodernism.'"[25] Such a postmodern landscape of ethnic identity includes two levels. First, the migrant experience revolves around memory patterns that are recreated or imagined about their pre-immigration lives in Mexico. Second, immigrants' experiences include not only the memories of Mexico but also the realities of ongoing sentiments, social relationships, and extensions of communities with Mexico through their actual migration back to Mexico and, equally important, their constant interaction with Mexican communities through persistent social relationships with family and fictive kin networks in Mexico and/or newly arrived immigrants in the United States. Thus postmodern Mexican immigrants remember Mexico, not only as it was when they left, but also in the way they (re)imagine it for themselves, in the way they carry on social relationships with Mexicans in Mexico and newly arrived Mexican migrants to their communities, and, most importantly for this study, in the way they (re)imagine it for their second-generation daughters.[26]

My study builds on Roger Rouse's conceptualization of the border's social landscape by incorporating an additional dimension. I suggest that immigrants may not necessarily experience and maintain social interactions and networks with their Mexican communities of origin. They may experience or imagine such social interactions and networks, which then become part of their everyday lives and those of their American-born children. The Mexican American women in my study recall family stories in which their parents revealed both actual and imagined immigrant discourses and interactions with their own communities of origin. Immigrant parents retain memories of their lives in Mexico, but only one family made yearly trips to Mexico. These Mexican immigrants reflect the post-1965 immigrants who came to the United States more as displaced urban workers than as displaced rural agricultural workers. These second-generation women remembered the ways in which their immigrant parents talked about leaving such cities as Morelia, Durango, Chihuahua, and even the largest urban metropolis of Mexico City, but their stories were largely neighborhood based. Their parents spoke in terms of their neighborhoods—their *vecindades*—and, more commonly, they told of their circle of family and friends left behind in their hometowns. Yet, their ties appear to be a more closely-knit web of interrelationships of blood and fictive kin. Their immigrant parents left behind personal links more powerful than their actual ties to physical localities in Mexico. Such sentiments, as recorded by their American-born children, increased over time, even though actual ties became tenuous, if not altogether lost. These parents saw themselves not as transnational migrants, but as immigrants whose return to Mexico was more in their rememberings than in their return. Julia captures these sentiments:

> My Dad and his brothers would start up and tell about how they grew up in Durango but then moved to Chihuahua before actually leaving Mexico to come here. They would talk about which cousin stayed in one place and then another left to go to some other city. His cousin went to El Paso, but he came to Los Angeles but stayed in Tijuana first. I would get all mixed up—it was like a geography jumble or puzzle. But he just kept telling us stuff about all these relatives. I really don't remember all the places, but I sort of remember these relatives because of how my Dad talked about them. He talked about his family and relatives in Mexico but not just Mexico as a place.

The immigrant's *memorias* emphasize people over places, family relationships over geographical communities. Mexico is inscribed on the life manuscripts of the second generation as family "portraits" preserved in the memories of their parents. They remember Mexico without a continued reinforcement of it from contact with newly arrived family members or revisits to Mexico. As Irene concludes:

> I thought it was funny, you know, all their [her parents'] talk about Mexico and their family and friends, and then they would say how long it had been since they had seen them and it didn't really matter. It was, I guess, like playing a videotape over and over. So I never thought I had

to go back to visit Mexico. I already had it here, well, you know what I mean, by listening to them tell it.

In general, researchers using a transnational framework maintain that immigrants participate in ongoing circular migration patterns which contribute to the development of new cultures, behaviors, and social relationships: an immigrant weltanschauung. Such a transnational migrant mindset relied on a physical movement, a persistent (re)crossing of borders creating new geographical spaces. Many argue that such a transnational framework cannot be used to fully understand the Mexican immigrant experience. Hondagneu-Sotelo criticizes such an immigration conceptualization by first pointing out that, although Mexican immigrants may continue to see their settlement in the United States as an impermanent one, the majority not only remain in the United States but also travel infrequently to Mexico. As an urban working class, primarily in the service sector, Mexican immigrants are employed year round, unlike seasonal agricultural work, making it difficult for them to make long trips back to Mexico.[27] Based on my interviews, Mexican immigrant parents told their children that they would like to go back to Mexico for an extended period of time but their jobs made this impossible. They wanted to return to their hometowns of Chihuahua, Torreon, Monterrey, and even Mexico City not so much to visit their parents, many of whom had either died or had joined them in the United States, but to recover some of what they left behind. These immigrant parents found it difficult to specify what they wanted to recover in a return trip to Mexico and, when pressed by their daughters, assumed an aura of melancholy. Isabel captures her mother's sense of longing for Mexico:

> My mom always said that she was here [the United States] and she knew that this was her new home, but I guess she always wanted to remember Mexico. But it wasn't like she actually made plans to go there for long visits or anything. I would tell her, "So why don't you go there if you keep talking all the time about how it was?" She would first get kind of sad and then say she was here to stay and she was OK to think about Mexico and tell us about it.

Similarly, Carmen, whose parents came from a Mexican middle-class background, said that her parents also expressed their feelings for Mexico but focused their energies on leading their lives in the United States:

My dad talked about the school he went to back in Mexico and his friends. Once I think he told us about his first girlfriend but my mom got mad. It would be like he was in another world. He talked about these people as if they were here with him, but they weren't and he hadn't seen them for a long time. He said he just liked to remember them and the times he had back there. I would get tired of hearing them over and over again, but, you know, it's a part of him and in some way of me, too.

These women reveal their immigrant parents' real and imagined ties to Mexico and the effect on the process of their own identities. My research findings suggest that for these immigrant parents, their country of origin remains in their daily experiences as a web of symbols and meanings, a tangible postmodern space and an imagined community passed on to their children who, in turn, add to it and shape it within the context of their own second-generation imagined communities. Carmen expresses her ties to Mexico through her father in a subtle yet powerful phrase when she says that Mexico was "a part of him and in some way of me, too."

Palimpsests of Patriarchy

These second-generation Mexican Americans were aware of another key dimension found within their family's immigrant stories. Adding a new twist to the traditional immigrant saga, immigrant mothers narrated their lives as gendered ones, making their daughters aware of their experiences with patriarchy and gender contestations. Immigration studies on the first and second generations have been criticized for diminishing the experiences of immigrant women by relegating them to the margins of this research. Recent studies on Mexican immigrants and their second-generation children have integrated a gender analysis into their theoretical frameworks and, in so doing, have moved the study of Mexican women immigrants "from out of the shadows" of American and, more specifically, immigrant history.[28] Researchers have documented the diversity of Mexican and Mexican American women's experiences as they navigate and negotiate between the worlds of Mexico and the United States.[29] Such scholars are challenging a postmodern transnational framework for not viewing the immigration process as a gendered one shaped by patriarchal constraints. This challenge consists of several major components. Transnational studies have focused almost exclusively on migration as a nongendered process and therefore have not been critical of their exclusion of women from their studies. Moreover, studies that focus almost exclusively on male migrants overlook the process through which men's lives are also gendered and shaped by the changing relations with women (for example, in their relationships with their wives and daughters). Women migrants are seen as invisible on two levels. At one level, their lives have indeed been relegated to the shadows of immigration history.[30] At a second level, their interrelationships with men have lacked systematic analysis. Together, such dimensions of migrant women's marginalization and invisibility have led to the rise of a "new scholarship" on transnational migrant or immigrant women. Informed primarily by feminist frameworks, this "new scholarship" focuses on the impact and consequences of gender on the everyday life experiences of immigrants and the dynamic power relations experienced in such contexts as the family. Hondagneu-Sotelo concludes:

> Most immigration research has ignored questions of gender, altogether, as if men were without gender. . . . [A]n appropriate research strategy requires more than either examining men's gender in isolation or simply "adding" women to the picture. Gender is not simply a variable to be measured, but a set of social relations that organize immigration patterns. The task then is not simply to document or highlight the presence of undocumented women who have settled in the U.S., or to ask the same questions of immigrant women that are asked of immigrant men, but to begin with an examination of how gender relations facilitate or constrain both women's *and* men's immigration and settlement.[31]

Three major themes related to gender and immigration crystallize in these second-generation narratives. First, their mothers told them about their struggles with their fathers regarding their immigration to the United States. Second, their mothers recounted their initial experiences in the United States. Lastly, second-generation daughters learned emerging "gender scripts" from their mothers whose interactions, both in Mexico and the United States, were with their immigrant husbands. All three themes represent variations along a continuum of patriarchal relations.

Moreover, although specific patriarchal relationships can be isolated within a specific period in the lives of immigrant mothers, their impact and effects appear and reappear throughout their lives, as evidenced in the stories they told to their daughters. Persistent patriarchy, overt and covert, shapes the lives of immigrant women and, in turn, contributes to the social construction of the gendered ethnic identities among the second generation.

Recent scholarship on immigration as a gendered process provides a framework for analyzing the different experiences of women during the process of immigration. One of the major critiques of the transnational approach to immigration can be used to understand the impact of gendered power relations within a system of patriarchy on the lives of these women. The border has been reconceptualized as a place and space of colonization and decolonization, processes that have been overlooked in general globalization literature because it has focused too heavily on the positive aspects of transnational interconnectedness at the expense of transnational conflict.[32] Gloria E. Anzaldúa conceptualizes the border and borderlands by stressing their dynamic and oppressive nature as places where the physical and the spiritual collide:

> The actual physical borderland that I'm dealing with . . . is the Texas–U.S. Southwest Mexican border. The psychological borderlands, the sexual borderland and the spiritual borderlands, are not particular to the Southwest. In fact, the Borderlands are physically present wherever two or more cultures edge each other, where people of different races occupy the same territory, where under, lower, middle, and upper classes touch, where the space between two individuals shrinks with intimacy.[33]

I suggest that a gender analysis of the immigration process adds another dimension to the conceptualization of the border as a site of cultural and, for women immigrants, gender contestations. The border is a symbol of both location and dislocation, of community and alienating individuality, of discovery and colonization. Borders as myths and realities do not merely stretch between countries; they create what Anzaldúa calls open wounds: the "heridas abiertas."[34] Borderlands are seen as more than mere sites of transnational movements and (re)movements; they are sites of oppositional culture where meanings are formed and (re)invented within the lived experiences of its inhabitants.[35] The border is redefined as a site of cultural contestation and resistance in which the first and the second generation live their "everyday lives . . . crisscrossed by border zones, pockets and eruptions of all kinds."[36] This is a contested process where the construction of social identity is a contingent one, not an essentialist one. The ethnic identities of immigrants, the second generation, and later generations involve "multiple encounters both within the ethnic culture and outside it. . . . Nothing in these relationships is static. There are no monolithic or essentialist or 'authentic' cultures. . . . Individual as well as collective identity is always in a state of flux, constantly being reinvented and always open and fluid."[37] Transnational migrants move through and within borderlands of space and spirit—a multidimensional real and imagined entity—a marker for Mexicans, Mexican immigrants, and second-generation Mexican Americans. Moreover, the borderland is a geographical space in which immigrant women struggle to redefine themselves. The border and borderlands become sites of gender contestation; they are a crossroads and *frontera* where identities are constantly in the process of (re)invention.[38]

Researchers have examined various areas in which women immigrants experience patriarchal gender constraints. Some focus on existing patterns of gender relations within their homelands by tracing their continued effect on immigrant families. Other studies examine emergent gender constraints that also develop within immigrant families because of their structural relations of inequality within American society and, specifically, those experienced by immigrant men as they work in the paid labor force. A growing number of studies have shown how immigrant women, such as Mexican domestic workers, redefine their identities as women, wives, and mothers. In general, cross-cultural studies of immigrant women are documenting a gender constraint continuum confronting these women, and, most importantly, this "new scholarship" on immigrant women is documenting their ability to create survival strategies that will help them cope with their lives in the United States. Lastly, the most recent works examine the interrelations between immigrant mothers and their American-born daughters, such as those in this study.[39]

The second-generation women I interviewed talked about their mothers' confrontations with patriarchy. These daughters retained stories of how immigrant women, like their mothers and other women, experienced specific gender constraints as they made the journey to and settled in the United States. I suggest that these stories represent ideational and behavioral components of a specific kind of social capital. Their mothers' immigrant stories are both narratives and didactic mechanisms capable of contributing to their daughters' gendered ethnic identity formation. These stories focused on the gender transformation that their mothers experienced as they settled in the United States.

All of the respondents' family "immigration stories" focused on their mothers' problems with their fathers and, to a lesser extent, with other male family members. Common themes among these stories were the ways in which these women challenged their husbands' gender ideology and behavior. They described how they were changing to their daughters. These changes represented an ongoing struggle to redefine themselves as women, wives, and mothers. As such, this struggle also involved a process of redefining men as husbands and fathers. Mexican immigrant women identified two major areas in their lives that led to gender tensions and, for most, gender transformations within their families. First, respondents pointed out that their mothers' lives changed dramatically when they started to adopt certain ways of living in their households. Second, their mothers identified their entrance into the paid labor force as a source of family discord and adjustment. Taken together, these factors trace a process of struggle, contestation, and survival strategies experienced by immigrant mothers. In general, these mothers included gender as a component to their family's immigrant saga, a component that became instrumental in their second-generation daughters' identity development.

Mexican immigrant mothers told their daughters about their struggles with their husbands who wanted them to "stay Mexican." These mothers were aware that crossing the border into the United States signified the beginning of a new life, but they told their daughters that they soon discovered that their lives as women would change dramatically. Immigrant women confronted another border—a border that once crossed would change their lives as they faced new situations and responded to them, eventually redefining themselves as women. The second-generation women learned that their mothers retained a sense of their "Mexicanidad," but they separated it from their attempt to resist various forms of patriarchy, such as male-dominated decision making and the unequal gender division of household labor. Both factors became most contentious when these immigrant mothers entered the paid labor force. Sonia, one of three Mexican American women introduced in chapter 1, describes the following story:

> One time my mom's cousin was over at our house and told my mom that she had really changed now she was working. He told my mom that she was now pretty "Americanizada" [Americanized]. I was really proud when my mom just blurted out something like, "So what, as long as we survive and my kids can stay in school." She even said, "esto es lo que tengo que hacer y si es Americano, que pues?" [this is what I have to do and if this is American, so what?].

Other respondents were more specific regarding the kinds of changes that their mothers went through once they became wage earners. Many focused on the tensions that developed between their mothers and the rest of the family. Once the mothers started working, they had to figure out how to take care of their children and the household. These immigrant women met their childcare needs in several ways. They had relatives, such as mothers or sisters, who were not in the paid labor force and who agreed to take care of their children. Others worked part-time while their children were in school. Some worked full-time once their children were in junior high and capable of taking care of themselves. All the immigrant women told their daughters that they had to change the way they saw themselves and the way their husbands saw them. Their mothers became wage earners for three major reasons. Several had unemployed husbands, others had husbands with medical disabilities, and some entered the paid labor force to supplement their husbands' wages. In general, they found jobs in the service sector (although two became clerical workers as a result of their English proficiency). All but one mother remained employed, if only part-time, even after their husbands returned to work.

Perhaps most interesting for this study is that the majority of mothers entered the paid labor force in order to increase the family's income. For many of my interviewees, this additional income was often used to improve their education, as Yolanda affirms:

> My mom said she went to work because she was trying to get us more stuff for school. She wanted to make sure we could keep up with all the other kids. She told us to buy books and a computer. But she would say

that her job caused troubled with my dad. You know, with her not taking care of the house like before.

Other students recalled that their mothers became cannery workers, waitresses, cooks, and domestic workers, not as a profession or career, but as a necessity. They told their daughters that they had to adjust to what they called "outside work" and housework. Working in the paid labor force was difficult, but the stories they passed on to their daughters stress the difficulties they experienced at home. Julia remembers her mother's story:

She told me that when she got her first job cooking at this restaurant my dad would get mad because she wasn't around to cook for him. He used to say he was better off if he went to eat at the restaurant and get his food there. My mom would say that this really got her mad, and once she told him if he liked her cooking so much, maybe he could learn how to do it himself. He never did but, you know, my mom said he was shocked that she said this, and what happened is that a few days a week she would bring home food from the restaurant and my dad would put stuff in the microwave the other days. But, on Sundays, if she didn't have to work, she would go all out and make this big Mexican meal. My mom said its wasn't perfect but it worked.

Other women employed similar strategies by negotiating a compromise designed to lessen gender tensions. Patricia Zavella's study found cannery women using similar tactics when confronted by their husbands for neglecting their families. The cannery women redefined family responsibilities to include their seasonal work. They succeeded in convincing their husbands that their participation in the paid labor force was a benefit to the family and that only minor adjustments to household labor was needed.[40] Beatriz M. Pesquera's study of Mexican American couples from professional, white- and blue-collar classes also underscores the family as contested terrain in which women negotiate the effects of patriarchal constraints, with some women emerging more successful than others.[41] My own study of Mexican immigrant and Mexican American women business owners also revealed a successful process of negotiation initiated by women in order to ease the tensions between themselves and their husbands over the division of household labor.[42] Nevertheless, immigrant women, like other women, enter the paid labor force only to return to what Arlie Hochschild calls a second shift, a double day of work in the paid labor force combined with one in the home.[43]

Although Mexican immigrant mothers experience periods in which they contest established gender relations within their families, they also go through other periods in which they choose not to challenge such constraints. In both cases, immigrant mothers employed in the paid labor force are aware of the strength of gender constraints but, under certain circumstances, withdrew their resistance. Although I agree that patriarchal constraints are challenged, often successfully, by immigrant women, as Hondagneu-Sotelo's work argues, I suggest that patriarchal constraints do not decline in a permanent, linear progression.[44] On the contrary, these constraints can resurface as family conditions change. Moreover, I am suggesting that an immigrant mother's lessons about patriarchy are passed on didactically to her second-generation daughter and represent a dominant force in the process of their gendered ethnic identity formation. Elena's discussion of her mother's gender strategies emphasizes how she grew increasingly adamant when her father challenged her Mexican identity:

> My mom would tell me that my dad would start criticizing her for not doing this and that around the house. He would say that if they had stayed in Mexico, she would be different, but here she had become some one else. My mom said she hated when he started at her like this. She told him, "Yes, I'm different. I have to work and I can't do everything around the house like before I went out and worked." But she would also say that she would always be the same—a Mexican—but it doesn't mean being bossed around or tied to the housework.

Similarly, Irene recalls the time when her grandmother (her father's mother) came from Mexico for a summer and started cleaning the house while her mother was at work, ironically as a domestic worker.

> My abuelita [grandmother] went around the house that summer when I was around 14 and just kept cleaning and cleaning. My mom was at work and I sort of knew that there would be some kind of family mess. Well, it did happen. My dad came home first and looked around and liked what his mom had done with cleaning the house. When my mom got home, she looked around and didn't say a word. My mom told me later that they had a sort of fight later. My dad said that this is the kind

of house he wanted—clean and neat like his mom had left our house after her cleaning it all. My mom said that he told her she had become like all the other women who come here from Mexico and then just become like American women. My mom says she really got mad but didn't want to fight. Well, my grandma left and our house went back to the way it was before—well, not dirty, but just not perfect. Later my mom told me she just let my dad talk because she knew that he knew she had to work and he didn't want to do much housework. So, he got used to a sort-of messy house. But what I really remember is that my mom said she got mad because my dad threw in that remark about her not being as Mexican as she used to be back in Mexico. She told me that, of course, she was different, it had to happen, but she always would be Mexican. She told me that she wanted me to change even more, get a good paying job, become a professional, and this would not change that I am from a Mexican background.

Mexican immigrant mothers, who themselves experience dramatic changes in their private and public lives, pass on various lessons to their daughters. Irene's quote captures a recurring motif in all of the respondents' interviews. Their mothers experienced challenges to their "Mexicanidad" based on their gender role transformations and the adjustments they made within their families. Their mothers contested various levels of patriarchal constraints by developing specific gender strategies that they, in turn, passed on to their daughters. An overarching theme within these gender strategies is the immigrant mothers' adamant belief that gender contestation and transformations do not signify a break with their ethnic allegiance—their "Mexicanidad." In so doing, these immigrant mothers taught their daughters that their ethnic identity was not a fixed one, particularly not one tied to gender constraints. "My mom said she would always be Mexican, but she wouldn't always be the same."

Overview

Second-generation Mexican American women, like their immigrant parents, (re)create and (re)imagine Mexico through various lenses. They (re)live their parents' memories of Mexico, both real and (re)imagined, and in so doing find themselves (re)negotiating the ethnic boundaries with their immigrant parents, with their own understanding of Mexico, and with the larger American society. Their narratives unfold, revealing tensions and ambiguities about the respondents' ethnic identities. In addition, they discover their immigrant mothers' struggles with patriarchal constraints and contestations. Daughters of Mexican immigrant parents learn to live in a second-generation borderland of identity in which boundaries are fluid, highly nuanced, and always emergent. At the same time that these women reflect on their parents' "*memorias* de Mexico," they undergo parallel experiences, forming additional layers in the social construction of their identities. Their parents remind them that they will always be Mexican, but they also want them to understand and, in fact, never forget that they are also American. The second generation appreciates and identifies with their parents' "Mexicanidad," yet they layer this dimension of their identity with an understanding that they are Mexican American. Nevertheless, they live with daily challenges to their emergent gendered ethnic identities—challenges that led them to identity reconstruction in ways that will be analyzed in the next chapters.

CHAPTER THREE
Palimpsests of Identities

Second-generation Mexican American women construct their ethnic identities by (re)negotiating the boundaries between themselves and their immigrant parents and between themselves and the larger American society. Their personal stories illustrate the complex process of identity construction in which cultures meet, blend, collide, and negotiate, creating a socially constructed second-generation self.[1] Such narratives reveal an emergent, unfolding, and contingent process of identity construction in which these women negotiate, contest, invent, and reinvent their ethnic, social-class, and gender identities. This chapter examines the meanings that women attach to their ethnic, social-class, and gender identities as members of the "new" second generation.

"One Thing I'm Sure of Is that I'm Mexican, Sort of"

The second generation's ethnic narratives reveal their attempts to construct group boundaries, a geography of their own ethnic identities. Their narratives contain a common trope: a recognition that a sense of "Mexicanidad" shaped by their immigrant parents' (re)imaginings of Mexico has been inscribed on their life manuscripts. This layer of Mexicanidad is formed by various aspects of material culture, including language, customs, religion, and kinship patterns. All these combine, in one degree or another, in second generation lives as reminders that their palimpsests of identity bear the imprints of a real and imagined Mexican culture, one which is itself unfolding as immigrants navigate their way through American society.

The second generation view language as a generational and ethnic marker. Without exception, my interviewees reported that the Spanish language resonated throughout their childhood. Their parents, relatives, and Mexican immigrant neighbors spoke, if not preferred, Spanish. As discussed in chapter 2, their Mexican immigrant parents carried language with them across the border, maintaining Spanish long after their U.S. settlement. Respondents described themselves as bilingual but considered themselves primarily English speakers, with most of them speaking English instead of Spanish. Yet, they viewed Spanish as a constant reminder of their Mexican heritage. As long as they could remember, they heard, and usually but not always spoke, Spanish within their homes. Indeed, many stated that their parents spoke metaphorically of their home as Mexico, with Spanish as its primary language, and the outside world as the United States, with English as the dominant language. Sonia, like other respondents, said that her mother spoke Spanish with her father and her grandmother. Many respondents referred to Spanish as the language of adults because the adults in their families were the ones who had maintained their language. This second generation, unlike their immigrant parents, navigated through American society from birth, while their parents and other significant adult family members entered American society as monolingual Spanish speakers.[2]

Respondents believe that language is a major factor shaping their ethnic identities. Nevertheless, they express mixed feelings about their Spanish language surroundings. At times, they appreciate the opportunity to learn a second language in such a natural setting. They see language as a direct tie to their sense of self, even though the link between the two is confusing. Respondents believe that both Spanish and English signify markers of their ethnic identities, as Diana explained:

> I can see how Spanish is not just part of some class I've taken in school. It's not just a textbook thing. It's part of me and even though I know I use and, well, even prefer English, I speak Spanish when I come home. But really I know that my world is going to be outside of this. Even my parents tell me that I have to be English-speaking first and then Spanish-speaking.

All of the respondents preferred English and said that their parents stressed the importance of mastering the language. Studies demonstrate that the majority of Mexican immigrants prefer to speak Spanish at home, while their second-generation children are bilingual but prefer English.[3] More recent studies report that children of Mexican immigrants have higher rates of bilingualism than other second-generation children. Still, researchers underscore the propensity of second-generation Mexican Americans to use both languages within specific contexts, such as their interactions with their grandparents, their own parents, and their peers. Moreover, a preference to use English does not reflect a decline in ethnic identity.[4] Pyong Gap Min and Joann Hong found similar patterns among second-generation Korean Americans who stated their preference for English but maintained high levels of ethnic attachment as Koreans.[5] The language issue has always been and will remain central to ethnic identity formation for children of immigrants, but the specific sociohistorical and cultural experiences of a given immigrant group provide a key factor in both the saliency of the preferred language and its effects on the second generation's identity formation. For example, second-generation Filipino Americans, particularly university students, are reclaiming their parents' use of Tagalog as a symbol of resurgent cultural nationalism.[6] The common practice in Filipino American communities is not to establish language and cultural schools for their children. Interestingly, although most Japanese and Chinese American communities did organize language schools, studies of the second generation have found that even among those who attended these school, parents preferred the exclusive use of English by their children.[7] Studies of other Asian groups, however, such as Korean Americans who have higher levels of residential segregation, suggest that close-knit communities increase the likelihood of language retention.[8] I suggest that a combination of individual choice and structural factors help to explain such divergent findings. Moreover, my study suggests that second-generation individuals learn to navigate between both languages.

Respondents found themselves surrounded by Spanish, the language of their parents and most of their adult relatives, but they expressed an understanding that their parents viewed English as a necessity for their children's success in American society and, in so doing, often attempted to increase their own English language skills. Still, the respondents made a direct tie between their Mexican immigrant parents' maintenance of the Spanish language and their own ethnic identity. For most, "being surrounded by Spanish" served as an identity touchstone, but one that often created confusion, leading to different ethnic identity attachments as daughters of Mexican immigrants.

Several women discussed an incident that took place on campus involving what they described as a "Mexican" food service worker. Respondents recalled a situation in which an Anglo student complained that he overheard two cafeteria workers speaking Spanish to each other when he was progressing through the cafeteria line. Since he was selecting prepackaged fast food items, he admitted that he did not need to communicate with either of the workers, but he still complained that this was the United States and workers should only be allowed to speak English even in private conversations with each other. The school newspaper carried this story, using direct quotes from their interview with the student who registered the complaints against the workers.

Several of my respondents referred to this issue during their interviews, illustrating the complexities surrounding language retention and usage. All of my interviewees who discussed this episode expressed their "disgust," "anger," and "surprise" that this incident took place. All concurred that English should be used in business transactions unless those involved agreed to speak Spanish. They pointed out that these workers were speaking Spanish in a private conversation that happened to be overheard by the student. María explained her reaction to this volatile issue: "If the workers needed English in order to do their job, well, OK, but this was a private conversation. Since when do we patrol this?" Julia was surprised that some of "my Anglo friends took the side of the student and the whole English-only thing." Those women who expressed their dismay at this incident accepted that English was "the language we have to know and that's the way it is," but they contested the acts and ideology that supported the exclusive use of English. Perhaps one of the most intriguing aspects of this story involved their parents' reactions, all of whom questioned the actions by the food service employee. Lucia's comments capture the complexity in understanding the role and symbolism of language retention for the first and second generation:

> I couldn't believe both my parents said that the women [food service workers] should only speak English at work. I told them it wasn't right. And that the school said if it was a private conversation then it was OK. But they [her parents] said that they should try to learn enough English so they wouldn't have trouble. I got mad at them and said that we have rights, but then they said what if they lost their job anyway. Their work

was more important. I can see this but everyone should be able to speak another language, even though, its funny, I don't really speak Spanish much except with my parents and relatives.

This passage reveals more than just an intergenerational debate over language usage. It underscores the immigrants' attempt to keep their jobs over their personal use of their language of origin. Another respondent recalled that her parents did not want the incident to lead to problems for her as a "Mexican student," illustrating her parents' desire for her to move away from an association with Spanish in order to avoid any difficulties within an English-speaking world. The second generation focused on language and equality without realizing that their opinions might result in difficulties at school. Still, respondents discussed their use of Spanish, however limited, with a sense of being "Mexican." For example, Anna expressed confusion about the various self-identification labels even though she attempts to identify as "Mexican."

I don't understand really a lot of the terminology like Hispanic or Chicano or Latino. Some people don't like to be called that, other people don't like to be called Hispanic or Chicano. Some of these names get too technical, and then I don't see the reasons for using all these names like Hispanic or Chicano. The only reason I call myself Mexican is because that's the only way that I am absolutely sure of the definition. I mean that I'm Mexican because my parents are Mexican, you know, actually born there. OK, so I was born here but I'm their daughter. Of course, I am American, but I have roots that are Mexican, deep down. I'm Mexican and of course my parents remind me of this all the time. I speak to them in Spanish and that's Mexican. It might sound all technical but I really do get it. I mean one thing that I am sure of is that I'm Mexican, sort of.[9]

Anna's simultaneous use of the words "sure of" and "sort of" captures two of the major dimensions of ethnic identity formation for the second generation. Anna, like the other respondents in this study and those in other studies of second-generation individuals, struggles with the use of language as a symbol for Mexican identity. Respondents expressed their confusion as they tried to negotiate within the worlds of their parents and the larger society. At the same time that they express some degree of assurance of who they are as second-generation Mexican Americans, they also recognize that they are "sure of" this, adding a qualifier signifying the reemergence of identity ambiguity. They say that they know who and what they are, but only "sort of."

While Carmen and other respondents describe themselves as Mexicans in terms of their family's ancestry and the use of Spanish everyday, their responses include confusion regarding their selection of Mexican as a term of self-identification. Ironically, this confusion often results from their interactions with their grandparents: a source for what they call their "Mexican-ness."

Elena explains her confusion with her own retention and use of Spanish: "I think I just took it for granted that all families had another language, not just English, but I probably always think in English even when I speak Spanish. I'm not sure how this works, but when I speak Spanish, especially with my abuelita, I am aware that I am speaking Spanish. It's not automatic like English." Interestingly, Elena refers to her grandmother by using the Spanish word *abuelita*. The taped interview does not capture any hesitation when she uses the Spanish word. Other respondents also used *abuelita* or *abuelito* when they spoke about their grandmother or grandfather. This suggests that the second generation do indeed use some Spanish "automatically," to use Julia's words, but they describe their language usage differently. Most of these Mexican American women increased their use of Spanish when their grandparents lived either with them or in close proximity. As with other second-generation groups, the presence of immigrant grandparents reinforces the intergenerational retention of language.[10] Although these Mexican American women speak Spanish with their parents, since their parents have different levels of English proficiency, they all said they spoke Spanish exclusively with their grandparents. Language represents a reminder of their "Mexican-ness," but it is an ethnic identity that they know is not the same as their immigrant parents'. In addition, the second generation believe that language adds a problematic layer to the confusion they were experiencing as they struggled to construct their own identity. Consuelo shared this memory of her grandmother:

> My abuelita died four years ago but I always remember her. She was always there waiting for me when I got home from grade school. She

always spoke to me in Spanish, and I would answer her in Spanish but not with my parents. I would sometimes answer them in English. I was different when I was with her. She was really Mexican. She came here when I was only about six or seven, and then my mom arranged for her to stay. My grandmother never tried to get used to the life here. She didn't have to work or learn English. She just kept being like she was in Mexico. This made her different from my parents, but it made her special for me. It was like going back to visit Mexico but staying here.

Consuelo refers to herself as "Mexican" but indicates that her grandmother was different: "she was really Mexican." Like other respondents, Consuelo constructed an ethnic boundary between herself and her grandmother, a boundary between a second-generation Mexican American granddaughter and her Mexican immigrant grandmother. In addition, she recognizes a difference between her parents who arrived in the United States as young adults and her grandmother who came when she was much older. Sonia describes her experiences living with her Mexican immigrant grandmother:

Even though my grandmother had been living here in the United States for a long time, she would still get upset about being here. I remember this time when she was really upset because my mom and dad had given me permission to go on this overnight camping trip with my Girl Scout troop. She told my mom that she didn't like this; it wasn't right. "How could she let me do this? Mexican girls just don't go off like this." She told my mom that this was an American thing. I couldn't believe it. Then, I was surprised because my mom told her that her kids were not in Mexico. I guess I'm not Mexican like my grandmother but really more American, but still, well, different from my parents, too.

At the same time that second-generation Mexican American daughters reinforced their Mexican roots through their daily lives with their grandparents, particularly their grandmothers, they also realized that they were different from both their grandparents and parents. Yet, Sonia's quote reveals that her mother was quick to identify her as not being raised in Mexico, underscoring that while her daughter shared similar experiences, her "Mexican-ness" existed within an Americanized context. Although many of the respondents agree with Anna, who said, "one thing that I am sure of is that I'm Mexican, sort of," they ultimately see this expression of ethnic identity as the source of ambiguities and contradictions, supporting the view that the second generation exists within the shifting and fluid postmodern boundaries of ethnic identities that are, as Joane Nagel argues, truly emergent, never fixed.[11]

"I Feel like I Am All of this All of the Time"

Second-generation individuals experience the differences between their immigrant generation and that of their parents through a process complete with ambiguities, contradictions, and unresolved issues. They occupy a kind of borderland of ethnicity, gender, and social class. Vicki L. Ruiz's study of Mexican American women who came of age during the 1930s and 1940s illustrates the Mexican cultural changes and continuities that exist within Mexican immigrant families and their American-born children. These daughters confronted the complex worlds of their family and the social milieu of the flapper culture of the Roaring Twenties. They developed a network of coping strategies in their attempts to reconcile these distinct cultural and social spaces. Yet, as Ruiz emphasizes, these survival strategies show that the women did not merely discard what they defined as traditional Mexican culture in favor of what they considered a liberating and modern flapper culture. Ruiz's respondents moved back and forth between two geographical cultures, attaching emergent meanings to their sense of ethnic selves—a major issues at the core of the research on second-generation individuals.[12] Building on Ruiz's analysis, I argue that these second-generation women did not move back and forth between two worlds, but rather they carried both with them, each inscribed on their own individual palimpsest of ethnic identity.

Research shows that individuals from different immigrant backgrounds adopt a variety of terms with which to refer to themselves. Many terms have been used to refer to American-born daughters of Mexican immigrant parents: Mexican American, Latina, Hispanic, Mexican, and Chicana. These terms carry sociohistorical and political meanings. For example, the term *Hispanic* includes a panethnic dimension by referring to individuals from Mexico, Cuba, Puerto Rico, and Central and South America. *Hispanic* has also been used by the U.S. Census Bureau as an umbrella category for all the groups listed above. For this reason, some groups reject the term *Hispanic*, seeing it as an arbitrarily constructed ethnic label. In addition, during the social protest movement of the 1960s, *Hispanic* was seen as an ethnic label adopted by those who wanted to stress their racially European Spanish heritage at the expense of their racially indigenous past. This brief overview of the ethnic label *Hispanic* is not meant to be exhaustive, but rather it is meant to give an idea of how such self-identification labels are best understood within a historical and contemporary context. Increases in biracial, bi-ethnic generations will add to this complexity of self-identification. Most importantly, this study is guided by a social constructionist perspective that focuses on the processes through which individuals negotiate their ethnic group boundaries and the meanings that they attach to their ethnic labels. This process includes the groups' perception of their social geography of ethnic selves in the United States, including their communities and other specific settings, such as a university. All of my respondents usually use the label "Mexican American" as a way of claiming their immigrant heritage and their birthright as United States citizens. Yet, they do not limit themselves to this self-identification level. They crisscross their way through such ethnic labels. Early studies on ethnic identification among Mexican immigrants, the second and later generations, found a straight-line movement from the term *Mexican* to *Mexican American*. Susan E. Keefe and Amado M. Padilla's work points toward this unilinear development of ethnic self-identification; however, like other studies conducted in the 1970s and 1980s, an overreliance on quantitative measures of ethnicity precluded a recognition and understanding of the process through which individuals use a variety of terms under specific circumstances or even, in a postmodern sense, the simultaneous use of terms.[13] Respondents did express panethnic sentiments, referring to themselves as "Latinas," but limited themselves with an ethnic attachment that did not cross Latin American boundaries.[14] Padilla's study of ethnic consciousness focuses on the situational context within which Mexican Americans and Puerto Ricans "became" Latinos in Chicago as they joined together in common political struggles.[15] Interestingly, respondents not only avoided an identification with the terms *Hispanic* and *Chicana*, they expressed a generally accepted interpretation of both terms. *Hispanic* was seen as an umbrella term, but they pointed out that it "sounds, well, like from Spain" and "just wipes out the Mexican part of me." Furthermore, they discussed the term *Chicana* as a political term from the sixties, with some providing a detailed overview relating the use of the term with militancy. They did not express a dislike for this ethnic label, but they knew their parents did not like the term because it did not convey the kind of American identity that they, as immigrants, wanted for their second-generation children. As the researcher, I have been referring to my respondents as Mexican American women since this is the ethnic label that they preferred and referred to at some point in their interviews.[16] The issue of self-identification with ethnic labels divides groups of second-generation individuals and represents a long-standing political issue. Nevertheless, my focus is on the respondents' discourse on ethnicity, the meanings that they attach to these, and the context for both.

The respondents described themselves in ways that strongly suggest they are constructing their ethnic identities to support both a social constructionist framework and a postmodern one. All of the women defined their ethnic self-identification by giving themselves a one- or two-word ethnic label, such as Mexican or Mexican American, but, given the open-ended nature of in-depth interviews, they also provided "thick descriptions" of the meanings that they attached to these labels. In addition, and perhaps more importantly as a contribution to the research on the second generation, respondents did not talk about their ethnic identities as fixed categories. Although they initially answered the classic question "What do you say you are or how do you describe yourself?" with answers that included a variety of terms such as Mexican, Mexican American, and American, they discussed their sense of ethnic identity in a classic social-constructionist manner. Their responses reveal that they identify with several different ethnic labels. For example, María, whose story is highlighted in chapter 1, identifies herself as Mexican American, but when she talks about her plans to become a lawyer, she refers to herself as a Mexican: "I want to go to law school, but I think it will be a hard thing. I don't think there are a lot of Mexican women lawyers, and so I guess being Mexican still makes things difficult, you know, with prejudice and stereotypes. But I want to do this." When María discusses her own ethnic identification in other parts of the interviews, her responses, like the majority of other respondents, uncover the tensions and ambiguities she experiences as a daughter of Mexican immigrants:

My parents wanted me to be American but still know that I am Mexican, but I have to admit this sometimes—it's pretty confusing. It didn't always click or blend. They are Mexicans because they were born over there but then came here. Pretty simple. Then us kids were born here, and we learn stuff from them, but we are in a totally different place, time, culture, everything. I still try to figure it out, especially since I have been here at school. But even when it's really confusing, I know that I am proud of my parents—who they are—but I am different, not better or anything, just different.

All the women share María's ambiguity, recognizing that they are different from their parents based on their birthplaces. Geography, nationality, and citizenship are all sources of difference between themselves and their parents, yet these differences are tempered by their parents' attempts to create a "little Mexico" within their families. "Well, let's see, I am Mexican American because I was born here not there, you know, Mexico. I haven't even been back to Mexico since I visited there when I was in sixth grade. But my parents have always tried to sort of make our home be sort of Mexican. We speak Spanish, especially when my aunts and uncle visit which is too often. I guess that's Mexican too." Elena also describes her ethnic identity as a fluid, emergent social construction:

I used to work every summer in a large wholesale store that employed high-school students from my neighborhood. I would hear a lot of different names used. I remember that one guy said his friends used Chicano, but his parents said they didn't like this. I sometimes use Mexican American. It's sort of a judgment call, I guess, I'm not sure, and it even depends where I am or how I feel. Sometimes I think I'm not aware of this, like I say different things. At home we use Mexican, especially around my grandmother, but its mostly to avoid arguments with her. She's from Mexico, you know, but has lived with us a long time. When I am with my friends from the softball team, I usually don't see myself like ethnic, but I do say I have a Mexican heritage, but I guess now that I talk to you, that I still see myself as different, you know, my skin is darker, but actually my cousin is lighter but is Mexican. But, well, it's confusing. I'm everything but I am not like my parents and really different from my grandmother, but we're all still Mexicans, somehow.

Phrases similar to "sort of Mexican" and "Mexicans, somehow" appear throughout all of the interviews, although in different forms, such as, "kind of Mexican," "like a Mexican family," and "more Mexican-like." The key word is, of course, "Mexican," used by these second-generation women to identify their parents and, in so doing, construct their own ethnic identification. They talk about their mothers putting up home altars with statues of the Virgin of Guadalupe, cooking Mexican food, and watching Mexican television *novelas* (soap operas). All of the respondents, even those few who do not live in predominantly Mexican and Mexican American communities, identify their homes as ones in which Mexico was, indeed, "all around" them. They experience the vestiges of Mexican culture, as reified by their parents, in their everyday lives, most of the time without even an explicit articulation of their cultural content. These women differ from Mia Tuan's Asian American respondents who described their families' attempts to revive their cultural heritage with what Tuan calls "ethnic snippets"—activities such as field trips to Asian heritage museums or cultural fairs.[17] On the contrary, my respondents, like second-generation New York Jews in the early 1900s, live in the world of their fathers and mothers.[18] They know that they live in an immigrant culture, although the content of that culture is a largely reinvented one constructed by the first generation almost as soon as they left their homeland. Studies of the second generation underscore the fluidity of identity even when second-generation individuals define themselves in juxtaposition to their immigrant parents. Based on her study of second-generation Jews in the early 1900s, Deborah Dash Moore concludes that second-generation individuals compare themselves to their immigrant parents, using them as a reference point for their own identity rather than a primary shaper of it. Indeed, Moore found that second-generation Jews recreate the world of their parents "into an object of nostalgia and idealize it, but they do not see themselves defined by it."[19] Both New York Jews and Mexican Americans construct their ethnicity in the way Barth argued ethnic identity is actually formed—as "the ethnic boundary that defines the group, not the cultural stuff that it encloses."[20]

Issues of geography and nationality intersect the interviews. The women raise the issue of their parents' place of birth and their physical movement as immigrants. They define immigration as a process of movement from one place to another, yet, at the same time, they assert that such a process did not "erase" their family's cultural "Mexican-ness," which they define in terms of language, customs, religion, and other visible reifications of culture. Nevertheless, respondents do not see their distinctiveness from their parents as one characterized by a rupture from their Mexican world nor one that gives them a clearly defined sense of ethnic self. Their socially constructed ethnic identity takes shape in a postmodern sense, revealing a second-generational identity full of tensions and contradictions, without clear-cut generational or geographic boundaries. Their ethnic narratives reveal that they are both similar to but different from their parents. They do not juxtapose themselves with their immigrant parents in constructing their own ethnic identities. They may not always be clear of who they are, but they know that they carry part of their parents with them even though they expose a marked confusion in explaining this "Mexican" inscription on their identity palimpsests. Isela's discussion of her ethnic identity begins by focusing on its situational aspect, but it concludes with a most revealing, insightful statement:

> I say I'm Mexican, but sometimes I say to people Mexican American. Other times I just tell people that I am American but part Mexican. Here at school [university], I tell my friends I like to call myself Latina because they are from other countries like El Salvador, so I share this with them. But then they say but I am Mexican not Latin American. But I usually say Mexican American, but not like Mexicans—I never lived there. My cousins from Mexico call me Pocha, you know, it means half-and-half Mexican and American. I get mad when they call me like this, but it's funny. I guess I am really half-and-half. And then I tell them that I feel like I am all of this all of the time.[21]

Research on the new second-generation documents similar expressions of feeling, such as "I am all of this all the time." James M. Freeman's study of Vietnamese Americans includes this passage from a student's essay, which eloquently captures her palimpsest of identity in a way that closely resembles Isela's:

> If one were to ask a Vietnamese in Vietnam if I were Vietnamese, he or she would undoubtedly say no. . . . If one were to ask a Caucasian in the United States if I were American, the answer would still be no. No matter how one views me, I am a Vietnamese American. . . . Though my ethnic origin may be from Southeast Asia, my essence and soul is the conglomeration of all cultures. To describe me as either Asian or Asian-

American would be grossly incomplete. I acknowledge Asian, Anglo, Hispanic and African influences to all be a part of my heritage.[22]

Similarly, Tuan's second-generation respondents grappled with the tensions inherent in experiencing life within two cultures or even more, as in the case of biracial or bicultural individuals. One respondent identified herself as primarily Japanese American, but then she expressed an ambiguity with this ethnic identification due to her Chinese heritage:

> I guess as an Asian American, I don't consider myself just Japanese, just Chinese. I don't consider myself just American. I don't know. I kinda like terminology like Asian American and African American because it's kinda messy. . . . By blood, I'm Chinese and Japanese. By culture, I don't know if I am so much of either. I don't know. . . . Mom would always tell me I used to get confused growing up. "How can I be Japanese and Chinese and American?" "Well, you are half Japanese, and Chinese, and all-American."[23]

The study of biracial and multiethnic individuals represents a new and rapidly growing area of investigation resulting in further revisions of concepts such as ethnic identity, ethnic group boundaries, and, in general, the social construction of ethnic identity. Studies on multiracial Mexican Americans point to differential outcomes related to ethnic self-identification and the meanings attached to combinations of ethnicity. In his study, Tomás Jiménez points out that, unlike multiethnic Asian Americans, multiethnic Mexican Americans living in California "stand at a crossroad in the process of assimilation: they are structurally assimilated due to their multiple ethnic origins [Mexican and Anglo], yet the social context that they negotiate is highly un-assimilated."[24] Moreover, these Mexican Americans continue to search for their ethnic narrative—one that captures the specific nature of the multiethnic selves. Further research will be needed to study the children of second-generation Mexican Americans who intermarry, creating a multiethnic third generation.[25]

Looking into a Second-Generation Mirror

Carmen echoes the sentiments of the other respondents, describing herself as if she were looking at her portrait and, with changes in lighting, noticing traces of other images, with some superimposed on others, while others are only visible as faint tracings. Her description calls to mind what artists call *pentimentos*—images from a previous painting whose traces reveal themselves in the present canvas. Like many of the other Mexican American women, Carmen's portrait reveals images of the past on her "identity canvas." Gloria Anzaldúa conceptualizes identity as a borderland, a place in the middle where multiple sources of identity meet, collide, and intersect. For Anzaldúa, identity is

> an arrangement or series of clusters, a kind of stacking or layering of selves, horizontal and vertical layers, the geography of selves made up of the different communities you inhabit. When I give my talks I use an overhead projector with a transparency of a little stick figure con un pie en un mundo y otro pie en otro mundo y todos estos mundos overlap; this is your race, your sexual orientation, here you're a Jew Chicana, here an academic, here an artist, there a blue-collar worker. Where these spaces overlap is nepantla, the Borderlands. Identity is a process-in-the-making.[26]

This borderland is similar but not identical to my use of the term *palimpsest of identity*. I suggest that the metaphor of a palimpsest of identity sharpens Anzaldúa's concept of the borderlands by allowing for conditions under which some sources of identity may not form part of the visible geographical layers of an individual's identity. Although I see identity as socially constructed, I also maintain that identity can be (re)imagined and (re)invented in a postmodern sense, in which each layer of identity is not defined solely as the "borderlands" but intersect or conflate. I propose adding an additional dimension to Anzaldúa's conceptualization of social identity. The passage quoted above shows Anzaldúa repeating the word *here*: "here an artist" and "here an academic." My view of social identity is closest to the first phrase Anzaldúa uses: "here you're a Jew Chicana." By joining these two sources of identity, Anzaldúa is using my metaphor of a palimpsest of identity. It is possible to conceptualize ethnic identity as "all of this all of the time," to quote one of my respondents. Furthermore, some aspects of identity may not be salient or visible for periods and then reemerge in a fluid and dynamic manner, demonstrating the possibility of movement between layers. Nevertheless, I agree with Anzaldúa's paraphrasing of Simone de Beauvoir's famous quote, "You are not born a woman, you become one," when Anzaldúa states, "You're not born a Chicana, you become one."[27] Based on a social constructionist perspective, identity unfolds as an individual "becomes," but I would quickly add that the process of becoming allows for a dynamic construction, not specifically layering of identities.

Carmen has constructed her own palimpsest of identity—her own autobiographical manuscript inscribed with many texts, some of which have been written earlier then superimposed by others but never completely replaced and, therefore, capable of reappearing again. In her description of her identity, Carmen reveals the unresolved tensions, ongoing conflicts, and persistent ambiguities that shape the dynamics of her emergent ethnic identity. In her autobiography, *Hoyt Street*, Mary Helen Ponce captures a similar identity palimpsest when she relates her coming of age as a second-generation Mexican American woman:

> Our church did not have a statue of the Virgin of Guadalupe. This really bothered me. After all, were we not Mejicanos? Father Mueller constantly assured me that the Virgin Mary and Guadalupe were one and the same, but I never believed him. How could they be? One was from Mexico and had appeared to an Indian named Juan Diego. And the other? She was American, with blue eyes and blonde hair. Although I accepted them both as holy women, I actually preferred the Virgin Mary; she at least understood English.[28]

Like Ponce, Mexican American women recognize that their ethnic identities consist of multilayered meanings, usually confusing and bordering on contradictory. On the one hand, for example, their narratives document a vague but still recognizable ethnic Mexican consciousness within their "Mejicano" families. Yet, on the other hand, contradictions and ambiguities are layered over a deceptively "fixed" Mexican immigrant identity. Their identity palimpsests contain traces of what this second-generation group refers to as their "Mexican heritage" passed on by their parents. Still, they usually add some description of themselves as American-born, using such phrases as "born here not over there," or "from here," or, in some cases, "American but kind of different." Second-generation Mexican American women do not show decreasing levels of ethnic identity as predicted by classic assimilation theory. These women find themselves in a process of self-discovery as they reflect on their parents' past and their present realities. This process involves much more than merely synthesizing the best of both worlds. In addition, I argue that these second-generation Mexican American women do more than reach into a "portfolio of possible identities," a concept used by Mary Waters to describe the process of ethnic identity construction among West Indian immigrants to the United States.[29] Richard A. García sees Anzaldúa and other Mexican American women as "calling for a revision of ethnic women/men relations, a balance of politics and status, a redefinition of the intellectual and academic codes that have held them in cultural and gender bondage."[30] My respondents do not see their ethnicity in terms of a selection process of either Mexican or American in the same way that the West Indians selectively avoided identifying themselves as "Blacks," preferring their citizenship or nationality as West Indian. Nazli Kibria reconceptualizes the second generation's ethnic identity as a changed one, different in kind from their immigrant parents but not necessarily diminished in degree.[31] I am suggesting, however, that their ethnic identity is not merely a changed one, but a changing, (re)imagined one, which, under some circumstances, may resemble their immigrant parents' and, under other circumstances, may change into something else only to emerge changed again.

An examination of my respondents' use of the Spanish language illustrates the process of their emergent identities. Language became a visible marker, with English representing the American part of their identities and Spanish symbolizing their parents' identities. Yet, these women also made a point to describe themselves as bilingual, even though, as described in chapter 2, they recalled how their relatives criticized their Spanish when they visited them in Mexico. In such circumstances, my respondents often stressed that English was their preferred language. Nevertheless, all of the women were aware of the ambiguity in using language to define a person's ethnic identity. Interestingly, several of the women described their frustration when others, including first- and second-generation individuals, assumed that they spoke Spanish. They challenged those who define *Mexican* and *Mexican American* in terms of Spanish language usage and skill. Marta explained this frustration: "I know Spanish, but I don't go around thinking that everyone who is like me knows Spanish. What if I didn't speak Spanish? I would still be Mexican." Clearly, Marta separates language from ethnic identity; she understands that a person can be Mexican but may or may not be a Spanish speaker. Ironically, some of the women related episodes in which others who were not Mexican or Mexican American questioned their English language ability. They described their experiences in a variety of ways. Some expressed surprise that people would even raise this issue. For example, during an interview for a part-time job at a department store, Irene was asked how many years she had been speaking English: "I don't have any usual or stereotype of a Spanish accent, and this guy still asked me about my English." Others with similar experiences admit that they learned to speak Spanish first, but they consider English their primary language even though they still speak Spanish at home. Again, these women resent questions about their proficiency in English, interpreting such incidents as affronts to their "American-ness." Irene expresses her frustration at such stereotyping:

> I wish people could see that I look different, have a Mexican last name, but why do some just not get it? I am American and speak English and am also Mexican and speak Spanish. But really my Spanish is not like my mom and dad. I mean they tell me I have an American accent and most of the time I speak English. My mom says it's best to speak the best English I can and keep Spanish but really focus on English. You know she even stood up for me when my aunt [her sister] said my Spanish was getting worse.

Other respondents related similar experiences, recalling the significance their parents placed on mastering the English language but retaining Spanish even at decreased levels of proficiency and even if others criticized them for their Americanized or accented Spanish. At the same time, respondents adamantly challenged those who doubted their English speaking proficiency, stereotyping them as recently arrived, non-English speaking Mexican immigrants. Almost all of the women who recalled incidents in which others questioned their ability to speak English also recalled questions regarding their immigration status. For example, Irene's interviewer not only asked her how long she had spoken English, but he also asked when she had come to the United States. Similarly, others recalled occasions when their high-school teachers and college professors asked them what their lives were like in Mexico before they immigrated to the United States. Perhaps the most egregious examples involved being stopped by a law enforcement officer who questioned their citizenship. The respondents were not so much embarrassed at being mistaken for Mexican immigrants as they were angered by an American society that defines those of Mexican heritage (but American-born) as, in Tuan's terms, "forever foreign."

Diana elaborated on this sentiment, using an angry tone:

> The buzzword is diversity. It's on TV, politics, and this school [university], but then people like me are seen as foreigners and worst, illegals. The logic is if you look Mexican you are an immigrant, don't speak English and are illegal. I get tired of saying that's not me, oh well, except for the Mexican part. I don't look at an Anglo with an Italian name and say, "Hey, do you speak Italian and when did you come to the United States?"

All the respondents made specific references to the issue of being treated as "illegal." Their specific stories share a common theme. Respondents expressed anger at being stereotyped and, most importantly for this study, their comments underscore an increased sense of ethnic allegiance. Their narratives made repeated references to their feelings of discrimination and "wanting to be more Mexican." They challenged those who stereotyped them as Mexican, yet their discourse did not emphasize their American selves but rather reinforced their imagined Mexican selves, which they link to their immigrant parents and all Mexicans in the United States. Elena recalls her "experience with this little racist guy:"

> I was shocked that my friend's uncle who was visiting from Boston asked me where I used to live in Mexico, and then even asked me if I had ever become an American. And then, I mean, it was really unbelievable, this guy asks if my parents came here by paying someone to cross them over. I knew people were still racist, but this was just so upfront. My friend was so embarrassed. For me, it meant that I wanted to defend myself for being Mexican and being just as American as this guy.

As I have pointed out in previous sections of this chapter, other respondents, like Elena, called themselves Mexicans in some parts of the interviews but pointed out their preference for Mexican American. Yet, when they recounted episodes with discrimination, they used the term *Mexican*. Nevertheless, Elena concludes her passage by stressing that she is both

Mexican and "just as American" as the person who defined her as Mexican. Diana echoes Elena's comments when she explained her use of the term *Mexican*:

> When people make some kind of remark about when I got here from Mexico or make a remark about how good I speak English, I just want to show that I am proud I come from Mexican immigrants. I am Mexican but I was born here and am as American as anyone born here. But, it's like you have to look like the traditional "American" [*uses hands to make gesture for quotation marks*] to be American.

All of these ethnic narratives share an underlying theme: second-generation individuals are aware that others often see them as "foreigners." This theme intersects other studies of the second generation, particularly research on Asian Americans. Tuan explores the most recent dimensions of racial prejudice and discrimination in the United States—Asian Americans being seen as "forever foreigners." Tuan follows Herbert J. Gans, who argues that some groups have racial and ethnic "leisure activities" with which they can to "opt" to be "ethnic," and Waters, who sees ethnicity as largely optional for white ethnic groups. Tuan concludes that "Asian ethnics, despite being longtime Americans, lack the option to cast aside their racial and ethnic affinities as European ethnics, who by birthright are part of the American mainstream, freely do."[32] Similarly, Pyong Gap Min and Rose Kim found that Asian American professionals, even those with low levels of ethnic allegiances, came to realize that they would never be treated as full-fledged Americans.[33] Based on their increased experiences with prejudice and discrimination, American-born Filipinos', unlike their immigrant parents, respond in ways that are "more assertive and demonstrative about [their] rights as a 'true Americans' in addition to being assertive about [their] racial, ethnic, and cultural roots."[34] Similarly, Ronald T. Takaki uses a personal anecdote to illustrate how racial stereotypes make it difficult for, in this case, Japanese Americans to be seen as American. A white Southern cabdriver comments on Takaki's excellent English, to which Takaki replies that his family has been in the United States for generations.[35]

The social construction of the second generation's ethnic identity reflects their experiences with external forces, such as discrimination.

Barth argues that such societal factors provide the context within which an ethnic group negotiates and redefines its group boundaries.[36] As Nagel concludes: "Ethnic identity is most closely associated with the issue of boundaries. Ethnic boundaries determine who is a member and who is not. . . . Debates over the placement of ethnic boundaries and the social worth of ethnic groups are central mechanisms in ethnic construction."[37] Barth and Nagel's views are further supported by Juanita's discussion of her relationship with other groups and her own construction of her ethnic identity. She is bothered that her Cuban friend wants to disassociate himself from Mexicans when he is mistaken for one. Her comments demonstrate her awareness of power relations between groups, and, in addition, she reinforces her preference for the term *Mexican* but, at the same time, calls herself American.

> I just say I'm Mexican. I don't say Hispanic because people can hear the word Hispanic but not know that I'm Mexican from Mexico. Well, my parents are not me. I knew this guy who was Cuban, and if people said, "Are you Mexican, are you?" he'd get so offended and say, "I'm Cuban." And I didn't like his attitude. I mean, so what? We both have darker skin than, you know, the all-American look. But he is actually lighter than me. But we're both American, but so why was he so upset that people called him Mexican? I mean, so I think he wants to make sure everybody knows he's Cuban, like this makes him more American. But I told him that I know that whites are whites and browns are browns. But I do not like to use colors. Like I said, I just say I'm Mexican.

The issues of race, power, and racial hierarchies cut across their narratives. Although Juanita later differentiated herself from her immigrant parents by stressing that she was born in the United States, she understood the shared significance of their skin color within American race relations. All respondents related stories in which they refer to their own skin color and that of others. Respondents discussed race as an unfolding and complex issue. The second generation defines *race* in terms of how their skin color sets them apart from what they believe others define as the "typical American." They position themselves near the margins of racial privilege, expressing sentiments that range from acceptance to anger. Their narratives include insightful accounts of what they call racially-

based episodes in which they respond to the negative stereotypes, prejudice, and discrimination imposed upon them by others. Their responses
are both ambiguous and contradictory but always reflect their understanding that race and ethnicity are socially constructed. They react to such
episodes by falling back on the civil rights and privileges of their American
birthright to challenge stereotypes and discrimination. Nevertheless, these
Mexican American women continue to be seen as racialized "others."

The women I interviewed grew up in predominantly Mexican immigrant and Mexican American communities. They were surrounded by a
cultural climate that they recognized as different, although not necessarily
on the margins, from the rest of American society. Their childhoods in
such largely residential segregated communities, most of which date back
generations as communities of Mexican immigrants, did not, of course,
isolate them from daily interaction with people outside their immediate
ethnic environment. Indeed, a vital part of their responses to the questions
regarding ethnic identification included references to socially constructed
terms. They inscribed a racial component to their identity but often with
words that included an understanding of how others saw them. They
spoke of how they believe others see them, which may or may not be the
ways they see themselves. This generation sees itself in a social mirror and
sees an image "colored" by negative stereotypes and created by the larger
society, which they define in terms of race hierarchies. Negative references
to skin color did not concentrate in one specific location but spanned
across their immediate neighborhoods, their high schools, and, as will be
discussed in the next chapter, their university settings. For example, Sara
likes her olive complexion, but she knows that

> in some places people treat me like I'm a foreigner or, really, like an
> illegal or something. I go into some stores in the mall near my school
> and the saleswoman looks at me like I am not there, but I think it's
> maybe she thinks since I'm young, I won't buy stuff. But then, guess
> what, I see her going right over to these blonde girls, well, white girls,
> who looked about my age.

Other respondents shared similar experiences, giving examples that
underscore how Mexican American women see their skin color as a

marker of their ethnic identity, one that forms the basis for prejudice and discrimination. One student described participating in her high school's marching band, and once, during a parade, some men yelled the disparaging phrase "little brown girls" to them. Yolanda describes this situation:

> It was so stupid. But I really got mad. I guess it was sort of sexual. They were older, sort of middle-aged guys, but I got mad because I had heard them whistling at the girls—well, you know, the Anglo girls, but they didn't say stuff about their being blonde or being white. I told my mom and she said something like that's how Americans are, and I said to myself, "Of course. Hey, but I'm American, too, but not white."

These two passages by Sara and Yolanda illustrate their understanding of a world inhabited by white or Anglo "others," a group that has often excluded them because of skin color. All respondents share an understanding that "race matters," with race usually, but not always, defined as skin color. They often conflate race with ethnicity as defined by culture, in this case, Mexican culture. They describe how others see them in racial and cultural terms. All of these sources of social identification emerge and reemerge across all incidents and within a single incident, underscoring how racial discourses reflect a highly nuanced navigation among emergent and shifting identities. Studying Mexican Americans is made even more complex based on the problematic nature of defining the group's race and ethnicity. David E. López and Ricardo D. Stanton-Salazar provide a succinct overview. According to the U.S. Census Bureau, Mexicans can be white, black Asian, or Native American, but, as López and Stanton-Salazar point out, Latino/a and Mexican are not racial terms by definition. Their historical experiences, however, underscore patterns of segregation, discrimination, prejudice, and they institutionalize racism, all of which may not affect individual Mexican Americans to the same degree, but do affect the group's collective American experience. Like their Mexican immigrant parents, these children are seen as racialized "others." Understanding these deeply embedded structures of inequality contributes directly to the social construction of ethnic identity.[38] A central theme threaded throughout the ethnic stories of these women is their recognition that, although they are seen as "the other," they never stopped referring to themselves as "American," particularly when confronting disparaging racial epithets. Their rebuttal to egregious racial slurs signifies an attempt to (re)define themselves at various levels: as a separate racial and cultural group with a different but equal position as American citizens.

Citizenship and civil rights emerge as a collective basis to fight racism, although not at the expense of eliminating pride in Mexican culture as they have defined it.

> I came home crying one day. I was with my girlfriends at the movies and some other girls, they were white, not Mexican, started pushing us out of line to get to the tickets. They said something like "these little Mexicans don't even understand us." Actually, we weren't speaking Spanish. I guess they looked at us and guessed we were Mexican and we are. We just looked at them and didn't say anything. We let them push their way up the line. See, we didn't want trouble. Now I think I should have complained because we have rights just like they do, like any American.

Again, the "other" is defined as "white," and the second generation's citizenship status is used to manage what they define as a racial incident. They identify the girls as "white, not Mexican." Interestingly, as in other examples, they define others in terms of color—white—but themselves as "Mexican." For these second-generation women, ethnicity signifies a cultural phenomenon, but one that is different from Italian, German, or Irish ethos. They do not refer to this sense of Mexican-ness— Mexicanidad—in explicitly racial terms. Instead, their most dramatic depiction of race is the word *white*, used in reference to European Americans. My interviewees see themselves as Mexican American women who are proud that their immigrant parents passed on a Mexican heritage, albeit a usually (re)imagined one. In her autobiographical essay, Christine Marín echoes such sentiments: "They [her parents] believed that I should retain our Mexican culture. I was also taught to be proud of being of Mexican descent. . . . While we knew that we were Mexican Americans and were proud of our heritage and ethnicity—a pride we learned from our parents—we also knew we were Americans."[39]

The ethnic biographies of my interviewees reveal an understanding of power relations and dynamics and that "race matters" in the United

States. Still, my subjects did not transform their ethnic cultural pride into a racialized component of their ethnic identity but, on the contrary, reinforced a sense of their rights and citizenship as the American-born daughters of Mexican immigrants:

> One day I told my mom that some girls, well, some white girls at school said that they didn't like Mexicans. It hurt me but know I can't change my skin, right? I could go but I would still be Mexican. And besides, I am just as good as anybody. My mom always tells me that I am Mexican from her but American because I just was born here.

Interestingly, for this student "Mexican" means skin color. The disparaging remarks made by "white girls" against "Mexicans" can be deconstructed to mean "my skin." At times, both skin color and nationality became conflated. One of these second-generation daughters, Angela, recalled an incident involving her father, a Mexican immigrant farm worker. She was with her father when he was pulled over for speeding. After the police officer gave him a ticket, her father told her that at least the officer did not question his citizenship. Angela recalls her conversation with her father:

> I told him I was glad that he didn't ask me if I was a citizen. My dad said that "Why should I worry since I was American and didn't have an accent?" My dad thought that I would be safe because I sounded different, you know, not like him. But I knew that I could be seen as an immigrant and in a bad way, like illegal. Why? Because I'm not, like, American looking, you know. I'm like my dad, dark. So, OK, I'm American, but others might not treat me like I belong here.

Angela sees herself as sharing her father's skin color, which for her and my other respondents serves as a basis for racial profiling. She recognizes that she may be a target for such profiling, which she detests, but she displays more indignation at the thought that she might be racially profiled because she is a citizen, unlike her immigrant father. Angela detests both positions but makes a clear distinction based on citizenship; yet, the similarity with her father's skin color is always present. None of the Mexican American women's discourses on race emerge along a linear trajectory in which they see the diminishing significance of race and ethnicity. They look at their reflections and see many things at the same time: their Mexican heritage, their citizenship, and the reality of persistent prejudice and discrimination. It remains clear, nevertheless, that a sense of citizenship has not diminished their understanding that race does indeed matter. Both dimensions are inscribed on their increasingly rich and intricately nuanced palimpsests of identity.

"Hacerle la Lucha" ["Take on the Struggle"]

Before attending college, all of the respondents but two lived in predominantly lower working-class communities with significant numbers of Mexican immigrants and Mexican Americans. Some neighborhoods experienced demographic changes over the past fifteen to twenty years, particularly with an influx of Asian immigrants such as Vietnamese. Nevertheless, these Mexican American women described their childhood communities as ones in which they were surrounded by others with similar ethnic backgrounds, immigrant experiences, and social class. They refer to social class by using a variety of sociological measures, including their parents' occupation, income, and education levels. The impact of social class on their everyday lives emerges with specific meanings for their ethnic identity. Respondents refer to their parents' struggles to succeed in the United States with their philosophy of always "haciéndole la lucha" ("taking on the struggle"). The second generation understands that their lives, like the lives of their parents, will be difficult due to their family's economic situation. Yet, this ideology strengthens the value of hard work and perseverance, although tangible upward social mobility remains largely elusive. In addition, these women contextualize their parents' economic survival strategies as an outgrowth of what they consider "Mexican culture." They understand the disadvantaged conditions within which their parents found themselves upon their U.S. arrival. As children of immigrants, these women are aware of the struggles their mothers and fathers faced as they attempted to make a new life outside of Mexico. Their experiences contrast sharply with those second-generation Filipino Americans whose parents immigrated to the United States as professionals seeking admission under specific immigration acts.[40] Respondents believe that the struggles of their parents and, above all, their determination to triumph over these struggles contributed to the development of their own ethnic identity. Sylvia expresses her pride in her parents' economic struggles:

> Life sure wasn't easy for them. When I was little I didn't really think
> about it. I mean I knew my family and other families like ours were
> different and had money issues, and, since I was just little, I didn't think
> about why. But I know now that they have worked hard, but because
> they don't have a lot of education, they can't get better jobs. But I can
> really see who they are now. Immigrants that try to make a better life
> for their kids. Now that I'm here at college, well, I had to take out a
> bunch of loans and work two jobs. I sort of see myself like them, sort of
> in a new place and struggling to get better.

Sylvia's remarks echo those of the majority of respondents who also compare themselves to their parents by drawing a parallel between their experiences as university students to those of their parents as immigrants. Their discourses on social class contain direct references to the constraints they view as part of their parents' immigrant experiences. This second generation knew that some immigrant groups came from different social-class backgrounds, ones that were more advantaged and ranked higher in economic standing than those of their parents. They described, for example, how Vietnamese immigrants had started businesses in their neighborhoods. They questioned why Mexican immigrants did not own similar businesses. Their everyday social interactions brought them face to face with people from different social classes, most of whom were not Mexican immigrants. Interestingly, respondents differentiated between the social experiences of immigrants like their parents and American-born individuals of Mexican immigrant descent. They talked about second-generation Mexican American adults with whom they interacted on a regular basis, primarily teachers, service workers, human services agency workers, and clerical workers. They described them as improving their lives because of their English language skills and education. Still, my respondents were aware of ongoing discrimination patterns and persistent inequality that maintains significant gaps between second, third, and later generations of Mexican Americans and the total U.S. population. Their parents had indeed found a better life than the one they had in Mexico, but it was permeated with the hidden and not-so-hidden injuries of social class.

My respondents' discourse on social class also focused on the lessons they learned from these experiences rather than the actual, often devastating, consequences of their family's precarious economic situations. They all discussed the significant impacts their parents' adversities had on them: a desire to work hard, to accept a life of struggle with dignity, and, above all, to maintain a spirit of optimism. A major trope that emerges across all the interviews is a powerful one: remember to "hacerle la lucha," as Julia explains:

> What I learned from my parents? That they had a hard life, but they never gave up hope for us. I know they are so proud that I was able to get this scholarship for college. It's like a final part of their life as immigrants, and, as their daughter, I know it's probably the beginning of a new kind of struggle. But, just like they didn't give up in their new surroundings, I won't either. I saw part of a film about farm workers, and my dad worked picking strawberries for a long time. It really meant something to me as a student when I saw the farm workers in the film carrying signs that said "Si Se Puede" ["Yes, it can be done"]. And I try to say to myself that my parents probably said something like this and now I will say the same. Yes, I can too.

Even though these daughters of Mexican immigrants were undergraduate students at the time of these interviews, they were aware that they represented only a very small percentage of the total Mexican American population. They expressed a serious concern that so few Mexican American students were in college. Those who had taken advanced courses in political science and sociology knew that less than 10 percent of the total Mexican American population were college graduates. Respondents identified social class constraints and discriminatory educational policies as the cause for low percentages of Mexican American college graduates. Discrimination was defined in terms that were primarily ethnic, as Marta describes: "I had teachers that didn't care about us. They made statements that I realize now were just plain racist. You know, they made comments about illegal Mexicans and how they should be deported. I just wanted to scream at her and tell her that she could be talking about my parents." Other students revealed an understanding of the structural inequalities embedded in the American education system. Several students had seen the film *The Lemon Grove Incident*, a docudrama about the 1930 attempt by the Lemon Grove California School Board to establish segregated schools for American-born children of Mexican immigrants.[41] They expressed their pride in seeing a film that showed how Mexican immigrant parents had fought against segregation. Yolanda's comments illustrate her belief, shared by many other respondents, that American institutions created and perpetuated systems of inequality for Mexican immigrants and their children:

> I saw *The Lemon Grove Incident* and it made me mad that this stuff happened, but when I saw how hard the parents fought for their rights, then I knew that I had to fight too. Other people, other groups, have to fight for their rights too. But I have to do fights like the ones in the film for my group, for Mexicans, like my parents. And more for me and others like me, who were born here. Americans but Mexican Americans.

Similarly, other students who had seen the film focused on the ethnic dimension and commented that the struggles depicted in the film were not just economic. Sara illustrates how she distinguished social class and ethnic inequality: "I saw this other film about poverty in the U.S. It showed how people in, I think, Appalachia, had no work or education. But it didn't show any racial discrimination. They were poor, but not like in *The Lemon Grove Incident* where the people were poor *and* Mexican." Margarita underscores Sara's analysis of multiple sources of oppression: "That school board didn't want a second school for poor people. I guess that there were poor whites in that place, in Lemon Grove, back then. No, the School Board said Mexicans had to be put in another school—rich, poor—all the same. But I know that all the Mexicans back then in that farm region were poor."

Another dimension of their discourse on social class focuses on the survival strategies their parents developed to deal with hidden and visible "injuries of social class."[42] Although the interviews show that respondents covered a wide variety of topics related to social class, they identified one overarching theme as a key to understanding ethnic identity. Their discussions of their families' economic status centered on the role that ethnicity plays in developing survival strategies to cope with such difficulties. The women explained the methods that their immigrant parents used to endure the ever-recurrent downward economic spirals. I suggest that these second-generation Mexican American women interpreted their parents' survival strategies as an important part of their parents' Mexican culture and way of life. Whether or not their parents share this view is not the point, but what is important are the meanings attached by the second generation to the development of specific survival strategies. These women believe that their "Mexicanidad" shaped key survival strategies adopted by their parents. That is, the second generation believes that ethnicity, in this case, Mexican heritage, led to the development of specific coping mechanisms. Thus, their responses to such coping strategies play a role in the formation of their ethnic identity.

Respondents observed the ways their immigrant parents and their compatriots responded to financial difficulties. For example, a common crisis involved lack of money near the end of the month. With payday a week away, many immigrant families found themselves without cash. Most had some kind of credit card and access to cash advances through these cards. In addition, families of my respondents lived in neighborhoods with "cash stores," providing customers with money at high interest rates using their next paycheck as collateral. Interestingly, only two respondents said that their parents had selected one or both of these options. The majority of parents borrowed money from relatives who lived nearby or coworkers who were also Mexican immigrants. Only five of the respondents owned their homes, while the rest rented houses or apartments. All of their parents were capable of negotiating within the American system of bank and loan companies, but the majority expressed a preference for informal networks for their personal loans. Not quite at the level of rotating credit associations as those studied by Ivan Light among Japanese and Chinese immigrants, Mexican immigrants operated loosely organized loan networks that served as safety nets in times of limited economic crisis.[43] Immigrants needing large loans for such things as appliances, cars, or other major expenses turned to formal lending agencies, but, according to their daughters, they preferred what respondents called *compadre* loans. Respondents described the *compadre* system of fictive kinship between Mexicans as a process by which their parents selected other couples, relatives, or friends to be co-parents for their children at various religious rituals starting at baptism with the selection of godparents. The relationship of co-parents, or *compadres* and *comadres*, is created between the two sets of couples: the parents of the child to be baptized and the godparents.[44] Although other ethnic groups, such as Italians, share this practice, my respondents referred to this custom and its basis for economic assistance between couples as a "very Mexican thing." María's description of this practice echoes that of the other Mexican American women:

> Sometimes my mom ran out of money before my Dad got paid. Some-times it was because something came up unexpectedly. Once when the car broke down and my mom called my godmother and they talked and arranged things. She gave us the money and then we paid it back in two months. This happened all the time and it's really interesting that with-out writing things down, they kept things straight. My mom told me that this is what they would do in Mexico, well, what her parents would do. I know I will never be that way, that Mexican, because I don't have the same kind of ties with people so I'll have to do it the regular Ameri-can way.

This passage is important because, as discussed earlier in this chapter, María constructs an ethnic group boundary around her parents and their "Mexican" ways by admitting her preference for "the regular American way." Similarly, Diana witnessed such lending practices as "Mexican ones" and, like María, said that she would probably never use such a sys-tem. Nevertheless, Diana made a significant and insightful comment toward an understanding of the social construction of ethnic identity among the second generation:

> Some of my friends' parents who are like mine—Mexicans well, immi-grants—do this kind of stuff all the time. One family borrows from another family and back and forth. No interest, of course. Well, this is definitely something from back in Mexico. But I can see how it might work for someone like me. I guess I can just keep it as something I could dig up if I ever wanted to, but it's still not really my way of doing things, but you never know what I might do.

Other respondents also defined their parents' survival strategies as an out-come of their "Mexican way" of dealing with their precarious financial circumstances. They referred to such cultural practices as a "Mexican way" of weathering a temporary economic crisis, but they also indicated that they would "file this away" "within me" or "in some place in me." Moreover, and most importantly for an understanding of social class's role in the formation of their ethnic identity, respondents made seemingly contradictory statements. On the one hand, they insisted that such economic survival strategies were too "Mexican" for them. Yet, on the other hand, they tempered such statements by recognizing that these survival skills were in fact tactics they might need in the future. Still, they were left with contradictions and ambiguities, as Elena concludes: "I know that this practice is a very Mexican-like practice. I know that I probably won't ever use it, but, if I do and others like me do, then is it still a Mexican thing or what? I'm getting really confused the more I answer these questions."

In general, by reflecting on their parents' immigrant experiences, the second generation revealed a process of self-reflection, one that revolved around a basic question: What lessons does the first generation pass on to the second and how do they affect the second generation? Ultimately, then, their discourse on their immigrant family's social class focused on the socially constructed meanings that they, as the American-born children of Mexican immigrants, attach to social class as a dynamic process of social relationships and power.

"I Know I Should Like the Way I Look, but Sometimes I Just Can't"

The second generation's "beauty image" narratives underscore that ethnicity is gendered and gender is ethnic. The women's definitions of human beauty do not include words such as "colors like mine, like darker, not blonde." Their narratives show that they possess a "geographic map" of their skin color, which they define in terms of power differentials and a hierarchy of privilege. Images of beauty confront these women every day. As these Mexican American women discussed their emergent ethnic identities, the issue of beauty standards unfolds as they comment on the lack of popular cultural images depicting Latinas, specifically Mexican Americans. All of the respondents talked about "the beauty myth."[45] In discussing their ethnic identities, many women referred to some aspect of the "way I look" and how "this, sort of tells something about me." The question remains: What is this "something" and how do the second generation respond to it? References to their physical appearance focus on their coloring, primarily their skin color but also their eye and hair color within the context of what they define as the "typical American look." Julia gave the following example:

> Once, in high school, I knew a Mexican girl, well, she was Mexican American like me, and she wanted to save her money to buy blue contact lenses. She didn't even need to wear them, well, she could see fine without them. But she said she wanted what she called cool eyes, prettier eyes than hers. She had dark eyes just like mine. I laughed and told her to save her money, but I should tell you, I might want to try some to see what it would be to have blue eyes. Odd, right?

The longing for "whiteness" or other characteristics of whiteness such as blue eyes is a common theme in the writings of Latina, African American, and Asian American women. Perhaps the most dramatic example remains Toni Morrison's *The Bluest Eye*, in which the protagonist, Pecola, dreams of transforming herself and having what she considers the most treasured feature, the one that she believes will make people love her— blue eyes.[46] My respondents all share this hidden desire to look, "you know, sort of white," by expressing varying degrees of anxiety about how they measure themselves using beauty myth standards.

Later chapters will show that respondents in this study present themselves as fiercely independent and active agents, yet they also possess another seemingly incongruous dimension to their identity: a racial insecurity associated with their attempts to attain idealized standards of beauty. Although they respond to racial slurs and behavior with a deepened sense of their civil rights as American citizens, at a more personal, intimate level, they also question their ability to measure up to the beauty standards imposed on all women. Their anxiety and anger concerning these beauty standards are eloquently captured by Chicana poet Inés Hernández in the first stanza of her poem "To Other Women who Were Ugly Once": "Do you remember how we used to panic / when Cosmo, Vogue, and Mademoiselle / ladies would Glamour-us out of / existence?"[47] Other ethnic poets echo the relationship between identity and beauty defined in Anglo European terms. In the first stanza of her poem, "In Magazines (I Found Specimens of the Beautiful)," Ekuo Omosupe looks for herself in magazines such as *Seventeen* and *Cosmopolitan* where "among blue eyes, blonde hair, white skin, thin bodies" she realized that she was indeed the "Other." Omosupe's poem also conveys a sense of self-hate; she hated the "shroud of Blackness that makes [her] invisible a negative print."[48] For Hernández, Omosupe, and second-generation Mexican American women, unattainable standards of beauty led them to question their sense of beauty. Some of my respondents, like Hernández who became "cold inside" and Omosupe who became "invisible a negative print," felt uncomfortable in their skin; however, in other parts of the interviews, they would express their equally strong sense of self in terms of achieving a higher education. Interestingly, all the Mexican American women were familiar with the magazine *Latina*, a "Latinized" version of *Cosmopolitan*, as one respondent described it. All agreed that at least a magazine existed that focused on Latinas, but most quickly pointed out that the magazine's ads were often the same as ads found in other beauty magazines. And even the ads with "you know, Latina-looking women, they are usually all stick skinny."

My respondents, like all women, are confronted with unattainable body images and the "color line." Their self-expressions include both a pride in their cultural distinctiveness and a concern, often turned into anger, with their skin color. Still, like all Mexican Americans, these women possess a wide range of skin coloring. Only two referred to themselves as "guerra" (light-skinned), with the majority using such terms as "morena," "dark," "sort of bronze," "kind of olive," and "chocolate."[49] Although all of the women expressed an understanding of the indigenous element associated with Mexico, none of them used the term *Mestiza* as a form of self-identification. Alicia defines *Mexican* as part Spanish and part Indian:

> Well, historically, Mexico is a racially mixed society. Spaniards colonized what is now Mexico and then intermarried and eventually everybody in Mexico has some Indian blood. It's what makes some of us darker. I can actually pass as not Mexican, as something like Italian, because I am light but not light enough for some. I still look different from . . . what people call "the all-American" look for ads and things But its weird, my cousins from Mexico still call me "la Americana" and make fun of my Spanish.

This definition of *Mexican* captures the usual racial definition: the mix of the Spanish and the indigenous produced the concept of *Mestizo* and *Mestiza* as racial terms. Alicia recognizes both the variation in skin coloring among Mexicans, pointing out her own "lightness." Nevertheless, she agrees with other respondents who describe themselves as "light-skinned" or "lighter," that her lightness is still darker than the "all-American look." These women, all of whom identify as Americans and as women of Mexican heritage, recognize the existence and impact of racial hierarchy within American society, and specifically within the development of racial standards of beauty. As in other examples, the passage quoted above includes a reference to the respondents being the "American 'other'" in comparison to their Mexican relatives, but this juxtaposition is one based on language, not skin color. Their Mexican relatives define these women as English-speaking Americans with limited Spanish skills, yet none refer to their skin color. Writer Mary Helen Ponce makes an interesting comparison in which she differentiates her ethnic self from an "American" Virgin Mary with Anglo features. The young Mary Helen ultimately identifies with the English-speaking image of the Virgin Mary. Ponce describes the Virgin Mary as blue-eyed and blonde and, in addition, refers to the "Indian" to whom the Virgin of Guadalupe is said to have appeared. Her preference for the "American" Mary, however, is based on language, not race.[50]

Body size represents an additional dimension to the discourse on the "beauty myth." As with skin color, body size varies among the women in this sample, but all of the women's narratives include some discussions of body images associated with their ethnic identities. Most importantly, discussions of body types and sizes emerge as a discourse closely intertwined with their ethnic selves. Anna explains her criticism of the magazine *Latina*:

> I like to read some of the stories especially about Latinas who are business owners or in other professions. But I don't like to have to see all those ads right next to them showing all those skinny women. You know, they are Latinas, like the name of the magazine, right? But they still look like all those in the other mainstream magazines. I don't like it. It's good to see role models for us, but then the magazine becomes one more example of trying to make women, not just Latinas, fit into a mold.

Like Anna, others recognize the contradiction of a magazine that includes stories about successful Latinas yet, at the same, includes advertisements replicating unattainable beauty standards found in mainstream magazines such as *Cosmopolitan* or *Vogue*. Mixed messages are being sent to these young women: take pride in your identity and, as one respondent said, "try to be, well, to look like us, the models in the ads."

The issues of body image and ethnic identify unfolded in ways that were not always clear to these Mexican American women. Their views on body image did not direct their reflections on their ethnic identities, rather, these views wove themselves into a discursive space as the women found themselves probing deeper into themselves. Their reflections on what they all agree are unattainable beauty standards contain stark contradictions and ambiguities, more similar to their discourses on ethnicity than to those on social class. Although they challenge socially imposed concepts of beauty and, in addition, recognize the racial component evident in the American beauty myth, these Mexican American women engage in behavior that could be construed as falling into the beauty myth trap. All admit that they have tried to "look more like the ads in the magazines," or "see what I would like if I did something drastic," or, even more dramatically, "see if I could be somebody else." They lightened their hair with blond streaks, stayed out of the sun so as not to "get even darker," and, most commonly, dieted, often excessively. They discussed the first two practices in a variety of ways; they wanted to experience being "guerra," or "almost blonde," or, most evocatively, to "look like one of those 'white skinny models.'" Their critique of beauty ads did not preclude them from participating in behavior influenced by them. They admitted being aware of such contradictions and reflected on them in an attempt to understand them. Sara conveys a deeply rooted frustration with falling into the "beauty trap" myth.

> I know I should know better. I know I should like the way I look, but sometimes I just can't. I look at those ads for mascara, for eye shadow, for lipstick, and I want to go buy them and try to look like that. So do my friends and, of course, we would never be caught without at least some make-up. I sound so, you know, critical, but then I go out and buy stuff. And then I also try and starve myself, or else what's the use of

having all this make-up if you are, you know, sort of gordita [diminutive for fat]?

Julia expressed similar contradictions. She wants to "look good" but added:

> I think if I don't look good all over, not just my face and hair, then I won't feel good. I think a lot of us Mexicans have trouble with weight, well, almost all my friends do. My mom says not to worry, it's something I can't control. She makes it sound like it's genetic, but I think I can be a thin person, but I haven't been able to see much results. I think it's a stereotype of Mexican women, being fat, or, well, bigger than white girls. So I feel more pressure. I want to be me, to be proud of my Mexican past, but I don't want to be fat. All the Anglo girls are thin and all the nice clothes seem to be made for skinny girls. I try and look skinnier by wearing baggy clothes, but I know it doesn't work. It makes me feel bad.

Interestingly, Julia recalled how her mother tried to lessen her concerns by intimating that Mexican women cannot control predisposed genetic propensities to be overweight. The voices of these Mexican American women resonate with feelings of confusion and anger as they try to refashion and remake themselves using traditional beauty standards. Their words capture both the agony that all women deal with in striving for unrealistic beauty, and they grapple with what they see as social stereotypes of what "Mexican women look like." "Starving" as a form of dieting is dangerous for anyone but becomes even more so when this is coupled with the pressure of avoiding ethnic stereotypes. At the same time that these second-generation women described themselves as strong and self-confident, they also demonstrated deep anxieties about racial hierarchies and standards of beauty. Both of these contribute to the process of their identity formation. They struggle to transform themselves into the accepted, classic standard of beauty, but they also struggled to challenge the beauty myth. The tension between the two is yet another dimension of their gendered ethnic identity. In addition, these women attach additional meanings to their sense of ethnic and social class identities as they navigated through the world of higher education, a world geographically and culturally removed from their own and, above all, that of their Mexican immigrant parents.

Overview

The emergent gendered ethnic identities of second-generation Mexican American women reveal various components, all of which are inscribed on what I have been calling their palimpsests of identity. They (re)negotiated the identity boundaries between themselves and their parents, their communities, American society, and Mexico. Respondents examined the meanings that they attach to their ethnicity, ones that emerge fluid and contingent. Their second-generation ethnic identities blend and collide with their parents' sense of "Mexicanidad." They move between their Mexican and Mexican American geographies, layering and maintaining both, with aspects of each reappearing throughout their narratives. In addition, they confront the external forces, such as stereotypes, prejudice, and discrimination, all of which result in renegotiating their ethnic group boundaries and emergent ethnicity. Their parents see them as children with a generational Mexican past, yet they reinforce their strong preferences that they embrace an American present and future. The second generation prefers a "Mexican American" ethnic attachment but moves between the two—a postmodern social construction of ethnic identities where boundaries are fluid, never fixed, and always emergent.

Nevertheless, the second generation confronts the process through which they are labeled and treated as *other*, a term full of tensions and contradictions carrying deep-rooted anti-immigrant sentiments. Finding themselves objectified as "foreign" and, at times, "illegal," these second-generation Mexican American women (re)negotiate their ethnicity by stressing their citizenship. This emphasis leads them to once again redefine their generational distinctiveness from their Mexican immigrant parents.

Studying the ethnic identities of the second generation requires a systematic analysis of social class and gender, variables critical to the emergence and construction of meanings attached to ethnicity. Their parents' daily struggles to "hacerle la lucha" represent a solution to understanding their identity formation. Their parents' ethic of hard work and their belief in the American Dream became ideational touchstones for the second generations' own struggles with their sense of self, culture, and society. Such identity struggles involve still another component: an unfolding gendered ethnic identity. These second-generation Mexican American women look at themselves through racialized beauty standards, ones that are more complicated by ethnicity. They contest these standards, but often find themselves embracing them anyway. These gendered ethnic tensions usually remain unresolved, but the process reveals their understanding that their identities are problematic and ambiguous, remaining sites of contestation that become more dramatic when confronted with their familys' patriarchal constraints.

CONFRONTING AND CONTESTING PATRIARCHAL CONSTRAINTS

Second-generation Mexican American women struggle to gain access to and succeed in higher education. They experience a combination of ethnic and gender-specific obstacles within their families, specifically with their fathers. Their mothers serve as role models by exposing their daughters to the various types of gender difficulties they experienced within their families. This chapter examines the patriarchal constraints placed on these women and the gender strategies and gender transgressive behavior they developed to contest such constraints.

Not-So-Dutiful Daughters

A common theme among my interviews with Mexican American women students involves their emergent identities as university students and daughters of Mexican immigrant parents. The majority of the students lived on campus, with only four living at home, but within fifteen miles of the campus. Of these campus residents, almost two-thirds of their families lived in the surrounding area, facilitating their face-to-face interactions with their families, usually on the weekends and school holidays, with some students returning home a few nights during the school week. The women recognized the differences between these two worlds, but they claimed both as their own. They spoke of going home on the weekends and brought their college life into the private world of their families, focusing on the tensions produced by this engendered cultural and generational collision. Carmen described her reaction to the contradictions between these two worlds:

> My parents didn't like the way I would spend time in my room with the door closed to study. Lots of my relatives would come to visit, especially on Sunday afternoons, and this is when I wanted to get some homework

done, before I went back to the dorms. But I could really feel the pressure to stop and go be with them. But then, you know, it was funny, my parents, more my dad, would make me feel guilty for not being with everyone, but then, if I finally gave in, you know what he would say? Well, he would go on and on about how proud he was of me, telling my aunt and uncle about how I got good grades.

Respondents discussed the various strategies they adopted to deal with such situations. In order to avoid family gatherings that usually started around lunchtime on Sundays, some students told their parents that they needed to return to the university on Sunday morning to use the computer labs, since the majority of my respondents did not have home computers. Respondent after respondent expressed ambivalence regarding the pressures of succeeding at the university, while at the same time they respected their fathers' views concerning the "proper" behavior for young women like themselves. Their actions clearly demonstrate concerted contestations of patriarchal authority. Julia related the following example:

Sometimes he [her father] drives me crazy. I am so pressured, but when I get really mad, I try to remember something. My mom and dad were always telling me and my brothers that they always dreamed of a better life for us. You know, they started out as farm workers when they got here from Mexico. And now my mom works in a factory and my dad works for a construction place. They don't want us to work at these kinds of jobs. My mom says her dream is for us kids to be "profesiónales"—professionals like a teacher, or doctor, or lawyer. Something like that. The whole American dream thing. But it still makes it hard for me to go home on the weekends and study and do what my dad wants. I'm not like that anymore. I've had to change.

The gender constraints experienced by these Mexican American women represent a common trope throughout their life stories. The women identified gender as a major constraint in their parent-daughter relationships, but specifically with their fathers. All agreed that their parents wanted a better life for them; the interviews contained an overwhelming number of passages in which they expressed their gratitude and love for their parents. Respondents became emotional, usually cried and even, in some case, asked the interviewer to stop the tape recorder in order to collect themselves. Yet, none of the women asked to end the interview, and, in many cases, they continued to talk about their gratitude for all their parents' sacrifices. Nevertheless, respondents made a smooth transition to a discussion of gender constraints. Although they expressed their gratitude for the sacrifices endured by their fathers, they also verbalized their negative experiences with the gender constraints placed on them by their fathers. Julia and others were critical of their fathers' expression of patriarchal ideology, expressing their contestation in terms of "blocking it out," "keeping it to myself," and "just sort of ignoring him." They were quick to point out that their silence did not reflect their lack of resistance to patriarchal authority but, rather, represented a nonverbal but judicious strategic gender strategy. Sonia explained her experienced with such a strategy:

> He would treat me like a little girl, not the way he treats my brothers, and I'm older. He still says that he hopes I find a nice guy and get married. But it's good that I go to college. He says something like "you just better stay in school in case something happens to your husband." I've heard this so many times I just block it out now.

Other women also received mixed messages from their fathers who, on the one hand, expressed pride that their daughters were attending college but then, on the other hand, tried to make their daughters accept traditional gender roles. Anna described a typical weekend during the school year:

> My dad would insist on picking me up at my dorm at around 5 p.m. on Friday afternoons, take me home, and then drive me back to school just before my first class on Mondays. He said that he didn't want me to be on campus over the weekend because he didn't think this was proper for a girl. I hated this. I told him I had actually stayed at school a few times and that I hadn't gotten in any trouble. He said something like he didn't know what's going on. Maybe it's a control thing. He just doesn't get it. I guess he means well, but I want to shout and say "I not a little girl anymore."

Another respondent, Yolanda, had just read Sandra Cisneros's *The House on Mango Street* for one of her English classes.[1] When she started to talk about her parents, she focused on her relationship with her father. This student reached for her copy of the book and pointed out one of her favorite passages: "Not a flat. Not an apartment in back. Not a man's house. Not a daddy's. A house all my own."[2] Another respondent described her dorm room as her own private place where she could "breathe on my own, away from my dad and his rules." Margarita used a family gathering to express her new "room of her own."

> It was my grandfather's birthday and my dad wanted it to be really special. It was his father. Anyway, he called me up at school and said that he would pick me up on Saturday morning so I could help my mom and sisters with getting the house ready. Of course, he didn't include my brothers in the housecleaning and cooking chores. I had a paper and a test on Monday and I needed to work on all this on Saturday since I would be home all day Sunday for the party. Well, my Dad got really mad and said that I had to do this. I didn't want to get into an argument so I did go along, but I knew that it was only a little victory for him because I did have my own little world now here at school where I come and go when I want to come and go. I do get homesick and my dorm room is crowded and I don't really like my roommate, but since she is usually gone all weekend I usually have the room to myself and I really just like to sit there and have the freedom to just do what I want.

Margarita adopts a gender strategy similar to those described in Vicki Ruiz's study of Mexican American women. Her research illustrates how Mexican cultural changes and continuities can exist within Mexican immigrant families. The second-generation Mexican American women in Ruiz's study, like those in my study, created spaces for themselves outside their immigrant homes, developing a network of coping strategies in their attempts to reconcile these distinct cultural and social spaces.[3] For Margarita, freedom from patriarchal authority enabled her to "sit" in her dorm room and "have the freedom to just do what [she] want[s]."

Like the women in Ruiz's study, all of my respondents discussed the various kinds of gender constraints that their fathers placed on their everyday lives. These patriarchal constraints took the form of both verbal exchanges and attempts to limit their behavior. During weekend trips home and on longer vacations, they received contradictory messages from their fathers who expressed pride in their college educations. Yet, at the same time, their fathers also hoped that their daughters would marry and settle down with children, often excluding the possibility that daughters could succeed at both a career and a family. As Lucia recalls:

> I would get really mad at my dad for telling me things about what girls can do or can't. I would just explode inside. I finally decided to try and tell him how I felt, but it didn't work out. He just went into this thing about it was great for me to be in school but that girls had to be sure that they didn't get a bad reputation. I just gave up. Besides, I knew I would be going back to my dorm and then I would just go on being what I want.

Lucia's concluding statement represents a powerful strategic gender strategy: deliberate silence designed as a sign of silent rebellion. Like Lucia, Elena spoke of adopting silence "to calm the situation but not to give in." Other respondents developed this gender strategy, knowing that they were already able, in Lucia's words, to "just go on being what [they] want." The university setting represents a feminist space of independence where second-generation women can (re)invent themselves, although not without conflict and ambiguity. This passage links the gender struggles of second-generation Mexican American women to an articulation of a gendered identity. Their struggles intensified their sense of independence as women and their transitional status as undergraduate women. Other women, like Margarita, talked about their dorm "space" as a place where they can "just like sit there and have the freedom to do just what [they] want to." Lucia and other respondents contested their father's authority and, in the process, became more aware of an unfolding, but often ambiguous, gendered layer of identity. Many of the women talked about their experiences with their fathers' patriarchal authority in an extremely animated manner, often recreating their anger and exasperation, which is not always apparent in my transcriptions. Diana, like several other women, spoke rapidly in an angry tone, demonstrating dramatically visible signs of her anger:

> I've gotten into so many discussions over the traditional Mexican woman role with him. He'll say that and I tell him, "So what do you want?"—I mean I am not going to do what he wants, I know that, but just to see what he'll say. I say, "You're saying you want me to go to

school, you want me to get an education, you want me to be financially secure so I won't have to depend on my husband, but then at the same time you want me to stay home to support him in the house, to be at home when he's at home, to have everything okay so he won't get mad, because if something is not right at home he's going to be upset and it's going to be my fault because I didn't follow along with the traditional role of the Mexican woman. I mean we've gotten in a lot of discussions about that. He says, "Well, that's how the Mexican woman was. That's how Mexican women should always be. That's what makes the man happy." I mean it's like, I don't know, there's no way that I will ever change his view. And sometimes it's kind of like, we can go on about it and I reach the point where it's kind of like, it's hopeless. There's no point in continuing this. His feelings aren't going to change. But I am. Actually I already have. I am not what he wants me to be. I'm not that Mexican woman and you know what? My mom isn't either anymore.

Diana's passage captures the feelings and emotions depicted by almost all of the respondents. She challenges, almost taunts her father in order to set a stage for a direct confrontation. Her strategy, direct and argumentative, was not adopted by all the women, but her self-affirmation as a woman (that is, "not what he [her father] wants me to be") resonates among all the respondents in one form or another. Moreover, her understanding of her gendered identity is explicitly grounded in an ethnic context. Her father refers to "how the Mexican woman was and that's how the Mexican woman should always be." Diana overcomes the angry confrontation with her father by concluding this story with a positive gender affirmation for herself and, surprisingly, for her mother. Sonia and the other second-generation women in this study moved away from what their Mexican immigrant fathers defined as a traditional Mexican woman and, recognizing that their mothers were also challenging such a gendered ethnic stereotype, began to (re)invent themselves into women who were not, or perhaps never were, "dutiful daughters."[4]

The literature on the dynamic relationship between the exertion of patriarchal authority and the repression of women's sexuality represents one of the fastest growing areas of scholarly research within Latina Studies. Earlier works focused explicitly on the issue of male domination—machismo—and its origin, development, and degree within Mexican and Mexican American families. A major theoretical and empirical debate addressed an overarching theme: the role of machismo—exaggerated masculinity—as men's response to the external constraints of prejudice, discrimination, and racism. The issue was both a scholarly and politically charged one, particularly in the 1960s and 1970s, during the social protest and cultural nationalist Chicano/a Movement known as "El Movimiento." Many argued, from a cultural nationalist perspective, that racism produced male domination within Chicano/a communities, and, therefore, the issue would be resolved with a decline in racism. In response to those who privileged the struggle against racism over sexism, Chicana feminists replaced a strictly cultural nationalist framework with an emerging Chicana feminist discourse that focused on the system of patriarchy and its concomitant patriarchal ideology and behavior as a universal phenomenon rather than a cultural one, specifically one originating with a Mexican cultural framework.[5] Chicana feminist scholarship addressed the patriarchal control of female sexuality, such as that expressed within the gendered ethnic narratives by the second-generation Mexican American women in this study. Chicana Studies scholars have established a discursive space within which to address, in a politicized academic context, the issues of patriarchy, sexuality (heterosexual and lesbian), misogyny, and other aspects related to the domination and suppression of women. Chicana and Latina creative writers and artists from all fields have contributed to this discourse, strengthening the "space" within which gender boundaries, sexual oppression, and gender transgression have been challenged. The groundbreaking works of scholars (such as Norma Alarcón, Gloria Anzaldúa, Cordelia Candelaria, Antonia Castañeda, Ana Castillo, Teresa Córdova, Deena J. González, Cherríe Moraga, Cynthia Orozco, Emma Pérez, Beatriz Pesquera, Sonia Saldívar-Hull, Chela Sandoval, Carla Trujillo, and many more) have all contributed to this critical area in understanding the experiences of Mexican, Chicana, Latina, and all women in general.[6] As Saldívar-Hull concludes: "To completely understand the complexities of the Chicana and Chicano subjectivity in the greater borderlands of the United States, discussions of gender and sexuality are central in our oppositional and liberatory projects."[7] These scholars' intellectual frameworks and ongoing research and cultural productions have provided me with "tools" to interpret the themes of patriarchal constraints recorded in my respondents' gendered ethnic narratives. Their narratives uncover the development of specific gender responses, provid-

ing further insight into their unfolding identities as they contest patriarchal authority, specifically its attempts to control their sexuality. The last
section of this chapter will return to these themes by analyzing their relationships with Mexican American male students in the university.

The respondents did not share the same specific experience or reactions to patriarchal authority, but they did share a generalized resistance.
Many described their reactions to their fathers' attempts to impose traditional gender scripts, with a combination of these responses moving back
and forth and, at times, manifesting combinations of responses during
specific family episodes. Gender contestation is one of the most common
reactions to traditional gender-specific constraints experienced within
their families, specifically with their fathers. Several women developed an
interesting form of contestation that involved writing a letter to their
fathers outlining their "gender contestations." Margarita, one of the only
respondents who played sports and had to travel to various events
throughout the state, vividly recalls the letter that she wrote to her father:

> I would have to travel with the team and, yeah, we would go out and
> party at the end of the meet. I would get into arguments with my dad
> when I tried to explain this to him. "Well, let me tell you, dad." One
> day, for I think it was Christmas, I didn't have any money basically, but
> I would always make cards. Well, I made him this card and I made him
> a letter and I said, "I don't understand why you don't let me go out with
> my guy friends." You know, they were like just friends, and I said, "I
> know that all the other girls do it, have sex, but it doesn't mean that I
> will too," but you just have to understand because guys would always
> come to my house, but it was always like, I'm better friends with guys
> than girls. The guys would always come knocking on my door, and my
> dad would throw a fit—"I don't want them in this house, how could
> they disrespect my house like this?" And I was like, "What are you talk-
> ing about?" Did I tell you that the last thing I said in that letter to my
> dad was "it was just normal for me to talk to guys and have them over"?

Interestingly, the respondents often used the idea of "normal" gender
roles and behavior as a common rebuttal to their fathers' patriarchal constraints and power dynamics. They contested patriarchal authority and
power by arguing that such relationships were not normal and, more
importantly, were detrimental to their success as college students. For

these women, patriarchal authority imposed gender roles and behavior that were "crazy, just crazy," "from another time," "ridiculous," and, "something that just doesn't make sense to me." Their challenges to patriarchal constraints and sexual repression corresponded to other studies on second-generation women. For example, Robert Anthony Orsi's work on Italian women established a direct relationship between a community's attempt to maintain its identity with its enforcement of rigid gender roles and boundaries, ones that attempted to "safeguard" the highly prized "Madonna of 115th Street," the title of Orsi's monograph.[8] Such a practice, according to Janet Mancini Billson, is an outgrowth of immigrant men seeing themselves as "keepers of the culture" of their countries of origin, in this study's case, Mexico. "Their" women were cast in a light that made them responsible for cultural maintenance in U.S. society. Impositions of patriarchal authority and a sexually repressive moral code for women originated as immigrants struggled to keep their cultural values and morality, and above all, their daughters' virtue "intact."[9] In her study of Filipina Americans, Yen Le Espiritu concludes that, "because women's moral and sexual loyalties were deemed central to the maintenance of group status, changes in female behavior, especially that of growing daughters, were interpreted as signs of moral decay and ethnic suicide and were carefully monitored and sanctioned."[10] Other studies reveal that immigrants value a close-knit family network in their new surroundings and, as a result, build the foundation for patriarchal control of their American-born daughters' sexuality.[11] My respondents documented such attempts by their families, specifically their fathers, to control their sexuality. Other letters of gender contestation echo this theme. Jackie described the letter that she sent to her father:

> I finally wrote this letter. "Why can't you understand? It's not like I'm going to do anything and, if anything, I'm a lot more moral." . . . [He referred to] my girlfriends who had gotten pregnant when we were in high school. I would hang around with them, but I wasn't living on the edge. I would always think, "I'm a leader not a follower." That was my main thing and I think that really helped me because if it weren't for that little attitude that I would have been right there with them. But anyway, back to my letter. So he would always bring up statistics like if you ever saw something in the newspaper, he would say, "Oh, they say

here that Latina women have a fifty percent chance of being pregnant by the time that they're a certain age." And like my dad totally threw that in my face and because he didn't know that much about me. I thought I was the model child and would tell him, "Why don't you trust me and accept me and understand?" But my Dad had no way of knowing that because he never saw the real me. But I just wrote this letter telling him like all the things I did and he was really surprised. I guess the letter worked sort of because he backed off after he read it but, you know, it was one way. He didn't say anything really to me and what I talked about in the letter. So I just figured, OK, I did it and that's it and next time when we go through this I will say, "Remember that letter I wrote you?"

Jackie defined herself as having a "little attitude" that, in her opinion, enabled her to overcome such problems as teenage pregnancy and her father's gender restrictions. Other respondents defined themselves using similar terms, such as "pushy," "outspoken," "kind of headstrong," "a fighter for what I want," and "someone who won't stand for people telling me what to do or what to be like." Time and again, these second-generation women associate who they were with what they learned from their mothers' power struggles with their fathers.

Immigrant Mothers and Gender Transgressions

The second-generation daughters I interviewed also contextualized their reactions to gender constraints by analyzing the relationship between their fathers and their mothers. They described specific examples of what many referred to as their fathers' "traditional stuff." By focusing on their parents' interaction with each other, respondents were able to reflect on their own gendered lives and identities. Diana describes her family's gender dynamics:

Growing up my mother would always have to have food on the table when my father came home from work or he would throw a fit. And I always told myself I want to tell my mom, "Why don't you care that he yells about this and why don't you yell back?" I couldn't understand why he'd get so upset just because he didn't have his food on the table.

Because he came home from work tired. So what? My mom got tired, too, taking care of us. He would say stuff like he's a man and she's a woman. And like growing up, I always contradicted my father and we would get to arguing because he's really not power hungry but, you know, he likes to have power and when I would go against [him], he would like really get upset. But, yeah, I saw my mother and she would cry. It still happens when I go home for the weekends. I tell myself all the time that I'm not going to be like my mom. I'm not going to be like her and let guys, people, nobody tell me what to do. I don't care what they say or think. That's it, I'm me.

Yolanda found herself in a similar situation as Diana, believing that "something's really wrong when a man expects things to be done for him all the time." Such passages illustrate a highly nuanced discourse. At one level, women display various responses to observed gender constraints placed on them within their families. Their accounts document their growing realization that, in the words of one woman, "something wasn't right." But, unlike Betty Friedan's generation of women whose "problem had no name," these women identified the source of the gender constraints within their families: their father's patriarchal ideology and belief in a masculine power hierarchy over women.[12] Second-generation women question their father's display of male dominance and attempts to consolidate patriarchal power. Their voices resound with explicit gender contestations that contributed to their emerging gendered identities. Their words resonate with self-affirmation and self-determination, both within their families as they challenged their fathers' power and within the larger society in general. For example, Carmen referred to *The House on Mango Street* by Sandra Cisneros.[13] In the chapter "Beautiful and Cruel," the novel's protagonist Esperanza conveys that she wants to start her own gender war by leaving the dinner table "like a man, without putting back the chair or picking up the plate."[14] Carmen, however, put a different spin on this often-quoted passage, one that is usually seen as an example of a woman's challenge to male dominance. Carmen stressed the need for both women and men to avoid sexist behavior: "nobody, not a guy or a woman, should leave stuff like that, you know, for someone else to pick up or clean. Everybody has to be equal. I want to push my chair back myself, you know, I don't want someone to pick up after me."

Although their contestations of gender emphasized a generalized feminist ideology that rejected privileging one gender over another, this did not minimize their strident challenges to their own immediate gender struggles with their fathers. Their stories document direct challenges to a patriarchal world, illustrating their emergence as active agents engaged in dramatic contestations over their identities as women and as daughters. Their gendered ethnic narratives illustrate their newfound ability to define themselves in juxtaposition with their fathers' version of an idealized Mexican woman whose identity becomes limited by such patriarchal constraints. Others in this study echo Julia's comments: "I'm me, lots of things. I'm still sorting stuff out about who I am, but I'm not somebody to be pushed around like I've seen my dad with my mom or others. Nope, not me, no way."

This process "of sorting things out" represents an internal dialogue in which Julia and the other respondents looked for answers to questions about their identity and strategies with which to overcome patriarchal constraints encountered with their Mexican immigrant fathers. Respondents identified "all the stuff my mom taught me" as a key to dealing with patriarchal authority. A common theme in their interviews involved their identification of their mother's role in molding them into strong, independent women conscious of a surrounding world, beginning in their families, in which they would experience gender constraints. They described their mothers as Mexican immigrant women who had spent the majority of their lives working in the paid labor force, almost exclusively in the service sector. None of their mothers had more than a high-school education. However, their immigrant mothers were teaching their daughters techniques to challenge existing gender boundaries. Given the economic demands of a working-class family background, their mothers, like most women, had always been forced to balance the demands of the family and the workplace.[15] In fact, studies of Mexican immigrant women have documented their contestations of traditional gender relations. While Mexican immigrant culture is far from culturally monolithic, research on Mexican immigrant families documents a continuum of gender segregated roles and varying degrees of patriarchal ideologies and behavior. Maxine Molyneux defines such strategic gender interests as actions intended to challenge existing forms of women's subordination, particularly within the family with an emphasis on childbearing and housework.[16] According to the respondents, their Mexican immigrant mothers found themselves accepting traditional gender roles while, at the same time, developing strategic gender interests which they, consciously or not, passed on to their daughters as ideational social capital. Respondents said that they learned their own transgressive gender ideology and behavior from observing their immigrant mothers. Lynn Stephen concludes, "in many cases women who inhabit these positions have found ways of coping, of redefining marginality of struggling and resisting, of encountering joy and happiness in human relations."[17] Second-generation daughters found themselves caught in a web of ambiguities in their relationships with their immigrant fathers. They expressed a great deal of respect for their fathers at the same time that they challenged their authority. They maintained a deep sense of gratitude for the sacrifices that their fathers endured as immigrants. Their attitudes toward their fathers reveal an admiration for their unwavering ability to "hacerle la lucha," a willingness to accept the challenge to work hard but usually with limited hopes for upward mobility. Still, they recognized that their fathers' worldviews were shaped by a patriarchal system of authority, which they, like their immigrant mothers, saw as a gender constraint in need of contestation.

Current research on immigration illustrates that immigration is a gendered social process, one that traditional research has largely ignored. Such a gendered process does not begin upon arrival to the host country, but rather it can begin in the country of origin. As men migrate to the United States, larger numbers of women step in as heads of households, usually on a temporary basis, until they can join their immigrant husbands. While in Mexico, these women experience a major gender-role transformation, becoming heads of households with various degrees of authority and decision-making power. Changes in gender relations are not only a result of immigration dynamics. Increases in participation in the paid labor force, a rise in single mothers as heads of households, and the ongoing constraints of a precarious Mexican economy are all factors that account for changes in Mexican women's traditional gender roles within a nexus of patriarchal authority.[18] These changes do not signal a reduction in inequality in the paid labor force as women continue to occupy marginalized locations in the secondary labor force. Nevertheless, studies suggest the possibility of changes in domestic gender relations in

Mexico and in Mexican immigrant communities in the United States. For example, research in Michoacán in the 1960s found that as young rural women entered the paid labor force changes in gender relations developed in their families.[19] Similarly, interviews with wage-earning rural women documented transformations, however limited, in their gender and power relations within their families, particularly with their fathers. Daughters of these fathers, who had left Mexico to work in the United States and who stayed away for long periods, showed an even greater propensity to devalue patriarchal authority by making their own decisions and even taking on what would be considered gender transgressive behaviors. Nevertheless, three critical points must be kept in mind. First, Mexican immigrant families vary in the nature and degree to which they undergo changes in gender relations. Indeed, it is a common mistake to assume that Mexican families are monolithic. Second, changes in the employment characteristics of Mexican women usually have an impact on gender relations, but these do not bring an immediate end to patriarchal authority. And third, men may themselves experience transformation in gender and power relations as women's roles, ideologies, and behaviors undergo changes.[20]

My study's findings concur with researchers who maintain that immigrant families retain some social and cultural family dynamics from their homelands while, at the same time, exhibiting changes produced by their sustained interaction with American society. Immigrant women not only show resiliency in meeting the challenges of their new lives in the United States, but they often articulate a range of survival strategies that may ultimately work to undermine male authority. Such a process is not limited to studies of Mexican immigrant women. Nazli Kibria's work on Vietnamese immigrants found that men experienced a significant loss of socioeconomic status within the United States, but women maintained a relatively similar position within their families, one that would eventually begin to change. Vietnamese women responded to changes in their husbands' power and authority by contesting gender relations in ways that they believed would be most beneficial to their families' survival. A common strategy involved their redefinition of ethnic kinship and community networks in ways that lessened some degree of patriarchal authority and decreased the power of their mother-in-laws.[21] Other cross-cultural studies have also documented similar changes in gender dynamics within immigrant families.[22] Pierrette Hondagneu-Sotelo summarizes a gendered migration process that can alter the dynamics of gender relations.

> In their daily lives and actions, immigrants draw upon social norms and traditional cultural frameworks, but they do so in this new, changing social environment. Immigrants arrive with cultural and ideological baggage, but in the new society, as they unpack and rearrange it, they discard elements and adopt new ones; women, for example, may take up new activities such as working for wages, attending meetings in the evenings, and driving and they may exert authority over family matters previously out of their control. Women and men may not always agree on these arrangements. Traditional social relations and cultural resources neither disintegrate nor continue intact, but are reshaped through processes of migrations and resettlement.[23]

Mexican American daughters told stories about their immigrant mothers that underscore the research on changing gender dynamics within immigrant households. Their interviews mesh stories of segregated gender roles with stories of their mothers' attempts to transgress these roles. Moreover, one second-generation woman revealed that her mother taught her how to "get around what everyone, like my dad, expected from her, and sort of do what she wanted to do." Many of my respondents described how their mothers struggled to navigate between two conflicting worlds, each with its own set of behavioral codes. Likewise, Patricia Zavella found similar gender conflicts among Mexican American cannery workers.[24] My respondents characterized their fathers as the head of the family and the decision maker, but they also saw their mothers as strong and very independent, capable of challenging their husbands' authority when they believed that, for the good of the family, they had to overrule their husbands' decisions. Esperanza recalled the gendered power dynamics that characterized her arguments with her father: "My father always tries to settle a family argument by saying that he is the one 'Que manda.' You know, that he is the one that rules or that gives the orders but usually my mother backs off, waits a few days, and then goes ahead with what she wanted to do. I bet my dad knows this but just goes along." Esperanza's quotation illustrates her mother's powerful, although nuanced, outwardly invisible contestation of her husband's authority. After a disagreement, her mother waits, then goes to do "what she wanted to do," thus challenging her husband's patriarchal opposition.

Studies on the second generation also examine the complex relationship between immigrant mothers and their American-born daughters. Research on immigrant mothers from diverse immigrant backgrounds documents their gender struggles within their families and their effects on their second-generation daughters. Like the Mexican American women in my study, a respondent in Susan Matoba Adler's work on Japanese Americans reflected on the gender conflicts between her immigrant parents and expressed the effect these had on her: "Probably the most prominent characteristic I've seen in her is her strength and her determination, her work ethic and her ability to just find a goal and design a solution and . . . reach the other side. . . . My mom didn't let those [cultural] preconceptions of who she was limit her."[25]

Similarly my respondents understood that their mothers' gender contestations had a profound impact on their emerging ideology and behavior. For example, their mothers challenge their husbands' attempts to restrict their daughters' newfound freedom in college. Curfew was a common theme. Those students who continued to live at home wanted more freedom to stay out later on the weekends and weeknights. Many had strict curfews imposed on them, almost exclusively by their fathers who monitored their activities. Interestingly, these "curfew battles" became one of the first visible signs of gender role contestation. All of the women in this study had at least one brother, and they complained that their brothers had been given more freedom. Respondents challenged the double standard imposed by their fathers while, at the same time, their mothers supported their daughters' transgressive gender ideology and behavior. They supported their daughters through a carefully crafted gender script written to contest their husbands' authority. Mothers challenged the restrictions placed by their husbands on their daughters' behavior, specifically curfew times. Mothers employed a very effective strategy: they explained that their daughters needed more freedom in order to succeed in college. In exchange for such mediation efforts, daughters agreed to spend part of their extended curfews in school-related activities, such as study groups, club activities, and, social activities. Their mothers' gender transgressive social capital—already developed in their own contestations with their spouses—now was used to assist their daughters. Immigrant mothers became the most important source of support for their daughters when they challenged their fathers' authority. This theme can be found in literature and oral histories. For example, in *Immigrant Daughter: Coming of Age as a Mexican American Woman*, Frances Esquibel Tywoniak recalls how her mother, who had only a few years of schooling, always supported her goal of obtaining a higher education. Even when her father expressed some resistance in giving her permission to participate in certain after-school activities, Frances remembers that her mother succeeded in changing her father's mind. Her immigrant mother recognized the importance of higher education and steadfastly supported her:

> My mother always gave her unswerving support to any school sanctioned activity. I trusted her and expected her to take care of getting my father's approval. Unlike other Mexican families who, I learned, prohibited their children from participating in certain school activities, my family never did so if they felt they would further my education. My mother always spoke fondly of her brief school experience. She was an advocate for education.[26]

Second-generation Mexican American women recalled how their mothers developed strategies to convince their fathers that school activities would benefit their daughters, even at the cost of spending less time with their families. For example, one woman joined a study group for one of her science classes during her first year at college. The group scheduled their weekly meetings on Monday evenings. A problem quickly developed when her father told her that he did not want her staying out until 10:00 P.M., the time that the study group would end. María describes her curfew war with her father:

> I overheard my mom tell my dad that this group would help me get better grades and that this would help me get a better job in the long run. She reminded my dad that they came here from Mexico to get a better life for their kids and things are different here. So, yeah, my dad put up a fuss, but in the end he said OK, but I had to call him a couple of times during the study session. I thought this was weird, but my mom said just go along with it. My mom also said not to tell him that my study group went out for pizza or some other stuff, so, you see, it was study but also social things. And yeah, of course, we didn't tell my dad.

Immigrant mothers and their second-generation daughters challenged patriarchal constraints together by designing and implementing carefully crafted gender pacts. Other students related their fathers' attempts to control their lives by setting limits on their "new freedom," "different lives," "new start," and "independence." They complained about their fathers' need for late night phone calls to ostensibly "just keep in touch" or "see if you need something from home."

Recent studies of Mexican immigrant families document similar dynamics in which gender roles are contested using gender strategies that redefine what is traditionally considered transgressive gender behavior into "acceptable" gender behavior, that is, gender behavior that would enable their daughters to be more successful in college. Mexican immigrant fathers believed that their journey to the United States developed out of a burning desire to improve their family's socioeconomic circumstances and, slowly but eventually, realize the American dream of economic security and upward mobility. Whatever patriarchal ideologies they held about women, specifically their daughters, Mexican immigrant fathers were capable of lessening patriarchal constraints, but only under a specific circumstance: the redefinition of gender transgressive behavior by their immigrant wives. Such a transformation was not always a smooth one, with conflicts and unresolved tensions surfacing between fathers and mothers and between fathers and daughters. Moreover, the women I spoke with viewed these gender battles as lifelong ones, knowing that at this point in their lives they were only beginning a process of (re)inventing themselves as second-generation daughters. Interestingly, these women believed that successful gender transgressions did not necessarily mean permanent changes in their fathers' behavior. A gender victory over attending study groups, for example, did not mean that future gender struggles with their fathers would be easier. Juanita describes an example in which her mother teaches her how to challenge patriarchy: "It was like every time I wanted to do something that involved staying late at school, I had to battle it out with my dad all over again. But, you know, my mother would say, just watch me and learn that this is how you get what you want. It's not magic; it's hard work."

In this way, second-generation Mexican American women demonstrate a crucial role played by their Mexican immigrant mothers. Grounded in the gender struggles between their parents, daughters of

Mexican immigrants accumulated ideational social capital that proved instrumental in their own gender transgressions with their fathers, and, as will be shown in later chapters, with others, specifically within a university setting. Their immigrant mothers represent a strong source of ideational social capital at two levels. First, they assumed the role of cultural mediators between their husbands and their second-generation daughters. They (re)signified Mexican gender behavior and ideology that immigrant fathers viewed as "correct" into what they believed their daughters needed: the ideational social capital to succeed in higher education and American society. Thus, Mexican immigrant fathers did not feel as though they were relinquishing their power or authority by giving in and allowing their daughters to engage in what they had once defined as transgressive gender behavior. On the contrary, fathers viewed such changed behavior as consistent with their motivation for coming to the United States: a search for upward social mobility. Second, immigrant mothers provided their second-generation daughters with a model, however limited, of feminist empowerment, one that developed as a survival strategy for navigating through higher education. Their daughters recognized that their exposure to this strategy contributed to their emerging feminist consciousness, a belief in their power of agency to challenge ethnic, class, and gender constraints. Their mothers' intervention in the conflicts between their husbands and daughters served as a feminist socialization tool. Daughters witnessed their mothers' challenges to traditional gender roles and, as a result, gained access to ideational social capital that they could draw on in gender struggles outside the home.

Emergent Feminist Discourses

At the same time that Mexican American women students were experiencing gender constraints within their families, they confronted gender constraints within the university setting. Emergent feminist discourses developed as a result of their experiences with gendered ethnic stereotypes and sexism on campus, with respondents expressing various degrees of frustration. As outlined in previous chapters, these women had been raised in communities consisting of a combination of Mexican immigrant, Mexican American (second generation, third, etc.), and other diverse groups. In addition, with only a few exceptions, all came from high schools with a diverse student body. At the university they studied and lived in an environment in which they were the numerical minority. They recalled their silent and vocal challenges to the gendered ethnic constraints they identified within the university setting. Their interviews provide insights into the meanings they came to attach to these episodes of gendered ethnic constraints.

For second-generation students from diverse immigrant communities, college represents new, yet often threatening, experiences. Based on the specific socioeconomic circumstances of their Mexican immigrant parents, these second-generation Mexican American women crossed the entrance gates of the university, bringing with them an array of ethnic, gender, and social class differences that distinguished them from the majority of students at this university. Throughout their interviews, respondents discussed their continued interactions with students sharing a similar Mexican immigrant family background. They formed such friendships in their dormitories, classrooms, and curricular activities. They found each other as they tried to find a "space" in which to feel safe from an often-hostile world filled with contradictions and ambiguities. Eventually, they began to expand their circle of second-generation friends, including third- and later-generation Mexican Americans and combinations of generations with whom they now shared similar realities. References to these groups included such statements as "students like me, Mexican but with parents born here," "Mexicans but without the immigrant parents," or "other kinds of Mexicans." A striking ethnic awareness developed as a result of the low numbers of Mexican Americans at the university. Sonia described herself as "sticking out. I look different, you know? I'm not white, like blonde." As with all of the other respondents, Sonia's ethnicity or "how [she] look[s]" became more salient in a setting that contained few Mexican Americans in comparison to European Americans. Their communities, as discussed in chapter 2, "looked like little Mexicos" and had "Mexico all around." The university was a stark contrast to their family and community environments. As Fredrik Barth and Joane Nagel would predict, these students eventually created ethnic group boundaries around themselves as daughters of Mexican immigrants which now included other generations of Mexican Americans.[27] Their experiences differ from Mia Tuan's study of Asian Americans who grew up in predominantly white communities. For them college became a site where they increasingly interacted with other Asian Americans.[28] Tuan's and other studies have shown that Japanese and Chinese American university students are more likely to develop a panethnic Asian American identity. They "become Asian Americans" largely because many of them grew up in white communities and college "often provided the first opportunity to meet and interact with a large cross-section of Asian Americans. What they discovered were others who had grown up under similar circumstances and who therefore understood their experiences in a very personal way."[29] While the college environment provided increased interactions among those Asian American students who were raised in white communities, second-generation Mexican American women increased their interactions with their counterparts as a result of the limited numbers of Mexican Americans at the university (and not because they did not live in predominantly white neighborhoods). Despite the differences between these two groups, European American students surrounded both. Nevertheless, Asian Americans came to college from higher socioeconomic backgrounds than the Mexican American women. Generational differences among Mexican American undergraduate women became diminished as they shared experiences with gender ethnic stereotypes and patriarchal constraints. Kibria's work on Chinese and Korean university students shows similar patterns on intergenerational alliances. Despite such differences, Kibria's respondents exhibited a growing solidarity with other groups based on a shared externally imposed position as "foreigners."[30]

My interviewees' narratives weave together various strands consisting of their encounters with and responses to gendered ethnic constraints. About half of the respondents referred to what Elena called "stupid stereotypes from people who should know better." One of the major complaints involved the attempts by white male faculty members to question their choice of a major, specifically if the Mexican American woman was a science major (many of the students expressed their hopes of pursuing a medical career). Interestingly, none of these students actually changed their majors, but all of them expressed dissatisfaction when faculty members exhibited prejudicial attitudes toward them. Juanita, for example, always wanted to be a doctor although her parents were not sure how she could accomplish this. Although Juanita's mother always supported this dream, her father thought that she would have a difficult time finding a husband if her occupation status was too high. When Juanita found herself in danger of failing one of her science classes, she approached her professor to discuss her situation, hoping to receive encouragement and, more importantly, advice on how to improve her grades:

> He didn't give me suggestions on improving my grades. The first thing he said was something like, why don't I change my major to something I can handle? I told him I wanted to be a doctor and he asked me why would I want to do that? Why would he ask me this? I know it's probably that he just figured that since I was having problems with the class, then I should change majors. But to me it didn't matter. It just made me want to show him and everyone that a Mexican and a woman can do it. I just want to come back and tell him something like "so there."

This passage illustrates the (re)invention of ethnicity within the context of perceived prejudicial attitudes. Juanita and other respondents who discussed similar types of experiences attached a specific "ethnic" analysis to these student and faculty interactions. They interpreted these events as a challenge to their ethnicity and gender. Juanita wanted to prove to the university world that "a Mexican and a woman can do it." Under different circumstances, Yvette, who was doing exceptionally well in her science class, recalled a classroom experience during which her professor asked her when she learned to speak English, because she spoke "such good English, with hardly any accent." Other students recalled similar experiences, which they interpreted as having overt or subtle stereotypes based on their gender and ethnicity. Several of these students expressed their dismay when a professor asked them when they had immigrated to the United States. Carmen and Sonia remembered that some of their white professors asked them about Mexican politics. Sonia's anger could not be hidden during our taped interview:

> What does he think? Just because I'm Mexican, I know everything about what's going on over there? I don't understand it. I really don't, and why does this still go on? It's just so frustrating for people to think that all Mexicans are immigrants or experts on Mexico. People look at anyone different like me and just can't see that I'm American but, yeah, my parents are immigrants, but I'm not.

Sonia's passage reveals an ongoing process through which she is constructing her gendered ethnic identity within a university setting. She expresses her anger with her words, illustrating the emergence of new inscriptions on her palimpsest of identity. She states, "I'm Mexican," but then contests ethnic stereotyping through her emphatic assertion "I'm American." Immediately after referring to her parents as immigrants, she quickly adds, "but I'm not."

Nevertheless, respondents did relate positive experiences with some professors who offered support, mentoring, and overall assistance in their studies when they asked for help. Their descriptions of such experiences underscore the importance of mentoring women in general and Mexican American women in particular: "I was lost until [an Anglo male professor] went out of his way to help. I really didn't know him, but my roommate [a Mexican American] said that she had heard he was great with students. So I just made an appointment and that was that." Others shared similar experiences with a particular faculty member, adding that they wished their college had more Mexican American faculty because "then I could have related even more, you know, with more things in common." In addition, several science majors hoped that more women faculty, including Latinas, could be available to serve as role models.

During the times that these interviews were conducted, between 1997 and 1999, the number of Mexican American and Latino/a faculty represented 4.7 percent, 5.6 percent, and 4.8 percent of the total university faculty. All but two of the respondents had taken courses from Mexican American faculty, but all of them explained that they planned to enroll in their classes. In addition, all of the respondents had interacted with some of these professors in more informal settings such as university functions or office visits. Respondent after respondent expressed two major sentiments. First, they wanted to increase their interactions with Mexican American faculty members in both formal and informal settings. Second, they expressed concern that there were so few instructors who shared the same ethnic backgrounds and believed that the university would make stronger efforts in their faculty recruitment efforts. Sara captured these sentiments:

I think it would be great to be able to look around here and see lots more Latino faculty, especially women. It makes me and my friends feel,

> I don't know, like glad or really proud to walk around campus and know that there are faculty who went through similar things to be here except they're faculty now and we're still students.

Similarly, Diana explained that on one occasion her parents came to a Cinco de Mayo dinner and were so excited to meet "the Mexican faculty members. My mom was really excited when she realized that she could speak in Spanish to them." All of the respondents stressed the importance of role models and, more importantly for them, the importance of mentors. Julia's comments reveal the potential relationship that can be forged:

> I'm not sure what I want to major in, but when I took this class with Professor [Mexican American woman], and she told the students how hard her life had been, but she always wanted to be a teacher. Well, I just remember this and when stuff here gets me upset, I just remember that she stuck it out and look what happened. She made it and got a degree, and that's what I want. And I won't let others tell me a woman, and Mexican, can't do it.

For Julia and the other second–generation women, having role models increased their feminist discourses because they were able to see the results of successfully overcoming gendered ethnic stereotypes. This proved to be strategic ideational social capital in their experiences with other sites of gender contestation, for example with dating behavior and patterns with Mexican American male students and participation in ethnic student politics. In both areas, respondents described their growing awareness of gender struggles in ways similar to those in their families, specifically with their fathers. At one level they recognized a set of double standards for male and female behavior within their student community. At a second and more important level, they emerged as active agents contesting these gender constraints.

Gendered ethnic narratives uncover my respondents' frustration with the Mexican American males who also found themselves in a university world vastly different from that of their communities. Their frustration was shared equally with third, fourth, and later generations of Mexican American women students. Emergent feminist discourses produced an additional layer to the social construction of their identities. They had more in common with other Mexican American women on the basis of gender, even though they were several generations removed from the immigrant experience. These women wanted to develop close friendships, specifically romantic ones, with Mexican American males. Although almost all of my respondents had attended high schools with a diverse student body and had dated men from various racial and ethnic backgrounds, they believed that dating Mexican Americans in a university setting where they were in the numerical minority would lessen their alienation. Ironically, their participation in college and community political causes did bring them into close interactions with their male counterparts, but it also forced them to confront and ultimately challenge sexist ideology and behavior.

Their experiences are not isolated ones; similar developments have occurred in the past between Mexican American men and women students, and, in both cases, women have developed feminist ideologies and strategies. For example, during the social protest movements of Chicano and Chicana students during the 1960s and 1970s, Chicanas, like other women of color, struggled to overcome sexism. Studies document a strong relationship between women's participation in revolutionary or mass sociopolitical movements and the development of a feminist consciousness and independent women's movements within such struggles. Respondents trace their "feminist awakenings" to confrontations with male domination.[31] Their personal experiences with sexism from their male counterparts at the university led them to analyze their gender oppression as a collective problem with a collective solution: a Mexican American feminist ideology and feminist activities that always reflected the interplay between gender and ethnicity. Respondents recalled the tensions and contradictions that they experienced in their attempts to establish close interpersonal relationships with Mexican American male students. Their parents did not try to influence their choice of boyfriends either in high school or at the university. Discussions about dating and marriage focused primarily on the importance of marriage and family rather than on the possible husbands. As discussed earlier in this chapter, fathers of these women often stressed marriage over career, while their mothers usually presented the possibility of balancing the two and even, in some cases, favored their daughters' careers over marriage. Tuan found slightly different results among Asian American parents who favored their children marrying coethnics, but ultimately they left the choice up to their sons and daughters.[32] Both differ from practicing Jewish parents who believe in the matrilineal line of Jewish descent and thus encourage their sons to marry Jewish women. Moreover, rising intermarriage rates have been a source of concern for Jews.[33] All of the respondents expressed their preference to date Mexican American men on campus, but they did not necessarily envision marriage as the ultimate goal. Elena explains this preference:

> My friend goes to Sac State[Sacramento State] and there are a lot of [Mexican American] guys over there. When I visited her I could see the difference. It's different here and I just think it would help me to have someone who understands me. I thought it would be best to go out with a guy that would understand why I felt left out at this school, and then I saw that they [Mexican American men] were going out with Anglo women. I guess I felt like what was wrong with me? But then I just got mad and said to myself, it isn't me. I'm OK, but mad.

Elena is displaying one of the earliest signs of what Gloria Steinem has called "outrageous acts and everyday rebellions" by moving away from a condition of self-doubt and self-blame to one of confidence in her own identity, stating in various parts of the interview, "I'm OK."[34] Moreover, Elena is angry at what she perceives as Mexican American males' preference for Anglo women as dating partners.[35] Respondent after respondent echoed Elena's belief that dating men with whom they shared cultural experiences who would provide them with a coping mechanism to survive in this hostile environment. They tried to seek out Mexican American male companionship, although they did not express anti-Anglo feelings. Their preference to date Mexican Americans does not suggest that they were reluctant to date Anglos, and many, ultimately, did.

African American women experience similar problems related to dating patterns with African American men. Several studies on dating patterns of African American university students stress that African American men are more likely to date white women than black women are likely to date white men.[36] The social science literature on dating patterns of students of color has shown that men of color are more likely to date Anglo women than their racial/ethnic counterparts.[37] One of the recent explanations offered for this trend, particularly among the new second generation, is the increased diversity and openness of American society where intermarriage taboos have been relaxed if not completely eliminated.[38] Intermarriage across ethnic groups but within the same "racial" group are also increasing. Studies by Espiritu and L. H. Shinagawa and G. Y. Pang explain this occurrence by a rising sense of panethnic identification that stresses the commonalities across groups usually stemming from shared experiences with prejudice and discrimination within American society.[39] A more long-standing explanation for men of color dating outside their own racial or ethnic group reverts back to standards of beauty which put a premium on "whiteness." This is, in fact, the actual meaning or explanation given by all of the respondents for their difficulties in dating Mexican American men at the university. They believe that Mexican American men see them as less acceptable. Finding it difficult to tolerate this, they reacted with a combination of anger and a growing feminist consciousness. They find it difficult to understand why Mexican American men on campus show a preference for Anglo women. Their feelings often revert back to the "beauty myth" issues discussed in chapter 3. Respondents' discussions about the dating patterns of Mexican American men were crafted using feminist frameworks. Sonia's explanation reflects a concrete use of feminist theory:

> It's not so hard to understand. Everywhere guys look they see ads, movies that glorify tall, blonde, white women. I suppose it's not all their fault. It's hard not to get sucked into this. But I want to stop it. It's not healthy and I don't like it. A bunch of us have talked about this, guys dating Anglo girls more than us. Well, we are seeing that it doesn't help to get upset, but we should try to make other Latinas see that they're not the problem. It's society's.

Emma Pérez analyzes the obstacles faced by Chicanas and all women of color regarding the postcolonial language of race and sexuality. Using Marguerite Duras's novel *The Lover*, Pérez analyzes the problematic relationship between a Chinese male living in French colonial Vietnam with an adolescent French girl. Pérez calls attention to the objectification and child exploitation of the young girl by her "lover" who, based on his own skin color, is seen as the "Other" by French colonialists, including the girl's brothers. Pérez adds another "lover" into this already problematic relationship: his Chinese wife who, as Pérez points out, must live her life with the knowledge that her husband from an arranged marriage is still longing for and in love with the "Other" woman, a symbol of colonial society with its system of racial privilege. Pérez sees the Chinese wife as the "extreme 'other,'" the marginal "other."[40] Without overextending the parallel with second-generation Mexican American women, I suggest that these respondents were articulating their frustration and contestation of being the "marginalized Other" in their relationships with Mexican American males in the university setting.

Reflecting the views of other respondents, Sonia felt hurt that she was not asked for dates by Mexican American men, but nevertheless she recognized the hurtful application of racialized beauty standards. Her passage is perhaps most insightful where it relates that "a bunch of us have talked about this." Other women had talked about similar experiences. Their narratives reveal an expanding feminist space in which second-generation women further (re)constructed their identities as they engaged in a feminist discourse with other Mexican American women who were not daughters of Mexican immigrants. As Inez explained: "We're all Mexicans, well, I guess *Mexican Americans* is a better term, well, it includes my friends whose parents aren't immigrants like mine are. I guess we are different in this but [Mexican American] guys treat us the same, they don't really prefer us, that's what I think, what we think and talk about." Inez learned that her problem was not a personal one but a collective one. Alicia captured the tension she experienced when she established a close friendship with a Mexican American male student:

> He's from a very traditional Mexican home where if he even washes a dish his mother will have an attack. He definitely expects me to do everything for him when he comes to visit me at home. Like when he comes over I have to get up and get'm a glass of water if he's thirsty. I do it but I'll be like, "Get yourself a glass of water." So, I mean, it's maybe not something that we flat out discuss, but it's definitely something that I won't put up with but sometimes I do. I get up and get him the stupid glass of water. Actually I do the same for my dad and so does my mom, but only sometimes. I guess we are just little by little, well, rebelling. First by thinking and then doing something about it. When I told my friends about this whole thing they said that they had gone through something the same.

Other respondents expressed similar reactions to such traditional gender expectations. Their contestation of gendered expectations that they "serve Mexican men," as Alicia called it, was not always verbal. They did "get up and get him the stupid glass of water," but their narratives capture the feminist development that was already "little by little, well, rebelling." When these women experienced close interactions with Mexican American male counterparts, they also revealed high levels of frustration produced by the gender constraints. Respondents discussed their participation in campus-wide activities such as the Mexican American student organization, a student-run center for cross-cultural and political activities, such as the anti-Proposition 187 rallies. The effects of politicalization on their ethnic identity will be discussed in the next chapter.

In general, these women students confronted varying degrees of sexism in their attempts to participate fully in specific student activities. They believed that their opinions were not taken seriously, that their leadership skills were not appreciated, and that their attempts to deal with issues of sexism resulted in lesbian baiting. Anita was ostracized from an organizational meeting to plan the Mexican Independence Day celebration. She had suggested a roundtable discussion of Chicana feminism from a historical and contemporary perspective, but she became disillusioned and eventually stopped attending these meetings. Julia also shared such treatment, recalling how she had suggested that the Mexican American student group organize a poetry reading by Latina poets as part of the Cinco de Mayo campus festivities. She was told that this was not an "appropriate kind of activity for a celebration of a Mexican historical event." Julia recalled trying to explain that some of the other planned activities, like the school dance, were not directly related to the original meaning of the Mexican national holiday. "I told them we could organize whatever we wanted. We couldn't exclude stuff like my poetry group for that reason. I knew that the guys just didn't want this. They said I was being difficult and that some of those poets were anti-male anyway. I really couldn't believe this." Interestingly, Julia used the terms *Chicana* and *Latinas* when she described this situation. Another respondent said that she and her "Mexican American" friends had discussed the term *Chicana* and liked to use it because "you know, it's radical, we think." Again, as in other parts of their entire narratives, these daughters of Mexican immigrant parents adopt a new, gendered, ethnic term, but they still reveal certain ambiguities in using it. Moreover, when other respondents talked about their using the term *Chicana*, they quickly added that their parents would not like them to use it, explaining that their parents considered the term radical. Ironically, both the immigrant generation and their second-generation daughters believed the term to be an expression of political radicalism.

Julia's words are also reminiscent of the circumstances for Chicanas active in the cultural nationalist movement of the 1960s and 1970s. As Chicana feminists became more alienated within the Chicano Movement, they outlined their areas of disagreement with the movement's politics. Their criticisms of the movement revolved around the following key issues: 1) the movement's leadership control by men and the exclusion of women from key leadership positions, 2) the politics of male domination that limited their full participation, 3) the movement's oppression of women in the same way that American society oppresses both Chicanos and Chicanas, and 4) the backlash against women for raising gender issues.[41]

Although their narratives contain very explicit manifestations of emerging feminist discourses, they also reveal ambiguities and contradictions regarding their new identities as feminists. At the same time that the women contested sexist behavior, many questioned the social class and racial/ethnic bias they experienced within the second wave of feminism. Their remarks reveal a tension between what they believed a feminist movement could do to reduce gender inequality and their experiences with both racial and ethnic prejudice within a feminist movement. Respondents, like Alicia, recognized some major limitations of feminism:

> The women's movement has done a lot. A lot, especially, or maybe more, for white women. But I think it hasn't done everything that it can do. Because I think even though white women, black women, Chicana women, Asian women, all of them are different, but I'm just not sure how to distinguish. Should the women's movement be all women or is that white women? It kind of depends on what you're talking about, but I think like in the U.S., the white women's movement needs maybe to focus on all women. I don't know what the problem is, but definitely it has not done enough. There needs to be more done for ethnic women. As far as like to bring the issue of rape, well, it has done a good job there, opening men's eyes.

All the respondents criticized the women's movement for its limited attention to issues specific to "ethnic women." Nevertheless, they expressed strong identification as feminists when they discussed such "women's" issues as rape and reproductive rights. Nevertheless, these Mexican American women tempered their identification as feminists by referring specifically to their ethnic and social class identity. Many linked a feminist identity with an ethnic identity. In the words of Margarita:

> I do say I'm a feminist, but I think some Chicanos and some Chicanas have a wrong attitude about just the word "feminist." I don't want men, you know, Chicanos or Latinos, to think I hate them. We're all the same. We're proud to be Mexican, you know our families are from Mexico but, well, not all of us have parents actually born there. Anyway, I do believe in what feminism means, but it's better for me to make sure I say Chicana feminist. It says more than just feminist. It's more like pride in yourself of being a woman and being Chicana at the same time. I have a more positive view from people if I say Chicana feminist, but still the guys sometimes just hear Chicana and not feminist because they just go on doing stuff that drives me crazy. Well, I don't mean crazy, I mean it drives me to really believe why feminism is needed. Well, I think this makes sense?

This passage underscores the tensions that developed as these women displayed an increasingly feminist outlook on their everyday lives and the power relationships that shaped them. Their statements reflect a discourse in which they talk themselves through a different layer of their emergent identities. As they found themselves vocalizing their attachments to a feminist social identity, they simultaneously considered the implications such an identity would have on their "ethnic worlds." The result was a resignification of the term *feminist* to include their ethnic identity. Their concerns with being seen as less than authentic ethnic echoes those of other women of color who have historically been cautious, if not skeptical, of feminism and the women's movement while at the same time sharing a concern with patriarchy.[42] Raquel captures the ambiguity of being a feminist:

> I know I am a feminist. I have read a lot about feminism. I learned about feminism in some of my classes here [in college]. But I don't want to be

141

set apart from my Mexican background and traditions. We're all Mexican, but I see how some of these traditions hurt women but some traditions like language and holidays are important. But I still want to show that I am different, too. I know that in the sixties they used the word "Chicano" and "Chicana" because it was, well, radical. I never have called myself that and my parents never. But I sometimes like the way "Chicana feminist" sounds radical, but I still have traditions. And by the way, I never use this in front of my parents. They hate the word and say Mexican is what they are and I am too, except I'm American, too. I do agree but I still like to sound radical, well, sometimes, when I get angry at guys treating us bad.

Raquel's passage highlights the essence of what I have been calling a palimpsest of identity. She recognizes that she is many things at the same time and that, in some instances, some traces of her identity surface in sharper focus. She says that she is Mexican, sometimes identifies as a Chicana feminist, but is an American, too. Her identity is not merely situational; it is one that is layered, inscribed on her life manuscript. Raquel, like the other women, attempts to redefine herself as a feminist, adding a new layer to her ethnic identity.

Their attempts were not completely successful because their attachments to a feminist perspective became a source of tension with their Mexican American male counterparts. Lesbian baiting represented perhaps one of the most disturbing backlashes against the respondents' attempts to place gender issues on the agenda of student politics. Respondents described incidents in which their vocal opposition to sexism and gender constraints led Mexican American men to label them "lesbians," an accusation that added to their undesirableness as dates. Students expressed not only their frustration but also their anger at being labeled "lesbians." Their narratives stress that they were not homophobic, emphasizing that their anger was aimed at their male peers for using such lesbian-baiting techniques to deflect from their male domination. Juanita's narrative captured the sentiments of many of the women. Alicia added that she became more interested in studying feminist writings and taking women's studies courses as a result of her experiences with male domination. Again, respondents shared gender constraints experienced by other Mexican American women in the early periods of Chicana feminism.

Chicana feminist lesbians brought an additional layer of critique to the sexism within the Chicano Movement of the 1960s and 1970s. Their writings reveal the societal contradictions that they had to contend with, and equally important, they reveal lesbian baiting as a tactic aimed to deflect attention away from issues of gender equality. African American and Asian American feminists have also been the targets of lesbian baiting for their efforts to eradicate male domination.[43] Responses to such attacks varied but, in general, women of color, including my respondents, emerged with a more fully developed sense of feminism and gendered ethnic identity.

In sum, their emergent feminist discourses originated from their lived experiences within the university setting and specifically within the context of their participation in Mexican American student politics, where they saw themselves as objects of criticism and ostracism. Ironically, respondents concluded that although they went through many painful moments, they survived, emerging stronger and more confident in themselves as Mexican American women. Yet, they knew that such struggles against gender constraints would follow them throughout their lives. Their hope was rooted in the belief that women, including themselves, would persevere in contesting patriarchal constraints. As María concluded:

> All this stuff made me tired, angry, and just, well, feel pretty bad at times. But, you know, I realized that all of us Mexican Americans, Chicanas, or Latinas, or whatever you want to call yourself, are in the same boat so we have to stick together. I tell myself, well, it's actually something my mom taught me. Women have to struggle to make it and to, you know, gain their place in the world and that, basically, not to give up and not to give in. And I won't. We won't.

Overview

In their Mexican immigrant homes, second-generation women received mixed messages from their fathers. While expressing deep pride in the accomplishments of their college daughters, immigrant fathers also exerted the pressures of patriarchal ideology and behavior, which they believed would mold their daughters into "dutiful daughters." Interestingly, challenges to their patriarchal authority originated with their wives, whose struggles with and contestations of patriarchal constraints provided models for their daughters who were engaged in their own acts of gendered rebellions and resistance which ultimately (re)defined their gendered ethnic identities. Their mothers created gender scripts with which they (re)invented themselves as women living in the United States, raising American-born children. Their gendered ethnic identity endured changes as a result of the immigration process that led to the renegotiation of gender roles between immigrant parents. Second-generation Mexican Americans learned to use their mothers' gender strategies, but in time designed their own. In combination, their repertoire of gender strategies transformed them into "not-so-dutiful daughters."

In the university setting, second-generation Mexican American women experienced additional patriarchal constraints. Although their narratives identify their university environment as a "space" in which they could develop as independent women, they continued to experience conflicts between their need for increased independence from their immigrant families, specifically their fathers, and their ongoing respect and admiration for their parents' sacrifices. Eventually, they addressed another gender and ethnic paradox which led to the development of emergent feminist discourses with other Mexican American women from second, third, and later generations. Respondents revealed strained relationships with gendered ethnic stereotypes within the larger university and, what they considered more serious, those with Mexican American male students. Both led them to put into practice their transgressive gender behavior, patterns of gender contestation that they learned from their mothers. Above all, the second-generation women, given the particular university setting, created a space for feminist discourses with other Mexican American women and, in so doing, moved toward a more universal definition of their ethnic identities that crossed generational boundaries. Given their small but highly visible numbers at the university, such discourse developed and was sustained on a regular basis. A second-generation Mexican American woman made the journey to the university, confronted a series of patriarchal constraints, and formed gender pacts with other Mexican American women, "like me, but not with immigrant parents." Their experiences and gender contestations were sources of conflict and contradictions. Yet, as they created spaces within which they engaged in feminist discourses with other Mexican American women, they emerged with an understanding that the personal is indeed political.

144

EMERGENT IDENTITIES IN A UNIVERSITY SETTING

Second-generation Mexican American women, like all undergraduate students, enter universities with diverse academic, cultural, socioeconomic backgrounds, and emergent identities. The women in this study broke through numerous social, structural, and cultural constraints to enter higher education, which, for most of their Mexican immigrant parents, seemed unattainable but was their dream for their children ever since they left Mexico. Their parents, specifically their immigrant mothers, instilled this dream in their American-born daughters, grounding them in their immigrant worldview—a belief in striving for a better life. These parents gave their daughters solid roots they hoped would guide them as they navigated through American society. As the second generation progressed through higher education, their parents' universe competed with their emerging one, playing an increasingly significant role in the unfolding of their ethnic identity. Mexican American women students found themselves defined as the "Other"—marginalized students in a predominantly white university. Their emergent ethnic identities reflect their responses to these experiences. Ultimately, the second generation's ethnic identity maintained not only their immigrant mothers' dreams of hard work and success but also their own developing worldview of American society—one they were beginning to see less as an immigrant's haven and more as an ethnic minority's problem. Each of these ideological strands remains inscribed on their ethnic identities, with the latter becoming more intense as they (re)negotiated their identity as both daughters of Mexican immigrants and Mexican American students. Second-generation women traversed these new "borderlands," a contested space in which they confront ethnic, social class, and gender barriers. This chapter will examine 1) the role a mother's support plays for her daughter(s), 2) the dynamic process through which second-generation individuals (re)negotiate the boundaries of their ethnic identity, and 3) the emergent politicalization of their ethnicity.

Immigrant Dream and Second-Generation Dilemmas

When each of the students set foot on campus, they brought with them specific views on the importance of a university education shaped largely by their relationships with their immigrant parents. Their immigrant mothers, none of whom had a college degree, represented the most dominant source of anticipation for their future lives as undergraduate students. Respondents referred to their mothers as their major supporters. As their parents had once crossed the border to enter the United States in search of the American Dream, these second-generation daughters crossed a symbolic and real border when they passed through the entrance gate to the university. Both parent and child found themselves in a "new world," struggling against the same adversities faced by generations of other immigrants. Both saw themselves bravely triumphing over many struggles. The parents gave their daughters roots, hoping to ground them as they bravely entered the "new world" of the university. The daughters learned to navigate their way, literally and figuratively, through the corridors of the university, and along the way they (re)invented themselves, creating new inscriptions on their palimpsests of identity.

Their mothers' hopes that their daughters receive a college education represent a major theme among their stories. Mothers told their daughters that a college degree would move them closer to the American Dream. Angela describes how her mother always encouraged her to pursue a college degree:

> My mom was always like she never had an opportunity to do a lot of things. You know, what she does is work, come home, take care of us, sleep, and go back to work at the cleaners. But she would start telling me, even in grade school, that she hoped I could go to college. She said she came here [from Mexico] to help her and when she had kids. And now, well, last July before I got here [to the university] she would tell me not to worry about the family but to concentrate on getting good grades. She would tell me she didn't want me to work at a cleaners. She wanted better things for me.

Second-generation women describe their Mexican immigrant mothers as hardworking women who were determined for their children, particularly their daughters, to have a better life than the ones they had experienced. As discussed in an earlier chapter, immigrant parents had little formal education in Mexico, and none of them had a college degree, although some had attended adult-education classes to learn English. Like other immigrant groups, second-generation college-bound children found it difficult to receive direct, practical advice from their parents, but not because their parents did not value higher education. Their parents' lack of experience with the American education system made it nearly impossible for them to assist their daughters with the steps required for college admission. Nevertheless, Mexicans and Mexican Americans emphasize the importance of education to their children, offering their encouragement during difficult times.[1] They use themselves as examples, especially their struggles as immigrants. Their narratives represent rich sources of ideational social capital transferable to their children.[2] Elena's story illustrates the kind of support her mother gave her:

> When I was admitted [to the university] my mom called my aunts and uncles. She was so proud. When I was applying she was happy but still a little worried. She had heard that it was hard to get into college. She said it didn't really matter to her where I got in. She just kept telling me that all she wanted for me was to, well, of course be happy and healthy but to get as much school and college. She just told me that she always knew I had it in me that I could succeed, but she wished she could help me. But she said she wasn't prepared—more like she needed to have gone through college to help me with college.

The immigrant mother's wish to "prepare" her daughter for college without being prepared herself is a recurrent topic, not only in these interviews but also in other studies and creative writings. Pat Mora's poem "Elena" stands as a poignant representation of a common dilemma facing immigrant mothers when their Mexican-born children immigrate with them and eventually attend school in the United States. Mora's poem can also be applied to second-generation children. Wishing that she could help her English-speaking children with their homework, the immigrant mother in Mora's poem tries to teach herself English, because if she does not, she "will be deaf when when my children need my help."[3] Although all of the undergraduate women I interviewed spoke Spanish, their levels of proficiency varied. It was not uncommon for those students with more limited Spanish proficiency to admit that they often found it difficult to fully express their gratitude for all their support and encouragement, in the same way that their mothers had difficulty giving them advice as they left for college. Julia shared her frustration at not always being able to express herself in Spanish. "Sometimes I would tell her she was helping me by always supporting me, but I sometimes can't get the right words in Spanish to tell her exactly what I mean. I know Spanish, but some words I can't find, you know in my head." Other respondents expressed these sentiments but shared an additional component: their frustration with the problems their mothers experience when dealing with agencies and bureaucracies where they need their daughters to act as their translators. Several women had to miss class in order to accompany their mothers to the bank, to the doctor, or to some human service agency. Irene recalls her reaction to one of these situations:

> I was studying for midterms, but my mom called because she needed to go to the doctor. She always wanted me to go with her, you know, she doesn't speak English and she didn't like the receptionist. My mom didn't like to have to try to talk to her, well, her English is not great. So, of course, I had to go, but I felt, well, just caught in-between my midterm stuff and this. I guess other students don't understand, well, their parents—the Anglo ones—speak English and aren't like my mom and dad. But I don't have a way around this. I have to, that's it.

Irene's story is similar to circumstances encountered by the other second-generation respondents. Irene feels caught between two worlds: her new college one and her Mexican immigrant mother's. She can navigate between the two worlds, but her mother cannot. She recognizes that the parents of her English-speaking Anglo peers do not place similar demands on their children. Still, Irene, like the other respondents, never waivers in her support for her mother but, nevertheless, feels ambivalent, bordering on guilt, because of the pressure in meeting both the demands of her immigrant mother and those of the university. Irene attempts to resolve this dilemma but cannot escape her mixed feelings. In her short story, "The Educated One," published in an anthology of writings by Latina students, Lucy Guerrero touches on this same delicate subject.[4] Guerrero describes her frustration, knowing that her new life as "the educated one" brings the responsibility of helping her mother make her way through an English-speaking society. However, she is frustrated at having to take time away from her university studies to fulfill this obligation:

> It was a definite struggle throughout school and there were many instances where I was afraid of not finishing. My fear of failure was clearly evident when I attended school. . . . I had to continue my struggle mainly because I owed my parents that much. My parents never had the same opportunities I had. Likewise, I would never be able to experience or comprehend the struggles they had shared in establishing themselves in a new country. . . . I have been given the priceless gift of education and, little by little, I have begun to understand why my parents gave it to me and what they wanted me to do with it.[5]

My respondents knew, like Guerrero, that they were moving farther away from their parents, but they also knew that they would always have the obligation, an ultimately welcomed one, to assist their parents with the English education they never received.

> I know I will catch up with my school things, but I will always have times that I have to do stuff for my mom and dad since they still have problems with English. I used to get really mad, but I know, but it's still hard, that this is right, to do this. They had a hard time and I have problems here at school, but I have more, like a better position.

Past studies reveal the important role played by Mexican immigrant and Mexican American mothers in encouraging and supporting their daughters' aspirations for higher education. In their 1985 path-breaking study, María Chacón, Elizabeth G. Cohen, Margaret Camarena, Judith González, and Sharon Strover confirmed the importance of a mother's support for a daughter's college education.[6] Several studies by Gándara further underscore the significance of parental support in general but points out that fathers often send mixed messages to their daughters.[7] Mothers, on the other hand, provide unequivocal support, leading Gándara to conclude that "mothers were most often the guiding force in the home behind their children's powerful educational aspirations."[8] Similarly, studies of Mexican American, white, and African American undergraduate women show that Mexican American undergraduates receive the strongest support from their mothers. These studies do not always include information on the generational status of the Mexican American mothers in their samples, and, as such, my study contributes to this research by focusing on the roles of immigrant mothers and their second-generation daughters.[9]

Respondents acknowledged that their Mexican immigrant mothers, although lacking a college education or, for that matter, formal education at all, always expressed their strong beliefs that education would open the doors for upward mobility—doors that had remained closed to them. Cross-cultural studies of immigrant mothers and the second generation reveal similar mother-daughter dynamics in which mothers, at the expense of upsetting traditional patriarchal relationships, express their support for their daughters' pursuit of education. Caroline Bettinger-López's study of Cuban Jews includes the particularly interesting case of Orthodox Jewish Cuban families that develop stronger patriarchal relationships than most because of the interplay between Jewish Orthodoxy and the traditional male-dominated Cuban culture. The mothers interviewed by Bettinger-López expressed their hopes that their daughters would live in a world where their specific patriarchal constraints would be relaxed, enabling them the freedom to pursue whatever career they wanted. Like my respondents' mothers, the second-generation Cuban Jews hoped for a better future for their daughters.[10] Socioeconomic, cultural, and, above all, language barriers represent formidable barriers that prevent Mexican immigrant mothers from transmitting direct and practical advice to their college-bound daughters.

In contrast, Lorene Cary's autobiography, *Black Ice*, illustrates the critical role of middle-class African American parents in their children's education.[11] Cary recounts her mother's intervention with her science teacher who almost succeeded in preventing Cary from participating in a science fair because she had forgotten a required cardboard box. Cary told her mother that this teacher allowed the white children who had forgotten their boxes to enter their projects in the fair. Cary describes how her mother intervened by arguing with the teacher who finally allowed Cary to enter her project in the fair where she won third place. Cary's life is the story of middle-class African American women with a legacy of college-educated English-speaking family members. "Mama had stood in front of that teacher defending me with a blinding righteousness, letting the teacher know that I was not as small and black and alone as I seemed, that I came from somewhere, and where I came from, she'd better believe, somebody was home."[12] Lorene Cary's world as an African American girl from a middle-class family is far removed from the world of this study's second-generation Mexican American women, yet this excerpt from her book echoes the same sentiments of my respondents' Mexican immigrant mothers. Lupe says that she will always remember her mother's long-standing advice:

> She would tell me to remember that I was just as good as anybody else, that I shouldn't think other students were better because they had money or had parents that had better backgrounds. She meant better jobs. She didn't really say it, but I think she was also trying to tell me not to be ashamed to be Mexican.

This passage demonstrates two important aspects. First, Lupe's mother and other immigrant mothers in this study molded their daughters into women who would be strong enough to withstand what they perceived as potential sources of conflict, specifically with the education system. Nevertheless, such ideational capital has not always combined with pragmatic social capital; immigrant mothers lack access to educational resources because of their low education levels. As David E. López and Ricardo D. Stanton-Salazar conclude: "The tragedy is that [parental] exhortation alone will not move today's Mexican American generation into the middle class."[13] Lupe adds "Mexican" to the list of characteristics used to differentiate herself from the outside world. Moreover, Lupe "reads" this into her mother's advice: "I think she was also trying to tell me not to be ashamed to be Mexican."

I suggest that as the second generation moved farther away from their Mexican immigrant family and community, their understanding of their mothers' American dream began to include a new dimension: an awareness of the increasing significance of ethnicity and social class. Elena's comments speak to the second generation's awareness of the growing significance of ethnicity in their lives as university students:

> My mom would always tell me to work hard, to study hard so that I
> could be in a better situation in life. But as I saw how things were here
> at school, I realized that, yeah, you can work hard, but some students
> have so much advantage. Those of us like me, well, Mexicans with par-
> ents who work and work and are just getting by, well, we don't start out
> the same and we don't end always end up in the same place.

Elena's story captures the negative effects of racial and ethnic inequality
as a constraint to her immigrant mother's dreams of success and upward
mobility. Still, Elena and the other respondents always return to one overarching theme: the importance of their mothers' role as a source of support even though they were not able to help them directly. Their mothers
lack what I call "*pragmatic* social capital," which is needed in order to
assist their undergraduate daughters. However, their immigrant mothers
did pass on "*ideational* social capital" to their daughters, providing them
with ideas, values, imaginations, and the necessary spirit to meet the challenges of higher education. Their mothers' struggles imbued Mexican
immigrant women with their own ideational mindset (described in earlier
chapters as the will to "hacerle la lucha" ["to take on the struggle"]). Due
to limited education and socioeconomic levels, Mexican immigrant mothers could not provide the pragmatic social tools that would directly facili-
tate their daughters' struggles in college. Unlike Lorene Cary's African
American mother, these Mexican immigrant mothers may not have been
able to march into their daughters' classrooms and confront their daughters' teachers if a problem developed, but they instilled a strong sense of
self-reliance and independence in their American-born daughters.

Without ignoring the persistence of structural barriers in their daughter's attempts to pursue higher education, a mother's support is critical for
college-educated Mexican Americans. These hopes and dreams may not
always be realistic or attainable, but the daughters see them as an important survival strategy. Anna provides the following example:

> I would be filling out applications and forms for this and that [college],
> and my mom would come over and bring me something to eat. I would
> say I was going crazy—I didn't know if I was doing this right. I wanted
> to quit, to, well, give up. My mom just said something like keep at it
> and you can do it, but maybe you need a rest or something. I finally got
> some and then did it, but my mom was there always. It might sound

strange but I can hear her right now saying it. I had to try. I had to get an education—I just had to.

Patricia Gándara studied students who succeeded in graduating from college and received professional degrees. She found that Mexican immigrant and Mexican American parents, especially mothers, create "a culture of possibility" responsible for instilling a belief and value system in their children that serves as a cultural map to their search for upward mobility in American society. Gándara states:

> In sum, the parents of these subjects, created, through their stories and through their own faith in the future exemplified by their own strivings, *a culture of possibility*. And, in so doing, they reinforced in their children a self belief in efficacy which resulted in intense achievement motivation. In spite of daily evidence to the contrary, these individuals grew up believing they did not have to lead the lives of their parents and others they saw around them. For them, anything was possible.[14]

A *"culture of possibility"* represents a crucial element in ideational social capital. Mexican immigrant mothers instill ideas in their daughters that function as a support network for negotiating through higher education.

Research studies on college-educated African American women have also examined gender specific support systems. African American women, like their male counterparts, have to deal with the pernicious effects of racism in their everyday lives and within the education system. Elizabeth Higginbotham's study of African American women in higher education shows that prior to the end of de jure segregation, African Americans were forced to attend black colleges, but gender played a significant role in the educational paths pursued by women and men. For example, women were more likely to be encouraged to pursue careers in teaching, nursing, social work, and library science. African American men were usually encouraged to enter traditionally male-dominated occupations such as medicine and business. Higginbotham points out that men in these occupations were more likely to start their own businesses, increasing their chances for upward mobility, however limited, but unavailable to African American women.[15] Studies of African American women in higher education during later historical periods further document the mother's role in providing support networks for their college-bound daughters. These women prepared their children for a society that continues to place social, structural, and individual personal constraints on African Americans.[16] Similarly, in her study of black professional women during the Jim Crow period of American history, Shaw traces the ways that African American mothers created a family space in which to teach their daughters the essential skills to succeed in an educational system embedded with racism. African American parents are mindful of the tremendous obstacles facing their children, but this does not stop them from encouraging their daughters to struggle for an education.[17] Studies of African American women in higher education in the post-1954 period underscore the importance between a mother's support for and a daughter's success in higher education. Mothers identified the gender specific stereotypes of African American women that their daughters would have to challenge, contest, and overcome. African American mothers, like my respondents' mothers, continue to assume the role of raising future generations of black women who will continue to live in a society they see full of racism and sexism.[18] Higginbotham's summary of the key components in the socialization of African American university women also applies to Mexican American women:

> Membership in a disadvantaged racial group shaped aspects of these women's lives, especially as they struggled to scale barriers. Social class was always an issue in terms of the women's own expectations for their lives, the material resources available to surmount racial barriers, and their reception by people in mainstream institutions. Gender also played a critical role, especially since their parents' gender expectations shaped how they raised their daughters. Further, as the women interacted with mainstream institutions, they found conflicting visions of their futures based on others' views of oppressed racial groups as inferior. Social class shaped these images of their futures; some Black women coming of age at this time were expected to be service and clerical workers, but these women shared the common experience of being outsiders, looking for a way through the institutional and interpersonal obstacles to their successful passage through the educational system.[19]

Mexican American women, like African American women, remember their mothers as sources of support and encouragement, self-reliance and self-efficacy—values that prepared them for a world filled with challenges. A parallel to the Mexican immigrant parents' guidance to "hacerle la lucha" is the advice given by Japanese parents to their children: the value of *gambare*, defined as "to persist" or "to do one's best" or "to endure."[20] Because Mexican American women's mothers believe in them, they in turn believe in themselves, even when things are not going well in school. Their stories capture the many ways through which they gain strength, a belief in the power of endurance, and a sense of independence. At the time of our interview, Elena had been reading *The House on Mango Street* by Sandra Cisneros, and she said she identified very closely with the poem read by Esperanza to her aunt:

> I want to be
> like the waves on the sea,
> like the clouds in the wind,
> but I'm me.
> One day I'll jump
> out of my skin.
> I'll shake the sky
> like a hundred violins.[21]

Consuelo, also having mentioned the poem in an interview, reflected on its impact: "I don't want to do things just because others, like my mom, want me to. My mom supports me, but it's my violin. She wants me to know that I can do, you know, accomplish whatever I want and just do whatever it is that I have in my mind."

(Re)Negotiating the Boundaries of Ethnic Identity

Mexican American women described their new lives as undergraduates as "ethnically charged" ones. Their narratives reveal two developments. First, their experiences with marginalization and alienation sparked a growing understanding that their ethnicity mattered more than ever before in their lives. Second, respondents expressed an increased political awareness regarding the impact of race, ethnicity, social class, and gender. An analysis of both will further illustrate how ethnic identity is emergent, depending on social structural conditions and the changing nature of boundaries and power relations among groups. Joane Nagel stresses the interaction between structural forces and individual agency in the construction of ethnicity:

> The construction of ethnic identity and culture is the result of both structure and agency—a dialectic played out by ethnic groups and the larger society. Ethnicity is the product of actions undertaken by ethnic groups as they shape and reshape their self-definition and culture.[22]

These second-generation Mexican American women redefined their identities as they responded to the university setting and its specific structural and ideological network of institutional and personal power relationships. Such power relationships led the second generation to reconstruct their membership boundaries as they began to see themselves as part of a marginalized ethnic group, both within the university and American society. Although they never lost sight of themselves and their Mexican heritage, the boundaries that surrounded their ethnic identities included Mexican Americans who were not second-generation children of immigrants. Fredrik Barth describes this as a (re)negotiation of ethnic identities involving a new imagining of the socially constructed meanings that individuals attach to their ethnicity. Respondents (re)negotiated their ethnic identities when they found themselves in a predominately white university setting, a site defined by these undergraduate women as an ethnically charged one. The second generation's membership boundaries and cultural meanings changed as they navigated their way through higher education. In doing so they (re)constructed their ethnic group boundaries by increasing their interactions with third- and fourth-generation Mexican Americans who defined themselves more as a racial/ethnic group struggling within American society and less as individuals with a Mexican immigrant heritage. Nevertheless, they continued to define themselves as individuals with a Mexican heritage. Barth explains this by stressing that "ethnic identity is associated with a culturally specific set of value standards."[23]

Respondents added a new layer to their ethnic identities, one in which they tempered their immigrant parents' belief that hard work would eventually bring success with one in which they saw themselves as an ethnic group subjected to embedded ethnic inequality. Clearly, their view of American society changed as their value system did, explaining how structural inequality collided with the immigrant's belief in the American Dream. As a very small percentage of the total Mexican American population, these undergraduates were moving closer to the ranks of the structurally assimilated but, contrary to Herbert Gans, they experienced a resurgence of ethnicity rather than its twilight or transformation into a leisure activity or an optional choice.[24] These second-generation women manifested ethnic identities, complete with ambiguities, contradictions, and unresolved issues, that affected both generations and, as a result, occupied borderlands of ethnicity, gender, and social class.[25] Ethnicity was a more salient issue when students became aware that they were being defined as the "Other" in a setting where, unlike their home communities, they were now in a numerical minority. In a largely white university, their visibility made ethnicity a central issue every day in ways that were vastly different from their past experiences. Likewise, Hung Cam Thai's study of second-generation Vietnamese Americans illustrates the role that experiences of marginality play on the formation, and most importantly, the saliency of ethnic identity.[26] My respondents' ethnicity had suddenly, as Carmen stated, "become blown up by there being so few of us here at this school." Although these women expressed gratitude for their mothers' role in establishing a deep sense of self-esteem and self-reliance, their interviews traced the dramatic effects of the prejudice and discrimination they experienced as undergraduates. They described themselves as self-confident, young, Mexican American women who, once they became university students, confronted the process through which they became defined as the "Other" in a predominantly white middle- to upper-class private university. Their narratives capture their realization and eventual contestation of "becoming the 'Other' "—a process that ultimately led them to (re)imagine their ethnicity.

Gloria Anzaldúa uses the term *New Mestiza* to describe postmodern ethnic identity formation among Latinas. Anzaldúa adds the prefix "new" to the word *Mestiza*—the traditional term for mixed-race persons such as biracial individuals of Spanish and indigenous heritage. Anzaldúa resignifies *Mestiza* as a symbol of mixed, racial/ethnic Mexican American women whose identity is both a blending and a collision of cultures. The New Mestiza is caught in a changing world in which individual identities are formed full of tensions and contradictions. The New Mestiza engages in a "struggle for borders, because [she], a mestiza, continually walk[s] out of one culture and into another because [she is] in all cultures at the same time."[27] As a result, the New Mestiza develops specific identity skills:

> The New Mestiza copes by developing a tolerance for contradictions, a tolerance for ambiguity. She learns to be an Indian in Mexican culture, to be Mexican from an Anglo point of view. She learns to juggle cultures. She has a plural personality, she operates in a pluralistic mode—nothing is thrust out, the good, the bad and the ugly, nothing rejected, nothing abandoned. Not only does she sustain contradictions, she turns the ambivalence into something else.[28]

Anzaldúa's New Mestizas live in a borderland of cultures and identities described by poet Pat Mora as a metaphorical space in the middle—a "Nepantla," an Aztec word meaning a place in the middle.[29] Respondents are indeed New Mestizas whose college lives cast them into a Nepantla, a middle geography of space and identity in which they are defined as the "Other." Anzaldúa (re)defines Nepantla by adding a twist to Mora's use of the word. Anzaldúa describes Nepantla as more than a "land in the middle." It is a mental state in which a person is torn between two paths; it is a dynamic space that creates dissonance in the lives of those who inhabit it. Occupying such an ambiguous, postmodern space, Mexican American undergraduate women struggle to navigate between their new world and their families' immigrant space.

My interviewees mentioned what they called "ethnic episodes" or "ethnic issues," uncovering a striking process through which they (re)imagined their ethnic identity, their Mexican ethnic culture, and the meanings which they attach to both. Earlier chapters have shown the ways in which respondents constructed their ethnic social identity, including their dynamic interactions with those outside their Mexican and Mexican American communities. Nevertheless, their entrance into a predominantly white university, specifically their experiences with being labeled the "Other," brought about significant changes in their socially constructed identities. Research on other ethnic minority students finds similar levels of alienation and marginalization.[30] Studies have compared levels of satisfaction among African American, Mexican American, and

Anglo undergraduates, discovering significantly different levels between students of color and white students, with the latter expressing higher satisfaction levels. Studies reveal general patterns of alienation among Mexican American and African American students, although both groups see the university as a place of academic excellence and an avenue for upward mobility.[31] In addition, research on undergraduate women shows that the experiences of women of color are characterized by even greater levels of alienation.[32] The latest baccalaureate origin studies focus on the dynamic relationship between a university's structure and climate and the graduation rates of undergraduate women, including their later achievements (such as a doctorate degree). By using the institution rather than the student population as the unit of analysis, baccalaureate studies provide an additional context for reports on the second generation by examining those institutional factors that contribute to decreased marginality levels for women such as African Americans and Mexican Americans. Lisa Wolf-Wendel's research raises a general question that is of particular interest to this book: What institutional factors best predict an undergraduate woman's success in professional schools, specifically the successful completion of a doctoral degree?[33] Although it was beyond the scope of this study to conduct a longitudinal study of my respondents, baccalaureate origin studies, such as Wolf-Wendel's, represent an important contribution to the research on undergraduate Mexican American women of both second and later generations. For example, Wolf-Wendel's work found a strong relationship between the Latina students and the total population of undergraduate students who wanted to pursue a professional degree, which, of course, is based on their achieving the baccalaureate degree. Institutions with a larger percentage of Latina students had higher rates of Latinas receiving doctoral degrees. In addition, Daniel Gilbert Solórzano's study found a direct relationship between Hispanic-serving institutions of higher education and the number of Mexican American doctorates in social science.[34] I suggest that a university's campus climate is instrumental in decreasing high levels of marginalization among respondents such as those in this study. Questions related to the development of ethnicity among such groups as the second generation will form an important component of future baccalaureate origin studies. Although the present study includes the role of institutions in providing a welcoming climate for second-generation women, research that com-

pares and contrasts the undergraduate experiences of women of color will
sharpen the specialized studies on their emergent ethnic identities and the
meanings that the second generation attaches to such identities.

These second-generation narratives reveal a complex transformation
through which respondents emerge with new layers added to their identity palimpsests. Respondents experienced a growing awareness of the
ways that ethnicity, gender, and social class matter, and, above all, they
increased their sense of their "Mexican ethnicity," or their "Mexican-
ness," beginning as early as their first undergraduate year. A recurrent
theme found throughout these interviews involves the experience of being
labeled as the "Other" by their Anglo undergraduate peers. Mexican
American women students described their pre-college ethnic self as an
integral part of their everyday lives, with most experiencing some level of
ethnic prejudice and discrimination. They explained that their responses
to such incidents had not usually resulted in discernible changes in their
everyday behavior. Their college experiences led them to create specifically "ethnic" responses and coping strategies. Students expressed
increased feelings of alienation in this setting. All of the second-generation women described their families and their surrounding communities
as ones in which aspects of Mexican culture surrounded them. In addition, respondents came from low-income families whose Mexican immigrant parents had a long history of occupations with little opportunities
for upward mobility. Although they were aware of ethnic and class differences in American society, living in a relatively closed environment (such
as a small university) led to changes in the way these women saw themselves and their Mexican immigrant families. Moreover, all of the respondents admitted that college was the first time they lived with "rich kids"
or "students with rich parents like lawyers."

Their narratives reveal two dimensions. First, respondents (re)imag-
ined their Mexican ethnic identity as a coping mechanism to being labeled
the "other." Second, their confrontations with prejudice and discrimination led to an unfolding political ideology of ethnic cultural nationalism.
As discussed in chapter 2, all of the respondents found themselves, in the
words of Lucia, "with Mexico all around." Their narratives trace a distinct
rearrangement of the meanings that they attach to their Mexican ethnic
cultural heritage. Without exception, respondents described a change in
their way of looking at themselves after repeated instances of prejudicial

treatment. The interview tapes often captured the women's anger and frustration as they recalled occasions when they had interpreted the words or actions of Anglo students, both men and women, as ethnic slurs. At times, they fought back tears of anger or hurt, usually both. Erica expressed such feelings:

> One thing that I hear a lot about is like when we were talking about affirmative action. Some students say to me, it's easy for Mexicans and other minorities to get into college right now. This kind of bothers me. One student in my dorm said that he knew someone who was valedictorian in high school and didn't get into Berkeley, but some Mexican classmates with less grade point averages got in. I could sort of feel the whole conversation get tense. It makes me wonder how many people around here [the university] are thinking the same thing about me. It's really hard for me to cope with this. I have found myself going back into a kind of Mexican thing. I play Mexican music loud in my dorm and I just know it gets the Anglo girls mad. I figure they think I am not supposed to be here. They see me like I'm a token ethnic. Then OK, I will be ethnic. Oh, yeah, it's funny, I don't even really like that ranchers music. I like jazz. Well, I guess I like it a little bit, my dad and uncles always play it at home.

This passage underscores the role of renegotiating boundaries and the social constructions of a person's ethnicity: "They see me like I'm a token ethnic. Then OK, I will be ethnic." Other women's responses were similar to Erica's. Juanita became visibly upset when she told the following story:

> I get so angry. Some of these Anglo students are so ignorant. Wherever I go I know that there will always be people looking down on me, you know, as different, as less because they see themselves better than Mexicans. I can't really explain it all, but I can tell when people just don't like to have people around them that are different, you know, minorities. I hear from other students of color that there's a big push here at this school for diversity, but you can't change people's minds automatically no matter how many of us come here. There will always be students who will say things like this one guy I overheard saying that some students get here because of special treatment and not because they are qualified like him. Well, I know it's not just in my head, right? He's talking about all of us students of color.

Juanita recognizes that many Anglo students associate diversity and affirmative action policies with the admission of less qualified students. Moreover, this student dismisses the possibility that she is just being overly sensitive by reading more into the words she overhears from the Anglo student and, instead, recognizes it as a reflection of prejudicial sentiments. In his study of Latino and Latina university students, Felix Padilla emphasizes the negative stereotypes experienced by Latinos/as: "Latino/a students are often viewed by professors and white students alike as academically unprepared and inferior, and as receiving an undeserved 'free ride.'"[35] Interestingly, Juanita uses the words "students of color," which is similar to the concept of panethnic identity that Yen Le Espirtu uses to describe an ethnic identification, such as Asian American, that encompasses several cultural groups, such as Japanese American, Chinese American, and Filipino.[36] The use of this phrase will be discussed later in this chapter when I explain the rise of a politicized ethnic nationalism among these Mexican American women, who were found to use the expression "students of color" within the context of campus politics. Juanita's passage also illustrates an awareness of power relations and dynamics within the university and reveals another dimension to her identity by using the terms "minorities" and "students of color."

The second-generation women I interviewed not only described themselves as "being more ethnic now," but they also attempted to explain what they meant by this. Their ethnic identity was unfolding as a coping mechanism to their surroundings, sites of contested terrain. They (re)invented themselves by creating an "imagined community" of Mexican ethnicity.[37] As a response to ethnic episodes, respondents reified Mexican culture as they defined it. Finding themselves placed in a marginalized space as the "Other," they (re)negotiated their socially constructed ethnic identities into a visible Mexican persona that transformed the cultural fabric of their everyday lives at the university. Respondents decorated their dorm rooms with what they believed were symbols of Mexican culture: ceramic replicas of Aztec calendars, brightly colored serapes, Mexican pottery, posters by Mexican muralists Diego Rivera and Clemente Orozco and posters of the Mexican revolutionaries Emiliano Zapata and Pancho Villa. Marta explained her dorm room and her father's ambivalent reaction to it:

I like to come into my room and feel proud of my Mexican background. It's a place where I feel I belong. But, it's funny, at home I didn't have any of this stuff. And, once, my dad visited after I had done this redecorating and asked, "What's all this?" He seemed really shocked. I told him that other of my friends, you know, Mexican, well, whose parents are Mexican, did the same. He said it wasn't a good idea, especially the pictures of Villa and Zapata. He said that they were Mexican heroes, not Americans, so why did I have to have them on my walls?

Other students responded in a similar way when asked why they had selected these particular symbols from Mexican culture and history. They explained that they wanted visible signs that were "really, really Mexican, but also really political."

These second-generation Mexican American women were engaging in what Eric Hobsbawm and Hugh Trevor-Roper call "retrospective invention" when they invented clothes and fashions that they defined as representative of an imagined Mexican ethnicity. Their reinvention of such cultural symbols provides them with visible signs capable of strengthening their imagined group solidarity and ethnic attachments.[38] Postcolonial and cultural studies scholars have explained such (re)invented ethnic identities as a function of a developing oppositional culture of resistance. Dominant discourses and power are resisted through a process of resignification by subalterned groups who, through their dynamic and fluid agency, (re)invent themselves, challenging these hegemonic structures. Such resistance, however, is in itself contingent, capable of assuming various types. According to Henry Giroux, "resistance often lacks an overt political project and frequently reflects social practices that are informal, disorganized, apolitical, and atheoretical in nature."[39] Acts of resistance represent the search for a personal and, I suggest, collective space within which to contest stereotypes such as those described by my respondents. Manifestations of resistance develop as (re)imagined, reified Mexican culture. Heidi Lasley Barajas and Jennifer L. Pierce's study of Latino and Latina high-school and college students underscores the importance of constructing spaces as sites of resistance to externally imposed stereotypes prevalent in predominantly white educational settings.[40] The women students in their study, like those in mine, carved out ideational ethnic spaces and geographies of (re)invented ethnic culture. In addition, such (re)invented culture flourished within the imagined communities of my study's second-generation Mexican American women. The formation of "fictive kinships," "survival strategies," "ethnic consolidation," and "politicized roots culture" all contribute to the understanding of such (re)invented communities, sites of resistance against dominance and its productions.[41] My respondents created their own ethnic world as a reaction to an alienating university world. Pepi Leistyna explains that:

> in order to maintain their identity, students exposed to racist conditions often create spaces within the school context, such as language, clothing, style, and behavior that reinforce their solidarity with their communities. In fact, the significance of ritual, style, and dress are often symbolic manifestations, that signify a rejection of racial stratification and the cultural capital of the dominant society.[42]

Interestingly, other scholars argue that such modes of resistance include the development of an oppositional culture and anti-intellectualism as specific survival strategies. Respondents in this study, however, demonstrated a combination of a culture of resistance and a culture of achievement and possibilities, a mixture that deepened the ambiguity of their sense of selves. Studies on the new second generation argue that later generations, farther removed from the immigrant world and its spirit of optimism, are more likely to create such an oppositional culture.[43] I suggest that this culture of resistance can develop alongside a culture of possibility, creating tensions and unresolved conflicts, as Angela explains:

> It's not hard to see that these posters and t-shirts were, well, radical, even if some Anglo students don't know who about Zapata or Villa, but they can see that they are radical. But I still don't want to become totally different. I know I have to make it here and sometimes it's hard to fight back against this stuff and still fit in and to make sure I do well. I know I can't be seen as too radical, you know, how could I get letters of recommendation? I want to be a lawyer. So, I am learning to play this game.

Angela and others demonstrated a solid understanding of the significance and impact of symbols, consciously selecting those which they believed would have the most, as Irene put it, "shock value," but always tempering them with an understanding that set boundaries around such patterns of resistance. Many said it was their immigrant parents who reminded them that "it's important to stand up for yourself, but remember that sometimes you have to hold back to get ahead." Nevertheless, shock value became a key commodity in their efforts to cope with marginalization, a response to an eternally imposed condition of "otherness." Lisa Lowe's analysis of the "making of Asian American culture" and the formation of ethnic identity can be used to explain patterns of reinvention among my Mexican American respondents. Lowe argues that Asian Americans (re)define themselves, in part through their relations with other groups, specifically through their responses to ethnic stereotypes.[44] Like the other respondents, Irene confronts the externally imposed condition of "otherness" by constructing a new layer to her identity, one that Sonia calls "a really Mexican, Mexican" one. As discussed in chapter 2, many respondents uncovered their parents' memories of Mexico and their own, real or imagined, fashioning a Mexican cultural bricolage. The impact of living in an environment like a university setting allowed them to reach into their historical memory as a means to cope with their environment, which they often defined as less than friendly. Elena described herself as being in "a place where I get these cold stares from students, you know, the Anglo students." Recent studies on African American and Asian American women have found that the university climate is also perceived as hostile to them. Researchers have focused specifically on the effects and responses by women of color to increased levels of alienation and exclusionary behavior.[45] My interviews uncovered one overarching response: the creation of an imagined ethnic community by second-generation Mexican American women undergraduates.

Respondents shifted from recounting their college experiences with ethnic prejudice to coping with their new environment. All of the women verbalized feelings of alienation and marginalization. They believed that others saw them as different and they, in turn, played on this difference, resignifying their "otherness" into a source of individual and collective identity and solidarity. Lucia captures this conscious act of resignification when she described that one of her friends, another second-generation Mexican American student, had put a small picture of Emiliano Zapata on the bulletin board in her dorm. A few days later, someone had used a black marker to cross out Zapata's face and had written, "This isn't Mexico." Lucia described her reaction to this episode:

> When I found out about this I got really mad. Some Anglo girls on my floor told me I shouldn't make such a big deal over this. I think it is a big deal. It's just another reminder that we are still seen different, well, looked as not real Americans. But some of us decided to go to the flea market and have some Zapata T-shirts made. You know, they had his picture right on the front. We all wore them around campus and, I think, to class. It was like wearing sorority letters, only Mexican style.

This passage is striking in that it reveals a dramatically proactive response to an overt episode of ethnic hostility—the defacement of and xenophobic writing on the picture of Zapata. Moreover, another interviewee, who bought the Zapata T-shirts, pointed out that she and the other students had to take several buses to get to the flea market. Their strategy was well planned and accomplished with considerable effort. Interestingly, several of these respondents said that their parents saw the T-shirts and expressed their displeasure at their wearing such clothing around campus. In general, their Mexican immigrant parents, who had always stressed the importance of cultural pride, did not accept the Mexican cultural symbols (re)invented by their daughters to resist being treated as the "Other." Second-generation Mexican American women constructed an imagined "Mexican culture" in an attempt to cope with the "ethnic episodes" at the university. Mia Tuan points out that Asian Americans "are expected to 'be ethnic' in spite of [a] loss of cultural authenticity accompanying extensive acculturation."[46] My respondents expressed feelings of "being ethnic" but, like other second-generation individuals, they remained confused about what meanings they attached to their ethnicity. Being marginalized as the "other" led them, as discussed above, to "show" their ethnicity, selecting symbols from Mexican culture. They selected symbols of a "revolutionary" Mexican nature, resulting from their politicalization of ethnicity. During these college years their ethnicity emerged as a radicalized one, fueled by their growing experiences with incidents of prejudice and their growing political consciousness and cultural nationalism.

Politicalization Of Ethnicity

The second generation exhibited both a reaction to their experiences with prejudice and discrimination and an understanding of the origins and dynamics of race relations. Their narratives illustrate their deepening understanding that race and ethnicity "matter" at the university and, more importantly, at the larger social level. Their interviews illustrate how the process of politicalization changed the meanings that they attached to their emerging ethnic identities. At one level, as discussed earlier in this chapter, the women reacted to ethnic slurs by imagining a reified Mexican culture which they incorporated into their everyday lives: "OK, then I'll be ethnic." At another level, respondents (re)defined themselves as they moved from a personal to a more collective understanding of issues of race and ethnicity in the United States. As a result, their ethnic identity became layered with a (re)imagined sense of ethnicity that differed from that of their immigrant parents. Respondents also discussed their politicized ethnicity in ways that challenge the assimilationist perspective; their movement away from the world of their immigrant parents did not signal a marked decline in their attachment to their ethnic identification.[47] Second-generation ethnic identities emerged as multidimensional, always changing, and contingent on interactions with their families, their university peers, and the university in general. Ethnic identity emerged through a renegotiation of ethnic group boundaries. They recognized that they were changing but, at the same time, they admitted maintaining many aspects of their identity that were shaped by their immigrant parents. Margarita's sentiments capture those of many of the others:

> It's not that I have just thrown out all the stuff my parents taught me about who I am and what is important for me. It's that I now can see other things that exist that they don't see. I have learned about the history of racism and inequality and theories to explain these. I see the world different but Mexico still explains me but I'm different from before this.

This statement is insightful at several levels. It expresses an awareness that the changes this respondent experienced have the potential to move her farther away from what she sees as the ethnic world of her immigrant parents and the meanings they have attached to their immigrant worlds. It also reveals an attempt to reconcile the two; she keeps some parts of her ethnic identity shaped by her parents and adds a new layer of a politicized ethnicity which she had constructed from her own daily experiences. Margarita attaches a personal meaning to being "Mexican" but, at the same time, distances herself by acknowledging a new dimension to her social identity: a deepening understanding of the structural obstacles confronting most immigrant groups but particularly Mexican immigrants. Second-generation Mexican American women knew that their immigrant parents believed in the American Dream, but they acknowledged that their parents' dreams of upward social mobility had not been fulfilled. Their parents' optimism was driven by witnessing their second-generation daughters' admission to college. Their daughters, however, expressed increased feelings of pessimism in the American Dream even though they saw themselves moving beyond their parents. They understood that their college degrees would, most likely, result in their own upward mobility, but a college education also provided them with the analytical tools needed to probe the significance of social structural inequality embedded in American society. Irene, like all of the respondents, believed that her college education was providing her with a better understanding of the socioeconomic conditions of Mexican immigrants like her parents:

> I never really knew a lot about the general economic conditions of Mexican immigrants. I knew that my parents tried to become middle-class, but it just never happened. I got some breaks with scholarships, but now I know that most of us Mexicans don't get lucky like me. I guess I'm learning how to see how society, well, American society works.

Other respondents demonstrated an intellectual development that provided them, as college students, with a better understanding of American society, although their explanations for inequality varied in depth and sophistication. Their increased awareness of the pervasiveness of socioeconomic discrimination underscored their gradual movement away from their immigrant parents' vision of American society as a land of opportunities. Ironically, like other children of immigrants who were first-generation college students, respondents represented the possibility of upward mobility, a dream that led their parents to become immigrants in the first place.[48]

Irene's analysis of social class dynamics in the United States is substantiated by the most recent demographic profiles of Mexican immigrants and their second-generation children. Leif Jensen's demographic work on immigrants found that although some immigrant groups do experience improved economic conditions, Latin American, particularly Mexican, immigrants are much more likely to remain below the poverty line than other immigrant groups. Children with two foreign-born parents, like my respondents, are at the highest risk. In addition, studies show that such high poverty rates continue into the third and fourth generation of children of foreign-born parents. Jensen points out the "stark reality that assimilation in America occurs within a society that is highly stratified by race and ethnicity, even among those whose roots in the country go back generations."[49] Respondents were aware of the various dimensions of structural inequality, a challenge to their parents' hopes for attaining the American Dream. A college education was bringing an understanding of such demographic profiles to these second-generation Mexican American women. Such an understanding included a heightened level of ethnic identification reflected in their political orientations. For example, Sylvia recalled her political awakening when she began to study the relationship between poverty and the experiences of specific ethnic groups, such as Mexican immigrants and their second-generation children.

> One thing that comes to mind was when I told you that we were really low on cash, like when my dad was out of work. And I remember, I totally remember going with my mom to the Salvation Army, and we used to get like a big old cheese and we had to get some clothes. And I remember thinking that I never want to be like this. I don't need to be rich, I don't need six cars, I don't need a mansion, but I want to be comfortable and I never want to be like this where are my kids are in torn up shoes. I think about this sometimes now and I know now that my parents were hard workers; my dad just was in a job that didn't give him a chance for getting ahead. They worked and worked but stayed the same, but they have hopes for me. But I see now that I have been taking classes, sociology and history, that for the majority of Mexicans their dream is just a dream. I got here but we're just a small handful. Knowing about this history makes me really mad and I want to show everyone, see? I am here. I'm here to stay and I am going to try and get more of us here.

Sylvia recalls a memory from her past, then revisits it, analyzing it in a way that uses a "sociological imagination" as she moves from her family's personal troubles to public issues of ethnic inequality.[50] Moreover, she concludes with an explicit statement of political activism, vowing to "try to get more Latinos here." Other respondents, such as Elena and Sylvia, contextualized their immigrant parents' lives and worldviews within the larger issue of U.S. race relations, and, as a result, they began to attach a new meaning to their ethnic identity: a collective ethnic solidarity designed to overcome the effects of embedded structural inequality.

Second-generation Mexican American women added a new layer to their ethnic identities as a result of their increased participation in student ethnic politics at the both the university level and that of the larger community. The process of identity formation was neither uniform nor automatic. Their interviews document varying degrees of uncertainty, ambiguity, and confusion regarding their relationship to their immigrant parents and the larger society, particularly its record of race and ethnic relations. Diana explained how she became involved in the campus activities against Proposition 187:

> My mom always told me to do my best, and always never give up and always just have faith in myself that eventually it will be better and it will be accomplished and not to let anything get in my way. If I work my hardest and give it my best try, I will accomplish anything I want. Well, I will always keep this a part of me, but I know now that it's not enough in this society. Look at Proposition 187. If it goes through, it will have very negative consequences for us Latinos. Hard work won't be enough. So I did take my mom's advice, I worked hard at trying to stop 187.

These students, who were sophomores in 1994, participated in rallies against Proposition 187 and, interestingly, described their experiences by combining their views on their own newly emerging ethnic politics and their mothers' worldviews. Carmen recalled this situation:

> I think I get a lot of my strong will from her [her mother], but she just always said that no matter how, you know, no matter how bad a situation is, things will always turn out. She's always the type, she's always told me that she thought that way when she came here to the United

States and her life was hard. She said that things got better. God will always provide if you have faith and work hard. But, well, I know this is true especially for her, it kept her going when she was, and my dad too, here as immigrants. But there are problems that are bigger than this. I didn't know if I should get involved in all the rallies [anti-Proposition 187] but then I figured it out. I have to. My parents are Mexican, they're immigrants. This kind of stuff affects all Mexicans, immigrants and me, others like me, Mexican Americans, all Latinos and Latinas.

Carmen, like Diana and several other respondents, retained key aspects of their immigrant parents' belief in their interpretation of the "American Dream," but they included a different twist by adding political activism as an integral component for the realization of this dream. Their participation in activities against Proposition 187, an attempt in 1994 to bar undocumented immigrants from receiving various types of social service, contributed to the development of their unfolding politicalization of ethnicity. Carmen's remarks further underscore a movement toward the use of various ethnic labels.

Alicia described a heated discussion she had with a dorm mate who told Alicia that she did not think students should be protesting against Proposition 187, arguing that it was not a student issue. Alicia recalled how this same student was also against adding courses for Latinos.

There was this one girl in my dorm and she said to me something like, "I don't understand why minorities get all the scholarships, and I don't understand why you want to take Latin History." I couldn't believe she kept calling it Latin History. She said that it wasn't right for "Latinos" to be able to take classes on their history and culture and we have to take something else. I was shocked and I told her she didn't understand what it means to be a minority, like I explained to her that I didn't grow up with learning about Mexican culture or history, only European history, and now that I'm in college I have the right to learn about my history. And guess what she answered me? She says, "Well, I'm from Ukraine and I should be able to take Ukrainian history and culture." Then I asked her what generation she was and she said she was the fifth and I said I am the second and this was Mexico long ago and California was never Ukraine. And that's what I told her. I told my mom and she was upset that I got into a fight with that girl and got upset. But you know what, I didn't get upset, I felt great, really great, and I told my mom that I thought she would have done and said the same thing. I told her I thought she would want me to stick up for Mexicans against Ukrainians or whatever.

Alicia's story defends her political activism and support for a diversified curriculum as a direct outgrowth of her mother's emphasis on pride in their family's Mexican culture. For the most part, however, the second generation's parents found it difficult to understand the new politicized ethnicity displayed by their daughters, manifested by attempts to reify Mexican culture by decorating their dorm rooms with posters of Zapata and voicing their concern with volatile political issues such as Proposition 187. Like the second generation in my study, children of Filipino immigrants express varying levels of ethnic identification and attachments that cannot be accounted for using an assimilationist perspective. Their ethnicity, like my respondents', did not decline or revert to one that was optional. On the contrary, it differed in degree of ethnic attachment, not in gradual decline. Espiritu's second-generation Filipinos strengthened their identification as Filipinos over their view of themselves as assimilated Americans because of increased instances of perceived prejudice and discrimination.

Through their participation in various college organizations, such as the Filipino American Club, these second-generation Filipinos experienced increased levels of politicized ethnic identities. Espiritu concludes that these college students redefined themselves through their newly developed roles as student activists dedicated to securing more equitable treatment and opportunities for Filipinos.[51] Respondent after respondent echoed Alicia's views. They also responded to those who challenged their legitimacy by increasing their attachments to their (re)invented ethnic identities, which they described in terms of asymmetrical power relations: "I told her she didn't understand what it means to be a minority." Filipino Americans found themselves in similar circumstance as they redefined their ethnic identities. Nevertheless, both groups did not completely give up their immigrant parents' belief in achieving the American Dream, but they reconceptualized it by acknowledging the persistence of structural barriers impeding upward social mobility.

My respondents saw themselves as changing, moving into a more politicized view of themselves and the world but never losing sight of their Mexican roots. Their emerging politicalization also grew out of their work in various community organizations and agencies that served Mexican immigrants and their children, most of whom were foreign-born not American-born like themselves. All of the respondents participated regularly in the university's community placements, either on an individual volunteer basis or as part of a course requirement. All of the students had worked in community placements that included work such as after-school K-12 programs, classroom tutoring, adult ESL classes, GED tutoring classes, and homeless shelters. The second generation's reflection on their experience in these community placements illustrate their growing sense of ethnic politicalization. Their discussions did more than describe their experiences; they provided various levels of political analysis on the conditions facing the different groups with which they worked. An analysis of these conditions produced a dramatic effect on the meanings they attached to their ethnic identity. As interns and volunteers in agencies serving immigrant families and their foreign-born children, these students increased their awareness of their persistent disadvantages. Elena expressed her concern for young immigrant children and the problems that they face in the American education system:

Someone needs to make sure that these kids [immigrants] are taken care of in school. I tutor in this school and all of the teachers are white and I started to realize, well, a lot of the times I would just get so upset that I would just try even harder to help the kids when I had them to myself on a one-on-one situation. Teachers have to know what kind of communities their students come from in order to understand where they're coming from so that you can help them in the right way instead of just putting it off and saying, "They're dumb and they'll never understand and get ahead." The teachers don't understand how these kids have trouble, like speaking Spanish at home and having parents that don't have much education or money. I feel like I have to do more than just be a teacher, you know? I've always wanted to be a teacher, but now I see that Mexican kids still need role models. It's still a problem not just something from the past. I think it would help these kids to see that it is possible for a Mexican to get educated, well, they are all mostly born in Mexico, but still we're the same in a lot of ways.

Elena's lifelong desire to become a teacher was transformed by her experiences with Mexican immigrant children. She stresses the need for all teachers to be sensitive to the special socioeconomic needs of these children but, in addition, accepts the challenge to serve as a role model for them as a Mexican American. She points out the difference between the foreign-born Mexican children and second-generation Mexican Americans but concludes, "we're the same in a lot of ways." Other respondents were equally as empathetic to the immigrants, both adults and children. They made comparisons between the adult immigrants they tutored in English and their own parents. Many began to speak up in class, arguing against anti-immigration sentiments and public policies, and, as a result, they became more conscious of themselves as, in the words of Irene, "a minority, a Mexican American." Josie referred to a discussion in one of her classes to illustrate how she was changing and how others were responding to this change:

> I began to feel more Latina. I'm not just from an ethnic group, I'm from a minority group. Others here [at the university] just don't get it. They think I should just be American. But I am, but I'm more. I mean, not better, but American and Mexican. That equals Mexican American. Anyway, I was in my English class and we began talking about multiculturalism and diversity. All the white students were for it, they said it was great to share cultures. But then I said something about how people didn't like immigrants. And all of a sudden the class was dead quiet until some started saying that immigrants needed to blend in and share their cultures but become American and be glad that they could get ahead in life here in this country. I told them about the kids I tutor and all the problems they have and their parents have, but it was no use. But it won't keep me from speaking up in the future.

Josie associated her greater understanding of the lives of recently arrived Mexican immigrants and children with her own evolving view of herself as an "ethnic." The specific experiences of second-generation Mexican Americans differ from findings in some studies of other second-generation individuals. In her study of Asian Americans, Mia Tuan concludes that with their increased experiences with prejudice and discrimination, second-generation Asian Americans exhibit increased levels of anti-immigrant beliefs. Tuan interprets this as an Asian American

response to the role played by recently arrived Asian immigrants in per-
petuating long-standing stereotypes of the Asian culture which, in turn,
has negative consequences on their lives since Americans find it difficult
to distinguish between foreign-born and American-born Asians. Tuan's
respondents believed that the existing stereotypes of Asians as a "model
minority" were positive and that newly arrived immigrants undermined
such positive images. Tensions between the two groups have developed in
various communities and have even led to hostilities with other groups,
such as Latinos who believe that both groups are contributing to increased
waves of anti-immigration feelings in general.[52]

Josie's passage further develops the theme of power relations in analyzing ethnic groups. Her comment that she is "not just from an ethnic
group, I'm from a minority group" suggests an understanding of a power
hierarchy based on race and ethnicity. In addition, this understanding of
power's role in shaping relations between ethnic groups leads to her skepticism about "diversity and multiculturalism" intimating their potential to
mask anti-immigrant views. Other respondents shared the skepticism that
a society's stress on diversity and multiculturalism would work fast enough
to change harmful anti-immigrant policies. Their work with recently
arrived Mexican immigrants reinforced their memories of their parents'
immigrant life stories and, as a result, they changed in two specific ways:
they demonstrated high levels of empathy with immigrants in general and
Mexicans in particular and they redefined themselves even more as Mexican Americans but with a new twist—a focus on the power dynamics
among groups in American society or what I have called "the politicalization of ethnicity." Isela provides an explanation that cut across all the
interviews:

> I see that all immigrants share similar conditions and face similar prob-
> lems like my parents did when they came from Mexico almost twenty
> years ago. Things have changed. I'm in college and I see others like me
> have reached this same place. So there is some improvement, but the
> statistics I learned about in my sociology classes point out that real prob-
> lems like racism and inequality are still here, and I want to do something
> as a Latina to help others, you know, Latinos not just from Mexico.

Fredrik Barth and Joane Nagel's research further explains the process of
the politicalization of ethnic identity. Barth stresses the ways that "identi-

ties are signaled as well as embraced."[53] Respondents (re)negotiated their second-generation membership boundaries based on a growing solidarity with recently arrived Mexican and Central American immigrants. They began to use the term *Latina* as an expression of a new imagined community.[54] Josie's comments are also significant for an understanding of the social construction of the second generation's identity. Josie captured the formation of a nuanced layer of identity that was shared by all the respondents. Josie described herself as beginning to "feel more Latina" as she participated in political rallies and interacted with newly arrived immigrants and their children. All the women's narratives uncover a similar facet in their identity construction. The politicalization of their ethnicity led them to redefine themselves in such a way that (re)imagined their identity. They began to use the label *Latina* as a cross-generational and Latin American term in order to display their solidarity with recently arrived immigrant families from Mexico and other Latin American countries. These second-generation women began to discuss the uneven power relationship between themselves and the larger society; they redefined themselves as "minorities like other ones, like African Americans."

(Re)Imagined Communities of Ethnicity

Second-generation Mexican American women responded to the external constraints of living in the "borderlands" of higher education by reconstructing their ethnic identities, a process through which they inscribed a new layer to their identity palimpsests. Their experiences as daughters of Mexican immigrants and Mexican Americans with "Mexican roots" remained important (re)emerging elements in their identity palimpsests. Research on first-generation college students documents the specific obstacles facing students whose parents do not have a university degree and the social capital that a college education produces, specifically for their children. Moreover, such class differences are exacerbated by race and ethnicity, since first-generation college students are less likely to be European American.[55] Interestingly, although respondents made various references to being the first in their families to enter college, issues related to their identity as first-generation students were not as salient as their ethnic and gender boundaries. They did not reveal a development to or an attachment with such a social marker.

The construction of an imagined and emergent ethnic community represents a common trope running through the interviews. As the respondents negotiated their way through the university, they attached new meanings to their ethnicity. Their interviews reveal the paths that led them to see themselves, under certain circumstances, as students of color, an ethnic label that they share with African American, Filipino, Japanese, and Chinese students. Nagel's work on ethnicity construction provides a theoretical lens with which to understand how these second-generation Mexican American women (re)invented themselves as students of color. A social constructionist view of the formation and development of ethnic identity focuses on the process through which "cultural construction is a method for revitalizing ethnic boundaries and redefining the meaning of ethnicity in existing ethnic populations."[56] The narratives of these second-generation Mexican American women suggest that their ethnic membership boundaries expanded as they began to "see how things are, how we are, all of us students of color." Their creation of an imagined community of color emerged as a direct strategy of collective identity and ideational mobilization in response to external forces. Their imagined ethnic group formations represented attempts to engage in a collective action.[57]

Respondents recognized a personal transformation that accounted for their growing identification with "other minorities." They explained that their experiences as "outsiders" in the university setting changed them, leading them to see their commonalities with other ethnic groups on campus. Their interviews capture their self-reflections on their changed reactions to episodes of prejudice. They recognized that they were developing new coping mechanisms, ones that led them to attach new meanings to their ethnic identities. Yvette displayed both her sense of frustration at being treated differently and her growing sense of intergroup ethnic consciousness when she related the following incident:

> I always felt a tension in class when we got around to discussing something about immigration or affirmative action. I would get so uncomfortable, but then I would hear something that I just didn't agree with and I couldn't take it anymore and I didn't feel intimidated. I know I probably can't change how others feel about some issues like more minorities on campus, and I know that when I get into it about some issue, other students are just thinking that I am saying all this because

> I'm a minority. Well, I am a minority. Sometimes I get kind of hopeless.
> But then I know that I'm not the only one. Others students of color
> have to go through this.

This passage is striking for three reasons. Yvette believes that others
see her as a member of a minority group and she expresses her own perception of herself as a minority. She also acknowledges that other "students of color" share her frustration. Attachments to an ethnic identity
have been explained in ways dating back to Charles H. Cooley's classic
"looking-glass self."[58] Ethnicity matters more when others treat you as if it
matters to them, usually under conditions of unequal power relationships.
Furthermore, Georg Simmel's theory of the "Stranger" outlines the
importance of the "Other" in the creation and maintenance of group solidarity. For Simmel, groups define themselves in relation to who they are
not and what others say they are.[59] This process is the heart of Mary
Waters's study of West Indian Immigrants who select their West Indian
identity in order to distance themselves from African Americans. Waters's
research and other studies of both immigrants and second-generation
individuals illustrate that "the construction and adoption of a racial and
ethnic social identity represent an ongoing negotiation between self and
other identifications which reflects the meanings attached to possible
identities and boundaries."[60] Such a process involves a group's understanding of racial and ethnic hierarchies within its society. Isela provided
a particularly in-depth account of her understanding of race and ethnic
relations in the United States when she confronted "these white guys that
were speaking about affirmative action and they seemed really bitter
because people less qualified get more money because they're minorities."
Isela continued her story, recalling her response to these two classmates:

> I said that historically we've been underrepresented, and I think some
> things are wrong with the affirmative action program, but that's the only
> thing we have as minorities to help us as a whole, as a whole group of
> people to help us all move up, and that's the only thing we have right
> now. And, until we get something that's better, we're going to have to
> deal with people saying we as minorities are getting more. And if this
> means some people don't get into the college of their choice, their first
> choice, a white person doesn't get into the college of their choice, that
> doesn't mean that they can't pursue their education somewhere else.

Like we have before, like historically, we haven't gotten into the best schools, but we've done the best we can with what little we have. And about the money, most of us Latinos who get a lot of money need that money, like other minorities.

Isela's detailed comments echo that of many of the other respondents. Her story reveals several layers all tied to a growing ethnic consciousness. Again, like Yvette, Isela responds to her perception of how "whites" see her. She responds with anger, as captured in the taped interviews, yet she goes beyond such expressions of anger and frustration by providing her own interpretation of what minorities have experienced historically. She uses the term *underrepresented*, revealing an emergent understanding of power relations in American society related to ethnicity and social class. Moreover, she underscores her understanding that a "white person" has the advantage to go to other colleges. Waters refers to the works of Alejandro Portes and Dag MacLeod to analyze the experiences of her study's West Indian immigrants who, like these second-generation Mexican American women, attach meanings to their ethnic identity by, in turn, attaching meanings to that of others. Portes and MacLeod summarize this process by emphasizing that "what they think your ethnicity is influences what you think your ethnicity is, to say nothing of what they think you think your ethnicity is."[61] Other respondents displayed similar understandings of ethnic and social class privileges. Irene captured the sentiments of most of the other second-generation women by her hope that she would succeed in college while, at the same time, expressing her frustration with the college environment:

I know that this is an excellent school, excellent academics, the recruiters gave me all kinds of information, you know, statistics about how great an education I would get. But they kind of, I wish, now that I think, I wish they could have kind of prepared me for what the reality of it is once you get here because, I don't know, I guess I really didn't think about it and I knew that the majority of students were white, you know, were Anglo, and so, but that never really bothered me. My high school had a lot of diversity including Anglos but a lot of minorities, not just Latinos. But here it was kind of like culture shock because I'm living on campus so, you know, I can't go home after school and, you know, that's home, you feel comfortable, but here it was a different story. I wish they could have warned me, forewarned me, about that. But I'm trying to make contacts with as many of us Latinas as possible to stick together. Actually, I am also hanging out with other minorities, you know, all of us students of color share a lot.

Isela overcomes her problems of studying and living in a predominantly white university by discussing her attempts to cope with these difficulties. Like most of the respondents, she describes a specific survival strategy: organize a support group of Latinos and other "students of color." Other second-generation groups have used the phrase students or people of color to declare their ties with other groups whom they identify as sharing similar circumstances of isolation and marginalization. Pyong Gap Min and Rose Kim's study of Asian American professionals revealed their growing imagined ties to both African Americans and Mexican Americans on the basis of shared experiences with prejudice and discrimination.[62]

Such coping strategies develop from a collective need to deal with the external structural factors placing constraints on these second-generation undergraduate students. Their deepening ethnic, gender, and social class-consciousness reflect an emerging response to their everyday circumstances. As discussed in earlier chapters, these daughters of Mexican immigrants displayed (re)emerging layers of their identities. Throughout this book I have used the metaphor "palimpsest of identity" to conceptualize the ethnic, gender, and social class dimensions of identity construction. The women I interviewed adopted the language of ethnicity which united them to other Latinos and Latinas, not necessarily from Mexico, and, moreover, they established imagined ties to other communities of ethnicity, specifically students whom they view as experiencing treatment as "the other." As they engaged in such a discourse on students of color, respondents witnessed an even deeper politicalization of their ethnicity. Furthermore, their words and actions as self-defined minorities and students of color reflect their perceived need to reconstruct their ethnic membership boundaries. The saliency of their ethnicity as second-generation Mexican Americans and students of color supports the view that the expansion of intra- and intergroup ethnic networks is most likely to develop under two specific situations: 1) increased experiences of interactions among members of ethnic groups and, perhaps most importantly,

2) an intensification of structural constraints impeding the fulfillment of a group's goals, such as surviving the demands of college life. The process by which respondents transformed their Mexican American ethnic consciousness into a more generalized consciousness as students of color reinforces William L. Yancey, Eugene Ericksen, and Richard Juliani's argument that ethnicity emerges and increases as groups experience changing societal conditions which may likely reinforce their need to maintain or (re)create kinship and friendship networks. The possibility of increased ethnic consciousness is contingent on the nature and degree of structural constraints and, as such, "ethnicity is largely a function of the structural situations in which groups have found themselves."[63] Nagel concludes that

> research has shown people's conception of themselves along ethnic lines, especially their ethnic identity, to be situational and changeable. . . . one's ethnic identity is a composite of the view one has of oneself as well as the views held by others about one's ethnic identity. As the individual (or group) moves through daily life, ethnicity can change according to variations in the situations and audiences encountered.[64]

Second-generation women maintained their ties to their Mexican heritage and the meanings their parents attached to this aspect of their identity, but their experiences with prejudice led them to reconstruct these meanings. They increased their attachment to their Mexican American ethnicity but, in addition, they moved toward an imagined community of students of color. Their narratives demonstrated a creative process through which their identities emerged and unfolded in directions that they had not anticipated, but ones that they eventually embraced as a survival strategy for their lives in the "borderlands" of their university setting. Elena summarizes the development of an imagined and emergent community of ethnicity:

> I never really clicked on this before I came here. In high school, most of my friends were Mexican American or some other Latinos like from El Salvador. But I did have Asian friends. But things changed when I came here. I think this school needs to get more Latinos and Latinas to come here, but I have changed. Most of my friends are minorities. It's weird, I never really felt like this. I stick out here. And so I'm like asking, why

do I feel like weird here, sort of like an outsider always? I'm developing a new mentality here. And more and more now, I see that other minorities are going through this, just like me. We are different, you know, diverse, but we come together for strength. I never understood exactly why some people called themselves students of color here, but now I know why they did and why I do now.

In another insightful passage, Sonia not only agrees with Elena about the need to "become a student of color" but also provides additional support for the position her mother took in providing her with ideational social capital as she embarked on her college career:

I hang around students like me, but more and more I am relying on African American, Hawaiian, and Asian American friends. We have specific issues at school, but we are learning to be a new group. I've asked myself why am I suddenly developing this mentality here [at the university]. But it's funny because when I started to tell my mom about me being involved with other students of color, she said she didn't really like this term but, and this is what I think is important, she said something like that now that I was in college, I was going to find that maybe all the minorities have to stick together for like reassurance. And I thought that's kind of funny 'cause that's actually what's happening, you know, whether it's Asian or whatever, it's like everyone has an understanding that we are all together. It's not just us Latinos that are sticking together, it's more all students of color.

Overview

The university setting represented a challenge for second-generation Mexican American women who were aware that they were in a different environment from their largely Mexican communities. Their mothers' support provided them with the ideational social capital needed to confront these new challenges. Lacking direct experiences with the college experience, immigrant mothers could not provide their daughters with pragmatic social capital, yet their daughters recognized their spirit and drive to "hacerle la lucha" as a motivating factor, leading them to contest the obstacles imposed on them in their own university "borderlands." Defined as the "Other," Mexican American women faced ethnic and gender contradictions within their university environment, which was a world far from that of their immigrant parents yet one in which these women would gain access to more of the benefits of American society. In turn, immigrants' daughters recognized the basis for their problems, emerging as active agents who contested the externally imposed constraints placed on them in a "place where some, or, I guess, a lot of people see as theirs and don't like us."

Respondents developed a deeper understanding of the role that their mothers played in shaping them into individuals who could defend themselves. Chapters 4 and 5 analyze the ethnic, social class, and gender strategies developed by both immigrant mothers and their second-generation daughters. The second-generation women eventually developed their own specific coping mechanisms, which ultimately led to a resurgence and resignification of their identities, further inscriptions on their palimpsests of identity.

These second generation narratives capture the ways in which they (re)imagine themselves, creating new ethnic boundaries within the university setting. They responded to the problematic treatment they experienced in conflicts with "the school and the Anglo kids, but also others like some faculty, even staff." They crafted new "gendered, ethnic scripts" that provided them with new patterns of behavior, eventually transforming them. They resignified their marginalization and alienation by undergoing a resurgent ethnicity, a (re)invented one that includes an understanding of the effects of power relations and dynamics on their everyday lives in the university. Their experiences with prejudice and discrimination may not have been different from those of their parents, but they responded in ways that surprised them. Respondents assumed a (re)invented ethnicity: "They see me like an ethnic, then OK, I will be ethnic." They became "ethnics" in ways that Barth, Nagel, and Anzaldúa would predict. These Mexican American women displayed their ethnicity in manners and fashions that represented a reification of Mexican culture: symbols of what they defined as a Mexican ethnicity—music, art, and dress—that they used to build an imagined ethnic community. Their ethnic spaces, like the feminist spaces discussed in chapter 4, became a haven for them, one that their parents, ironically, considered questionable. Their parents expressed concerns that such signs of ethnicity could eventually become obstacles to their daughters' success.

The resurgence of ethnicity changed the second generation's weltan-schauung, leading them to deepen their understanding of race and ethnic relations in the United States. Although their preferred term of self-identification remained *Mexican American*, their narratives trace their simultaneous attachment to a large, more encompassing identity that forged a link with other groups such as African Americans and, most importantly, Mexican Americans from third and later generations. Respondents used the socially constructed phrase "student of color," an outcome of the politicalization of their ethnicity driven by a combination of their response to their treatment as outsiders (in Simmel's view) and their gradual but heightened sense of embedded structural discrimination. Second-generation Mexican American women remembered their cultural heritage roots while (re)imagining new and emergent ethnic identities.

NARRATIVES OF THE SECOND GENERATION: CONCLUDING REMARKS

The opening chapter of this book introduces María, Sonia, and Carmen and their second-generation narratives, ones that set the stage for this qualitative study of a growing sector of the U.S. population that is shaping American society and will do so for years to come. As Oscar Handlin writes: "I thought to write a history of the immigrants in America. Then I discovered that the immigrants were American history."[1] In the traditions of other research on the "new" second generation, this study has rephrased Handlin's now famous passage: the new second generation is a major part of American history, representing one of the most important forces that will have a dramatic impact on the social fabric of the twenty-first century United States. The stories of the new second generation underscore the continued saliency of ethnicity issues, a social construction that matters and will continue to matter.

My in-depth interviews produced a collection of ethnic narratives that I have analyzed using a social constructionist and postmodern perspective. I chose a university setting for my research because, as other researchers studying children of immigrants have explained, such a site represents a truly "new world" for the second generation, specifically those whose parents arrived in the United States with limited educational and economic resources. In a way, American-born children share an "immigrant" experience with their parents when they enter the university, an alien environment. In the traditions of qualitative sociological research, this study is, by nature, neither exhaustive nor representative of all second-generation Mexican American women. Yet it has captured, in an ethnographic-like manner, the "thick descriptions" of the process through which ethnic identity and meanings shape their everyday worlds.

The life history sketches of María, Sonia, and Carmen reveal the tensions and contradictions present in the lives of the Mexican American women in this study. Their parents came to the United States in search of the American Dream: the opportunity for better lives than the ones their families had in Mexico. They struggled to provide their children with the means to achieve upward mobility, such as obtaining a university degree. The women in this study, like other children of immigrants, face questions and issues that affect their relationships within their families and the university, and these concerns form the basis for this book.

- How is the ethnic identity of second-generation Mexican American women shaped by the experiences of their Mexican immigrant parents?

- How does the second generation navigate through the worlds of its immigrant parents, the university setting, and the larger American society?

- What meanings do the second generation attach to their ethnicity, and what kinds of ethnic group boundaries do they (re)negotiate?

- What is the relationship between specific social structural factors, specifically within a university setting, and the social construction of ethnic membership boundaries by the second generation?

- How does ethnic identity emerge over time for second-generation individuals?

- How do gender and social class shape the emergent identities of second-generation Mexican American women?

- In general, how do these women (re)invent their ethnic identities?

Palimpsests of Identity

Ethnic identity is contingent and emergent, capable of changing over a lifetime of collective memories. I suggest that the process of identity formation can be seen metaphorically as writings on a palimpsest, where traces of past identities can (re)surface under certain circumstances, alongside new ones. My interviews revealed the unresolved tensions, ongoing conflicts, and persistent ambiguities that continue to shape my respondents' identities. These students found themselves in a symbolic borderland where they were always (re)inventing themselves by creating spaces in which they could contest the constraints of ethnicity, immigrant heritage, gender, and social class. They struggled to reconcile the world of their parents with their own, both of which were constantly evolving, never static. (Re)imagined memories of Mexico became an organizing trope in their lives as they "became" American yet "remained" part Mexican, confronting the unfolding tensions inherent in this process. Their parents recalled a Mexico that they left behind when they came to the United States; their children (re)invented Mexico. The second generation carry with them a sense of their "Mexicanidad," but they also recognize their differences from their parents, stressing their future lives in the United States. The women value their special affinity with their Mexican cultural heritage and respect their parents' attempts to retain their cultural memories. They experienced a collision of cultural and gender identities as they came of age as university women. Their fathers took pride in their educational achievements yet confronted them for becoming "Americanized" women who were not "dutiful daughters." Their fathers tried to impose traditional Mexican gender roles on them. Their mothers provided a resolution to this tension. They taught their daughters to confront and contest patriarchal constraints. Both generations of women crafted gender scripts and pacts in response to the contradictions of living in the male-dominated worlds of Mexican immigrant families and American society. Mothers and daughters live in a borderland of self, culture, and society, where ethnic and gender ambiguities shape their palimpsests of identity.

Emergent Ethnicity

Respondents described themselves in ways that capture the meaning of emergent ethnicity. They have Mexican surnames but are Americans, speak English and Spanish, prefer life in the United States, and only occasionally visit Mexico where their relatives often criticize them for being Americanized. They live in predominantly Mexican immigrant and Mexican American neighborhoods where, as one student said, Mexico "was all around them." They redefine their ethnic identities when they confront ethnic group boundaries. The women realize that they are different from their parents and grandparents but are, in many ways, similar to them. The meanings they attach to their ethnic identity shift, change, and blend, producing unresolved problems. As one respondent stated, "I feel like I am all of this all of the time." Their geographies of selves are Mexican, Mexican American, and American. The women do not synthesize these into one integrated identity. Their ethnic identities have boundaries that are fluid, malleable, and contingent. Joane Nagel concludes, "one's ethnic identity is a composite of the view one has of oneself as well as the views held by others about one's ethnic identity. As the individual (or group) moves through daily life, ethnicity can change according to variations in the situations and audiences encountered."[2] These women's narratives reveal the shifting nature of ethnic identity by using various ethnic labels interchangeably. They call themselves Mexicans, Mexicanas, Mexican Americans, Americans, and Latinas in specific situations and interchangeably. They use "Latina" when they find themselves in a group of women from other countries in Latin America. They use "American" when they describe instances of ethnic profiling by school administrators and law enforcement officers. They adopt the ethnic label of "Mexican American" to distinguish themselves from Mexican immigrants. Sometimes they use a combination of all of these ethnic labels. The women recalled that as "Mexican Americans," they wanted to fight for their civil rights as "Americans," but know that they are "Mexicanas" living in an American world, one that sees them and their parents as "Mexicans" and "foreigners" or "illegal aliens." Respondents stressed their "American" identities when treated as the "Other." Ethnic identity unfolds through this process of ethnic labeling. My interviewees responded to ways others defined them by attaching new meanings to their ethnic identity, reinventing their ethnicity as a contestation of such labeling. Yen Le Espiritu summarizes this process by stating that since ethnicity represents a cognitive worldview, "it is important to understand the manner in which [second- and later-generation] individuals imagine and construct their ethnicity—the meanings they attach to their ethnic background and the degree of importance they give to these meanings."[3]

Bravely Entering a New World of Higher Education

Daughters of Mexican immigrants experience a greater need to (re)invent themselves when they enter college. The daughters I interviewed left their families to become undergraduate students in a predominantly white university. They gained admission to the university without being fully aware of the social difficulties they would confront. Their mothers provided them with a spirit of optimism and independence, championing their transgressive gender behavior as a means to succeed in school. These values served as ideational social capital for these women. They learned the importance of believing in themselves and their ability to break through obstacles. They compared their lives as students to that of their mothers who believed in a philosophy of "hacerle la lucha" ("to take on the struggle"). My students see themselves as immigrants entering a new, contested terrain that will lead them to reinvent themselves.

Their university experiences mirror the ethnic prejudices and discrimination prevalent in the United States. The students recalled painful ethnic episodes that increased their feelings of alienation. They (re)constructed their identities as a coping mechanism. They created a Mexican American student community of shared identity. They adopted visible signs of imagined ethnicity: language, dress, lifestyle, music, art, and other aspects of Mexican material culture. Their attempts to cope with a hostile university environment led to confrontations with their parents who did not understand their daughters' emergent identities.

The women's experiences with marginalization and alienation created new politicized dimensions to their identities, shaped by their understanding of embedded social-structural inequalities. They challenged their parents' view of American society and began to participate in social justice activities. They shared similar experiences with third and fourth generation Mexican, African, and Asian Americans. They began to call themselves "students of color" while identifying as Mexican Americans. Their participation in political activities fueled their growing frustration with the American Dream, which, unlike their parents, they now consider an elusive one. Their increased politicalization also led to feminist discourses that contested patriarchal ideologies and gender specific stereotypes. They challenged the sexism demonstrated by Mexican American male students by creating a geographic and discursive space for feminist dialogues. The students (re)invented their gender identity using their mothers as role models because they challenged patriarchal constraints imposed by their husbands. An emergent feminism combined with their politicized ethnicity to establish sites of resistance within the university setting.

The students did not resolve the tensions and contradictions of second-generation Mexican American women. They saw themselves as Americans when others stereotyped them as foreigners. They saw themselves as foreigners when with Mexican-born family and friends who, in turn, saw them as Americanized Mexicans. As women, they defined themselves as independent and equal when their fathers exerted patriarchal authority over them. In sum, an unfolding process of constructing emergent identities and negotiated spaces shaped their lives.

Future Considerations

In my preface I expressed my long-standing concern for the recruitment and retention of Mexican Americans to colleges and universities in the United States. This book traces the ethnic identity development of Mexican American women who struggled to overcome many obstacles in their pursuit of higher education. Their narratives explain their adjustments to the university setting and their relationships with their parents. My findings are not representative of all second-generation women students, but it can be used to guide new studies. I hope this research will promote reforms in the educational system and will contribute to the success of future second-generation students from all immigrant backgrounds.

Demographic changes will affect the ethnic identity development of the "new" second generation. The U.S. Census Bureau reports that Mexican Americans are the largest minority group in the country. High immigration and fertility rates indicate even greater population growth. Intermarriages are increasing among foreign-born and American-born citizens. Continued obstacles to upward mobility include concentrations of Mexican Americans in the lower rungs of the occupational ladder, high poverty levels, and low education levels. Increased access to colleges and universities represents a critical factor for improved Mexican American living standards.[4]

Research studies on Mexican American college students have documented the problems they experience and have helped to design policies that will improve universities.[5] During my interviews, students offered suggestions to increase recruitment and retention rates for Mexican American students. They provided various policy suggestions to improve the academic and social environments for future students. Students believe that university administrators, faculty, and staff would benefit from a deeper understanding of their family backgrounds. The process of their parents' immigration and adjustment represents a constant source of stress and tension. My respondents' integration into higher education differs from that of students whose parents are not immigrants. Many of their parents prefer to speak Spanish and have lower educational attainment levels than other parents. Many had never been to the university and were hesitant to attend parent activities. These parents value higher education and dream of a better life for their children. While they lacked sufficient pragmatic social capital to help their children adjust to college, they valued a spirit of hard work and optimism. The students supported the development of bilingual workshops designed to help parents learn about the university and student life. They wanted these workshops to attract other Mexican American students who have completed two years of college, because they could explain how they coped with problems. Students suggested mother/daughter support programs, which could transform their mothers' ideational social capital into a pragmatic one. Students believed that the more their mothers understood the demands placed on them, the better they could support them. Students felt that first-year student orientation programs needed to include special bilingual sessions. Many students established informal support networks with third- and fourth-year students, particularly with students in their majors, but they believe that such networking should be formally organized to insure that all students have this opportunity. Respondents also wanted more opportunities to network with Mexican American alumni who could counsel them on career choices and job searches. Alumni could also organize internships at their workplaces.

Students also suggested the development of student-faculty mentorship programs to create closer academic relationships, which, studies show, increase retention rates. They wanted a mentorship program allowing students to assist with faculty research projects. I have had the opportunity to work with student research assistants and have seen the tremendous difference such a relationship can have. Several of my research assistants who were second-generation Mexican Americans told me several years later that they had considered dropping out of school. However, they decided to remain in school once they had the opportunity to work on my projects. They gained more self-confidence and learned about university student support services that assisted them with some of the academic problems that they were experiencing. These mentorship programs require funding commitments from the institution and, above all, the participation from faculty. It is also important that faculty from a variety of ethnic backgrounds serve as mentors.

Students also recommended regularly scheduled meetings with Mexican American students from other universities with whom they could establish support systems. They believed that making connections with students from universities with a larger percentage of Mexican American students would assist them in their personal development. These ties would also bring them into contact with Mexican American faculty who could also serve as mentors. My interviewees value cultivating and maintaining a larger circle of students, faculty, and staff who share similar backgrounds. They wanted opportunities to work on co-curricular projects, such as high school outreach programs, to recruit students to their university. I found that during those parts of the interviews, when students discussed emotionally difficult situations, they also talked about working with incoming students who faced similar problems. They explained that they wanted to work with students from all immigrant backgrounds. As Elena points out, "We're all in it together, and what good does it do if we succeed and then don't help others? We have to and I really want to."

These narratives of Mexican American women reveal a spirit of community and responsibility for the welfare of other students. Their journey through higher education has been a difficult one, but they always keep their eyes on the prize, never forgetting their parents' touchstone of "hacerle la lucha."

NOTES

Chapter I

1. Alejandro Portes and Min Zhou, "The New Second Generation: Segmented Assimilation and Its Variants among Post-1965 Immigrant Youth," *Annals of the American Academy of Political and Social Science* 530 (November 1993): 74–96.

2. Min Zhou, "Growing up American: The Challenge Confronting Immigrant Children and Children of Immigrants," *Annual Review of Sociology* 23 (1997): 63–75.

3. Pyong Gap Min, *Second Generation: Ethnic Identity Among Asian Americans* (Walnut Creek, Calif.: Altamira Press, 2002), 3–4.

4. Alejandro Portes and Rubén G. Rumbaut, *Legacies: The Story of the Immigrant Second Generation* (Berkeley: University of California Press, 2001), 44.

5. See Robert E. Park and Ernest W. Burgess, *Introduction to the Science of Sociology*, 2nd ed. (Chicago: University of Chicago Press, 1924); W. I. Thomas and Florian Znaniecki, *The Polish Peasant in Europe and America* (New York: Knopf, 1927); and Louis Wirth, *The Ghetto* (Chicago: University of Chicago Press, 1928).

6. W. Lloyd Warner and Leo Srole, *The Social Systems of American Ethnic Groups* (New Haven, Conn.: Yale University Press, 1945).

7. Seymour Martin Lipset, *The First New Nation: The United States in Historical and Contemporary Perspective* (Garden City, N.Y.: Doubleday, 1963).

8. Milton Gordon, *Assimilation in American Life: The Role of Race, Religion, and National Origin* (New York: Oxford University Press, 1964); Zhou, "Growing up American," 72–73.

9. Warner and Srole, *The Social Systems*, 2–15.

10. For a full analysis of thick and thin ethnicity, see Stephen Cornell and Douglas Hartmann, *Ethnicity and Race: Making Identities in a Changing World* (Thousand Oaks, Calif.: Pine Forge Press, 1998), 72–80. For studies on the relationship between ethnic attachments and intermarriage, see Herbert Gans, "Symbolic Ethnicity: The Future of Ethnic Groups and Cultures in America," *Ethnic and Racial Studies* 26 (January 1979): 1–20; Richard Alba, "The Twilight of Ethnicity among Americans of European Ancestry: The Case of Italians," in *Ethnicity and Race in the USA: Toward the Twenty-first Century*, ed. Richard Alba

(London: Routledge and Kegan Paul, 1985): 134–58; Richard Alba and M. B. Chamblin, "A Preliminary Examination of Ethnic Identification among Whites," *American Sociological Review* 48 (1983): 240–247; and Stanley Lieberson and Mary Waters, *From Many Strands: Ethnic and Racial Groups in Contemporary America* (New York: Russell Sage Foundation, 1988).

11. Mia Tuan, *Forever Foreigners or Honorary Whites? The Asian Ethnic Experience Today* (New Brunswick, N.J.: Rutgers University Press, 1998), 24.

12. Zhou, "Growing up American," 70–72.

13. For general critiques of the assimilation paradigm, see Robert Blauner, *Racial Oppression in America* (New York: Harper and Row, 1972); and Ronald Takaki, *A Different Mirror: A History of Multicultural America* (Boston: Little, Brown and Company, 1993).

14. See Richard Alba and Victor Nee, "Rethinking Assimilation: Theory for a New Era of Immigration," *International Migration Review* 31.4 (1997): 826–74; Jean Bacon, "Constructing Collective Ethnic Identities: The Case of Second-Generation Asian Indians," *Qualitative Sociology* 22.2 (1999): 141–60; and Yen Le Espiritu, *Asian American Pan-Ethnicity: Bridging Institutions and Identities* (Philadelphia: Temple University Press, 1992).

15. María de los Ángeles Torres, "Transnational Political and Cultural Identities: Crossing Theoretical Borders," in *Latino/a Thought: Culture, Politics and Society*, eds. Francisco H. Vásquez and Rodolfo D. Torres (Lanham, Md: Rowman & Littlefield Publishers, 2003): 370–85.

16. Vicki L. Ruiz, " 'Star Struck': Acculturation, Adolescence, and the Mexican American Women, 1920–1950," in *Building with Our Hands: New Directions in Chicana Studies*, ed. Adela de la Torre and Beatriz Pesquera (Berkeley: University of California Press, 1993): 109–29; and George J. Sánchez, *Becoming Mexican American: Ethnicity, Culture, and Identity in Chicano Los Angeles, 1900–1945* (New York: Oxford University Press, 1993).

17. J. A. Richman et al., "The Process of Acculturation: Theoretical Perspectives and an Empirical Investigation in Peru," *Social Science and Medicine* 25 (1987): 839–47.

18. R. C. Delucia and J. Balkin, "Ethnic Identification among Second- and Third-Generation Italian-American Police Officers: Its Presences and Significance," *Ethnic Groups* 7 (1989): 283–96; K. A. Hill and D. Moreno, "Second-Generation Cubans," *Hispanic Journal of Behavioral Sciences* 18 (1996): 175–93; and Bacon, "Constructing Collective Identities," 144–45.

19. Espiritu, *Asian American Pan-Ethnicity*; Yen Le Espiritu, "The Intersection of Race, Ethnicity, and Class: The Multiple Identities of Second-Generation Filipinos," in *The Second Generation: Ethnic Identity Among Asian Americans*,"

ed. Pyong Gap Min (Walnut Creek, Calif.: AltaMira Press, 2002); and Deborah Dash Moore, *At Home in America: Second Generation New York Jews* (New York: Columbia University, 1981).

20. Bacon, "Constructing Collective Identities," 143.

21. Herbert J. Gans, "Second-Generation Decline: Scenarios for the Economic and Ethnic Futures of the Post-1965 American Immigrants," *Ethnic Racial Studies* 15.20 (1992): 173–92.

22. Joel Perlmann and Roger Waldinger, "Second Generational Decline? Children of Immigrants, Past and Present—A Reconsideration," *International Migration Review* 31.4 (1997): 893–922, esp. 904.

23. Gans, "Second-Generation Decline," 173–74.

24. Portes and Rumbaut, *Legacies*, 45.

25. Portes and Rumbaut, *Legacies*, 46.

26. Portes and Zhou, "The New Second Generation," 74–80; Min Zhou and Carl L. Bankston III, "Social Capital and the Adaptation of the Second Generation: The Case of Vietnamese Youth in New Orleans," *International Migration Review* 28 (1994): 821–45; Min Zhou, "Segmented Assimilation: Issues, Controversies, and Recent Research on the New Second Generation," *International Migration Review* 38.4 (1997): 975–1008; and Rubén G. Rumbaut, "The Crucible Within: Ethnic Identity, Self-Esteem, and Segmented Assimilation among Children of Immigrants," *International Migration Review* 31.4 (1997): 748–93.

27. Zhou and Bankston, "Social Capital," 821–25.

28. Mary C. Waters, *Black Identities: West Indian Immigrant Dreams and American Realities* (New York: Russell Sage Foundation, 1999), 197.

29. Rumbaut, "The Crucible Within," 790.

30. Sánchez, *Becoming Mexican American*, 38–83; and Manuel G. Gonzales, *Mexicanos: A History of Mexicans in the United States* (Bloomington: Indiana University Press, 1999).

31. Sánchez, *Becoming Mexican American*, 8 and 11.

32. Ruiz, "'Star Struck,'" 129.

33. Roger Rouse, "Mexican Migration and the Social Space of Postmodernism," in *Between Two Worlds: Mexican Immigrants in the United States*, ed. David G. Gutiérrez (Wilmington, Del.: Scholarly Resources, 1996), 247–263, esp. 248.

34. Sánchez, *Becoming Mexican American*, 12.

35. Tuan, *Forever Foreigners*, 37–47.

36. Pyong Gap Min and Rose Kim, "Formation of Ethnic and Racial Identities: Narratives by Asian American Professionals," in *The Second Generation: Ethnic Identity Among Asian Americans*, ed. Pyong Gap Min (Walnut Creek, Calif.: Altamira Press, 2002), 153–181.

37. Tuan, *Forever Foreigners*, 40–41. Tuan suggests the following two sources which address the issue of Asian Americans depicted as "foreigners." See S. M. Nishi, "Perceptions and Deceptions: Contemporary Views of Asian-Americans," in *A Look Beyond the Model Minority Image: Critical Issues in Asian America*, ed. Grace Yun (New York: Minority Rights Group, 1989), 3–10; and W. Wei, *The Asian American Movement* (Philadelphia: Temple University Press, 1993).

38. Tuan, *Forever Foreigners*, 44.

39. David J. O'Brien and Stephen Fugita, *The Japanese American Experience* (Bloomington: University of Indiana Press, 1991).

40. Nazli Kibria, "Power, Patriarchy, and Gender Conflict in the Vietnamese Immigrant Community," *Gender and Society* 4 (March 1990): 9–24; and Nazli Kibria, "Migration and Vietnamese American Women: Remaking Ethnicity," in *Women of Color In U.S. Society*, ed. Maxine Baca Zinn and Bonnie Thornton Dill (Philadelphia: Temple University Press, 1994): 247–261.

41. Gloria Anzaldúa, *Borderlands/La Frontera: The New Mestiza* (San Francisco: Spinsters/Aunt Lute, 1987); Patricia Zavella, *Women's Work & Chicano Families: Cannery Workers of the Santa Clara Valley* (Ithaca: Cornell University Press, 1987); Pierrette Hondagneu-Sotelo, *Gendered Transitions: Mexican Experiences of Immigration* (Berkeley: University of California Press, 1994); Vicki L. Ruiz, *From out of the Shadows: Mexican American Women in Twentieth Century America* (New York: Oxford University Press, 1998); and Mary S. Pardo, *Mexican American Women Activists: Identity and Resistance in Two Los Angeles Communities* (Philadelphia: Temple University Press, 1998).

42. Karen A. Cerulo, "Identity Construction: New Issues, New Directions," *Annual Review of Sociology* 23 (1997): 385–409, esp. 387.

43. Fredrik Barth, "Introduction," in *Ethnic Groups and Boundaries: The Social Organization of Culture Difference*, ed. Fredrik Barth (Boston: Little, Brown and Company, 1969), 9–38, esp. 15. For an overview of the relationships between social conflict and group boundaries using the theoretical framework of George Simmel, see Lewis Coser, *The Functions of Social Conflict* (New York: The Free Press of Glencoe, 1956).

44. William L. Yancey, Eugene P. Ericksen, and Richard N. Juliani, "Emergent Ethnicity: A Review and Reformulation," *American Sociological Review* 41 (June 1976): 391–403, esp. 391.

45. Yancey, Ericksen, and Juliani, "Emergent Ethnicity," 400.

46. Cerulo, "Identity Construction," 387.

47. Joane Nagel, "Constructing Ethnicity: Creating and Recreating Ethnic Identity and Culture," *Social Problems* 41 (1994): 152–176, esp. 152.

48. Lisa Lowe, "Heterogeneity, Hybridity, Multiplicity: Marking Asian

American Difference," *Diaspora* 1 (Spring 1991): 24–44, esp. 39. See also Lisa Lowe, *Immigrant Acts* (Durham, N.C.: Duke University Press, 1996).

49. Elaine H. Kim, "Beyond Railroads and Internment: Comment on the Past and Future of Asian American Studies," *Association for Asian American Studies Newsletter* 10.4 (1993): 3–7; and R. Radhakrishnan, "Ethnic Identity and Post-Structuralist Difference," *Cultural Critique* 6 (1987): 199–220.

50. Paula M. L. Moya, "Introduction: Reclaiming Identity," in *Reclaiming Identity: Realist Theory and the Predicament of Postmodernism*, ed. Paula M. L. Moya and Michael R. Hames-García (Berkeley: University of California Press, 2000), 1–26.

51. Patricia Hill Collins, *Black Feminist Thought: Knowledge, Consciousness, and the Politics of Empowerment* (Boston: Unwin Hyman Press, 1990); and Maxine Baca Zinn and Bonnie Thornton Dill, "Difference and Domination," in *Women of Color In U.S. Society*, ed. Maxine Baca Zinn and Bonnie Thornton Dill (Philadelphia: Temple University Press, 1994): 3–12. See also the essays in Maxine Baca Zinn, Pierrette Hondagneu-Sotelo, and Michael A. Messner, eds., *Through the Prism of Difference: Readings on Sex and Gender* (Trenton, N.J.: Prentice Hall, 1997).

52. Anzaldúa, *Borderlands/La Frontera*, 77–98; Bonnie Thornton Dill, "Race, Class, and Gender: Prospects for an All-Inclusive Sisterhood," *Feminist Studies* 9 (1983): 131–50; Collins, *Black Feminist Thought*, 19–39; Jane Flax, "Postmodernism and Gender Relations in Feminist Theory," in *Feminism and Postmodernism*, ed. Linda J. Nicholson (New York: Routledge, 1990), 39–62; and Judith Butler, *Gender Trouble: Feminism and the Subversion of Identity* (New York: Routledge, 1990).

53. Moya, "Introduction: Reclaiming Identity," 4–9.

54. Collins, *Black Feminist Thought*, 23.

55. I would like to acknowledge Richard A. García for helping me develop the concept of "palimpsest of identity."

56. Kathleen Day Hulbert and Dianne Tickton Schuster, eds., *Women's Lives through Time: Educated American Women of the Twentieth Century* (San Francisco: Jossey-Bass Publishers, 1993).

57. Hulbert and Schuster, *Women's Lives*, xxi.

58. Paula Giddings, *In Search of Sisterhood: Delta Sigma Theta and the Challenge of the Black Sorority Movement* (New York: Quill, 1988); Stephanie Shaw, *What a Woman Ought to Be and to Do: Black Professional Women Workers during the Jim Crow Era* (Chicago: University of Chicago Press, 1960); and Elizabeth Higginbotham, *Too Much to Ask: Black Women in the Era of Integration* (Chapel Hill, N.C.: The University of North Carolina Press, 2001).

59. María Chacón, Elizabeth G. Cohen, Margaret Camarena, Judith Gonzá-lez, and Sharon Strover, *Chicanas in Postsecondary Education* (Stanford, Calif.: Center for Research on Women, Stanford University, 1982); Patricia Gándara, "Passing through the Eye of the Needle: High Achieving Chicanas," *Hispanic Journal of Behavioral Sciences* 4.2 (1982): 167–79; Patricia Gándara, *Over the Ivy Walls: The Educational Mobility of Low-Income Chicanos* (Albany: State University of New York, 1995); Denise Segura, "Chicanas and Triple Oppression," in *Chicana Voices: Intersections of Class, Race, and Gender*, ed. Teresa Córdova et al. (Austin: Center for Mexican American Studies, 1988): 47–65; and Denise Segura, "Slipping through the Cracks: Dilemmas in Chicana Education," in *The Division of Household Labor, in Building with our Hands: New Directions in Chicana Studies*, ed. Adela de la Torre and Beatriz Pesquera (Berkeley: University of California Press, 1993): 199–216.

60. Segura, "Slipping," 210–14.

61. Rodolfo O. de la Garza et al., *Latino Voices: Mexican, Puerto Rican, and Cuban Perspectives on American Politics* (Boulder: Westview Press, 1992), 96.

62. Samuel Bowles and Herbert Gintes, *Schooling in Capitalist America* (New York: Basic Books, 1976); Harriet D. Romo, "The Mexican Origin Population's Differing Perceptions of their Children's Schooling," *Social Science Quarterly* 65 (1984): 635–50; Harriet D. Romo and Toni Falbo, *Latino High School Graduation: Defying the Odds* (Austin: University of Texas Press, 1996); and Daniel Gilbert Solórzano, "A Study of Social Mobility Values: The Determinants of Chicano Parents' Occupational Expectations for their Children" (Ph.D. Diss., Claremont Graduate School, 1986).

63. Gándara, "Passing Through," 169–71.

64. See Segura, "Slipping Through," and Gándara, *Over the Ivy*, 1–10.

65. Romo and Falbo, *Latino High School*, 20–69.

66. Paul DiMaggio, "Culture Capital and School Success," *American Sociological Review* 47.1 (1982): 189–201.

67. United States Census Bureau, "Table 215: Educational Attainment by Race and Hispanic Origin, 1960–2000," in *Statistical Abstract of the United States* (Washington, D.C.: U.S. Government Printing Office, 2000), 139.

68. United States Census Bureau, "Table 215," 139.

69. Clifford Geertz, *The Interpretation of Cultures: Selected Essays* (New York: Basic Books, 1973).

70. Geertz, *The Interpretation*, 5–7.

71. Nazli Kibria, "College and Notions of 'Asian Americans': Second-Generation Chinese Americans and Korean Americans," in *The Second Generation: Ethnic Identity Among Asian Americans*, ed. Pyong Gap Min (Walnut Creek, Calif.: Altamira Press, 2002), 183–207.

72. Sherna Berger Gluck and Daphne Patai, eds., *Women's Words: The Feminist Practice of Oral History* (New York: Routledge, 1991).

73. Katherine Borland, "'That's Not What I Said': Interpretive Conflict in Oral Narrative Research," in *Women's Words: The Feminist Practice of Oral History*, ed. Sherna Berger Gluck and Daphne Patai (New York: Routledge: 1991), 63–75.

74. Susan Matoba Adler, *Mothering, Education, and Ethnicity: The Transformation of Japanese American Culture* (New York: Garland Publishing, 1998), 169. For other essays addressing the issue of retaining feminist ethics in qualitative research, see: J. A. Cook and M. M. Fonow, "Knowledge and Women's Interests: Issues of Epistemology and Methodology in Feminist Sociological Research," *Sociological Inquiry* 56 (1986): 2–29.

75. Gloria Hull, Patricia Bell Scott, and Barbara Smith, eds., *All the Women are White, All the Blacks are Men, but Some of Us Are Brave: Black Women's Studies* (Old Westbury, N.Y.: The Feminist Press, 1982), 17.

76. Gwendolyn Etter-Lewis, "Black Women's Life Stories: Reclaiming Self in Narrative Texts," in *Women's Words: The Feminist Practice of Oral History*, ed. Sherna Berger Gluck and Daphne Patai (New York: Routledge, 1991), 43–58, esp. 56.

77. Maxine Baca Zinn, "Field Research in Minority Communities: Ethical, Methodological, and Political Observations by an Insider," *Social Problems* 27.2 (1997), 209–219, esp. 210.

78. Gluck and Patai, *Women's Words*, 1–5.

79. Rima Benmayor, "Testimony, Action Research, and Empowerment: Puerto Rican Women and Popular Education," in *Women's Words: The Feminist Practice of Oral History*, ed. Sherna Berger Gluck and Daphne Patai (New York: Routledge, 1991), 159–74.

80. Julia Curry-Rodriguez, "Reconceptualizing Undocumented Labor Immigration: The Causes, Impact, and Consequences in Mexican Women's Lives" (Ph.D. Diss., University of Texas at Austin, 1998).

81. Alma M. García, "'I Work for My Daughter's Future': Entrepreneurship and Mexican American Women," *California History* (Fall 1995): 262–79.

Chapter 2

1. Benedict Anderson, *Imagined Communities: Reflection on the Origin and Spread of Nationalism* (New York: Verso, 1983), 6.

2. Anderson, *Imagined Communities*, 7.

3. Anderson, *Imagined Communities*, 6. Recommended by Anderson, see

Hugh Seton-Watson, *Nations and States: An Enquiry into the Origins of Nations and the Politics of Nationalism* (Boulder: Westview Press, 1977), 5.

4. See Richard A. García, *The Making of the Mexican-American Mind, San Antonio, Texas, 1929–1941: A Social and Intellectual History of an Ethnic Community* (San Antonio: Texas A&M University Press, 1991).

5. Hondagneu-Sotelo, *Gendered Transitions*, 29–33.

6. Hondagneu-Sotelo, *Gendered Transitions*, 31.

7. Rubén G. Rumbaut and Alejandro Portes, eds., *Ethnicities of Children of Immigrants in America* (Berkeley: University of California Press, 2001), 7.

8. Rumbaut and Portes, *Ethnicities*, 9.

9. Alejandro Portes and Alex Stepick, *City on the Edge: The Transformation of Miami* (Berkeley: University of California Press, 1993).

10. Caroline Bettinger-López, *Cuban-Jewish Journey: Searchings for Identity, Home, and History in Miami* (Knoxville: University of Tennessee Press, 2000). See also Deborah Dash Moore, *To the Golden Cities: Pursuing the American Jewish Dream in Miami and L.A.* (New York: Free Press, 1999).

11. Barth, "Introduction," 15–16.

12. James M. Freeman, *Changing Identities: Vietnamese Americans, 1975–1995* (Boston: Allyn and Bacon, 1995), 120–121.

13. Sandra Cisneros, *Caramelo* (New York: Alfred A. Knopf, 2002), 17–18.

14. Adler, *Mothering*, 65–66; Espiritu, *Asian American*, 4–5.

15. Yen Le Espiritu and Diane L. Wolf, "The Paradox of Assimilation: Children of Filipino Immigrants in San Diego," in *Ethnicities of Children of Immigrants in America*, ed. Rubén G. Rumbaut and Alejandro Portes (Berkeley: University of California Press, 2001), 157–86.

16. Ronald Takaki, *From Different Shores: Perspectives on Race and Ethnicity in America* (New York: Oxford University Press, 1987).

17. Mario T. García, *Desert Immigrants: the Mexicans of El Paso, 1880–1920* (New Haven: Yale University Press, 1981).

18. García, *The Making*, 223–33.

19. Mario T. García, *"La Frontera*: The Border as Symbol and Reality in Mexican American Thought," in *Between Two Worlds: Mexican Immigrants in the United States*, ed. David G. Gutiérrez (Wilmington, Del.: Scholarly Resources, 1996), 90.

20. García, *"La Frontera,"* 91.

21. María Castañeda, "Mexican Immigrant Cannery Women Workers: Work, Family, and Culture" (Unpublished Senior Sociology Thesis, Santa Clara University, 1998).

22. Castañeda, "Mexican Immigrant," 16.

23. García, *Desert Immigrants;* Hondagneu-Sotelo, *Gendered Transitions,* chapter 1.

24. Mary Helen Ponce, *Hoyt Street: An Autobiography* (Albuquerque: University of New Mexico Press, 1993); Sandra Cisneros, *The House on Mango Street* (New York: Vintage, 1989); Cisneros, *Caramelo;* Pat Mora, *House of Houses* (Boston: Beacon Press, 1997); and Cristina García, *Dreaming in Cuban* (New York: Knopf, 1992). These are just a few of a growing number of such autobiographies. These authors were specifically mentioned by the respondents. For an introduction to Chicana literature, see the excellent anthology by Tey Diana Rebolledo and Eliana S. Rivero, *Infinite Divisions: Anthology of Chicana Literature* (Tucson: University of Arizona Press, 1993).

25. Rouse, "Mexican Migration and the Social Space of Postmodernism," 248.

26. Rouse, "Mexican Migration," 247–53.

27. See chapter 1 in Hondagneu-Sotelo, *Gendered Transitions.*

28. Ruiz, *From Out*, 127–46.

29. For one of the earliest anthologies on Mexican immigrant women, see Margarita Melville, ed., *Mexicanas at Work in the United States* (Houston: Mexican American Studies Monograph No. 5, 1988); Anzaldúa, *Borderlands;* Hondagneu-Sotelo, *Gendered Transitions;* Ruiz, "'Star Struck.'"

30. Ruiz, *From Out*, 127–46.

31. Hondagneu-Sotelo, *Gendered Transitions*, 3.

32. For an excellent overview of the relationship between transnational migration and gender conflict, see Hondagneu-Sotelo, "Overcoming Patriarchal Constraints," 393–400. For a primarily theoretical discussion, see Norma Alarcón, "Chicana Feminist Literature: A Re-Vision Through Malintzin: Putting the Flesh Back on the Object," in *This Bridge Called My Back: Radical Writings by Women of Color*, ed. Cherríe Moraga and Gloria Anzaldúa (New York: Kitchen Table-Women of Color Press, 1983): 182–90; Emma Pérez, *The Decolonial Imaginary: Writing Chicanas into History* (Bloomington: Indiana University Press, 1999); and Sonia Saldívar-Hull, *Feminism on the Border: Chicana Gender Politics and Literature* (Berkeley: University of California Press, 2000).

33. See entire preface in Anzaldúa, *Borderlands.*

34. Anzaldúa, *Borderlands*, 35.

35. For an analysis of the "border" and Anzaldúa's reconceptualization of "border" and "borderlands," see Theresa A. Martínez, "Storytelling as Oppositional Culture: Race, Class, and Gender in the Borderlands," *Race, Gender, and Class* 6.3 (1999): 33–51, esp. 45–50; Richard A. García, "Towards a Theory of Latina Rebirth 'Renacimiento de la Tierra Madre': The Feminism of Gloria

Anzaldúa," *Race, Gender, and Class* 6.3 (1999): 29–45; and Jose David Saldívar, *Border Matters: Remapping American Cultural Studies* (Berkeley: University of California Press, 1997).

36. Renato Rosaldo, *Culture & Truth: The Remaking of Social Analysis* (Boston: Beacon Press, 1989), 207.

37. Mario T. García, "Introduction" to *Migrant Daughter: Coming of Age of a Mexican American Woman* (Berkeley: University of California Press, 2000), xvi.

38. García, "Introduction"; Martínez, "Storytelling," 34–38.

39. See the following and their bibliographies: Hondagneu-Sotelo, *Gendered Transitions*; Ruiz, *From Out*; Mary Romero, *Maid in the USA* (New York: Routledge, 1992); and Pierrette Hondagneu-Sotelo, "Overcoming Patriarchal Constraints: The Reconstruction of Gender Relations among Mexican Immigrant Women and Men," *Gender & Society* 6 (1992): 393–415.

40. Zavella, *Cannery Women*, 159–61.

41. Beatriz M. Pesquera, "'In the Beginning He Wouldn't Even Lift a Spoon': The Division of Household Labor," in *Building With Our Hands: New Directions in Chicana Studies*, ed. Adela de la Torre and Beatriz Pesquera (Berkeley: University of California Press, 1993), 181–195.

42. García, "I Work," 270–72.

43. Arlie Hochschild with Anne Machung, *The Second Shift: Working Parents and the Revolution at Home* (New York: Viking, 1989).

44. Hondagneu-Sotelo, "Overcoming Patriarchal," 19.

Chapter 3

1. Anzaldúa, *Borderlands*, 78–80.

2. For a similar discussion on language usage among immigrants, see Jean Bacon, *Life Lines: Community, Family, and Assimilation among Asian Indian Immigrants* (New York: Oxford University Press, 1996).

3. de la Garza et al., *Latino Voices*, 41.

4. David E. López and Ricardo D. Stanton-Salazar, "Mexican Americans: A Second Generation at Risk," in *Ethnicities: Children of Immigrants in America*, ed. Rubén G. Rumbaut and Alejandro Portes (Berkeley: University of California, 2001), 57–90, esp. 64–68.

5. Pyong Gap Min and Joann Hong, "Ethnic Attachments among Second-Generation Korean Americans," in *The Second Generation: Ethnic Identity among Asian Americans*, ed. Pyong Gap Min (Walnut Creek, Calif.: Altamira Press, 2002), 125.

6. Linda A. Revilla, "Filipino American Identity: Transcending the Crisis,"

in *Filipino Americans: Transformation and Identity*, ed. María P. P. Root (Thousand Oaks, Calif.: Sage Publications, 1997), 95–111, esp. 104–7; and Theodore S. Gonzalves, "The Day the Dancers Stayed: On Pilipino Cultural Nights," in *Filipino Americans: Transformation and Identity*, ed. María P. P. Root (Thousand Oaks, Calif.: Sage Publications, 1997), 163–82, esp. 174.

7. Tuan, *Forever Foreigners*, 107–10.

8. Min and Hong, "Ethnic Attachments," 125.

9. Note that this last sentence is the subtitle for this section of chapter 3.

10. Lisandro Pérez, "Growing up in Cuban Miami: Immigration, the Enclave, and New Generations," in *Ethnicities: Children of Immigrants in America*, ed. Rubén G. Rumbaut and Alejandro Portes (Berkeley: University of California, 2001), 111–14. See also Lisandro Pérez, "The Household Structure of Second-Generation Children: An Exploratory Study of Extended Family Arrangements," *International Migration Review* 38.4 (1997): 736–47.

11. Nagel, "Constructing Ethnicity," 152–155.

12. Ruiz, "'Star Struck,'" 129–31. For a further discussion of the second generation negotiating its group boundaries, see Richard Alba, *Italian Americans: Into the Twilight of Ethnicity* (Englewood Cliffs, N.J., 1985); Richard Alba, "Cohorts and the Dynamics of Ethnic Change," in *Social Structure and Human Lives*, ed. Matilda White Riley, Bettina J. Huber, and Beth B. Hess (Beverly Hills: Sage Publications, 1988), 211–28; and Mary Waters, *Ethnic Options: Choosing Identities in America* (Berkeley: University of California Press, 1990).

13. Susan E. Keefe and Amado M. Padilla, *Chicano Ethnicity* (Albuquerque: University of New Mexico Press, 1987).

14. Espiritu, *Asian American*; Tuan, *Forever Foreigners*, 118–22.

15. Felix Padilla, *Latino Ethnic Consciousness: The Case of Mexican Americans and Puerto Ricans in Chicago* (Notre Dame: University of Notre Dame Press, 1985).

16. For a discussion of the relationship between the researcher's ethnic self-identification and those of the study's respondents, see Patricia Zavella, "Feminist Insider Dilemmas: Constructing Identity with 'Chicana' Informants," in *Feminist Dilemmas in Fieldwork*, ed. Diane L. Wolf (Boulder, Colo.: Westview, 1996), 138–169.

17. Tuan, *Forever Foreigners*, 51.

18. Moore, *At Home*, 3–58. For a classic study of Jews in America see Irving Howe, *The World of our Fathers* (New York : Harcourt Brace Jovanovich, 1976).

19. Moore, *At Home*, 9.

20. Barth, "Introduction," 15.

21. Note that this last sentence is the subtitle for this section of chapter 3.

22. Freeman, *Changing Identities*, 112.

23. Tuan, *Forever Foreigners*, 134.

24. Tomás Jiménez, "Negotiating Ethnic Boundaries: Multiethnic Mexican Americans and Ethnic Identity in the United States" (John F. Kennedy School of Government, Harvard University, Working Paper Series, January 2001).

25. See María P. P. Root, ed., *The Multiracial Experience: Racial Borders as the New Frontier* (Thousand Oaks, Calif.: Sage Publications, 1996).

26. Gloria E. Anzaldúa, "Writing A Way of Life," in *Interviews Entrevistas*, ed. Ana Louise Keating (New York: Routledge, 2000): 235–49, esp. 238–39.

27. Anzaldúa, "Writing," 239; see Simone de Beauvoir, *The Second Sex*, trans. and ed. H. M. Parshley (New York: Modern Library, 1952).

28. Ponce, *Hoyt Street*, 143.

29. Waters, *Black Identities*, 91.

30. García, "Towards a Theory," 40.

31. Kibria, "College," 190–99.

32. Tuan, *Forever Foreigners*, 28.

33. Min and Kim, "Formation," 174–77.

34. Antonio J. A. Pido, "Macro/Micro Dimensions of Pilipino Immigration to the United States," in *Filipino Americans: Transformation and Identity*, ed. María P. P. Root (Thousand Oaks, Calif.: Sage Publications, 1997), 21–38, esp. 33.

35. Takaki, *Different Mirror*, 1–4.

36. Barth, "Introduction," 22–28.

37. Nagel, "Constructing Ethnicity," 154.

38. López and Stanton-Salazar, "Mexican Americans," 60.

39. Christine Marín, "The Power of Language: From the Back of the Bus to the Ivory Tower," in *Speaking Chicana: Voice, Power, and Identity*, ed. D. Letticia Galindo and María Dolores Gonzales (Tucson: The University of Arizona Press, 1999), 85–89, esp. 89. For similar autobiographical essays, see Karin Rosa Ikas, *Chicana Ways: Conversations with Ten Chicana Writers* (Reno: University of Nevada Press, 2002).

40. Espiritu and Wolf, "The Paradox," 158–63.

41. *The Lemon Grove Incident*, prod. Paul Espinosa (Espinosa Productions, 1985), videocassette.

42. Richard Sennet and Jonathan Cobb, *The Hidden Injuries of Class* (New York: Vintage Books, 1972).

43. Ivan Light, *Ethnic Enterprise in America: Business and Welfare among Chinese, Japanese, and Blacks* (Berkeley: University of California Press, 1972).

44. Alma M. García, *The Mexican Americans* (Westport, Conn.: Greenwood Press, 2002), 67–78.

45. Naomi Wolf, *The Beauty Myth* (New York: W. Morrow, 1991).

46. Toni Morrison, *The Bluest Eye* (New York: Plume Books, 1993).

47. Inés Hernández, "To Other Women Who Were Ugly Once," in *Infinite Divisions: An Anthology of Chicana Literature*, ed. Tey Diana Rebolledo and Eliana S. Rivero (Tucson: The University of Arizona Press, 1993), 93–94, esp. 93.

48. Ekuo Omosupe, "In Magazines (I Found Specimens of the Beautiful)," in *Making Face, Making Soul/Haciendo Caras: Creative and Critical Perspectives by Feminists of Color*, ed. Gloria Anzaldúa (San Francisco: Aunt Lute Books, 1990).

49. For a discussion of skin color, see the classic essay by Cherríe Moraga, "La Guera," in *This Bridge Called My Back: Radical Writings by Women of Color*, ed. Cherrie Moraga and Gloria Anzaldúa (New York: Kitchen Table Press, 1983), 27–34.

50. Ponce, *Hoyt Street*, 143.

Chapter 4

1. Cisneros, *House*, 7–50.

2. Cisneros, *House*, 100.

3. Ruiz, "'Star Struck,'" 127–28.

4. Simone de Beauvoir, *Memoirs of a Dutiful Daughter*, trans. James Kirkup (Cleveland: World Publishing Co., 1959).

5. Alma M. García, "The Development of Chicana Feminist Discourse, 1979–1980," *Gender & Society* 1 (1989): 217–38. For an anthology of primary documents written by Chicana feminists during this historical period, see Alma M. García, *Chicana Feminist Thought: The Basic Historical Writings* (New York: Routledge, 1997). For similar developments among Asian American women, see Esther Ngan-Ling Chow, "The Development of Feminist Consciousness Among Asian American Women," *Gender & Society* 1 (1987): 248–99; see also Collins, *Black Feminist Thought*, 19–40.

6. The following list is by no means a comprehensive one. Authors are listed alphabetically. Alarcón, "Chicana Feminist Literature"; Norma Alarcón, Ana Castillo, and Cherríe Moraga, eds., "The Sexuality of Latinas," *Third Woman* (Special Issue) 4 (1989): 169–78; Anzaldúa, *Borderlands*; Cordelia Candelaria, "La Malinche, Feminist Prototype," *Frontiers* 5 (1980): 1–16; Antonia Castañeda, "Sexual Violence in the Politics and Policies of Conquest," in *Building With Our Hands: New Directions in Chicana Studies*, ed. Adela de la Torre and Beatriz Pesquera (Berkeley: University of California Press, 1993), 15–33; Ana Castillo, "La Macha: Toward a Beautiful Whole Self," in *Chicana Lesbians: The Girls Our Mothers Warned Us About*," ed. Carla Trujillo (Berkeley: Third Woman

Press, 1991), 24–49; Deena J. González, "Masquerades: Viewing the New Chicana Lesbian Anthologies," *Outlook* (Winter 1992): 80–83; Cynthia Orozco, "Sexism in Chicano Studies and the Community," in *Chicana Voices: Intersections of Class, Race, and Gender*, ed. Teresa Córdova et al. (Austin: University of Texas Center for Mexican American Studies, 1986), 11–18; Emma Pérez, "Sexuality and Discourse: Notes from a Chicana Survivor," in *Chicana Critical Issues*, ed. Norma Alarcón et al. (Berkeley: Third Woman Press, 1993), 45–69; Saldívar-Hull, *Feminism on the Border*; and Chela Sandoval, "U.S. Third World Feminism: The Theory and Method of Oppositional Consciousness in the Postmodern World," *Gender* 10 (Spring 1991): 1–24.

7. Saldívar-Hull, *Feminism on the Border*, 33.

8. Robert Anthony Orsi, *The Madonna of 115th Street: Faith and Community in Italian Harlem, 1880–1950* (New Haven, Conn.: Yale University Press, 1985).

9. Janet Mancini Billson, *Keepers of the Culture: The Power of Tradition in Women's Lives* (New York: Lexington, 1995).

10. Yen Le Espiritu, "'We Don't Sleep Around Like White Girls Do': Family, Culture, and Gender in Filipina American Lives," *Signs* 26 (Winter 2001): 415–40, esp. 428.

11. Yvonne Y. Haddad and Jane I. Smith, "Islamic Values among American Muslims," in *Family and Gender among American Muslims: Issues Facing Middle Eastern Immigrants and Their Descendents*, ed. Barbara C. Aswad and Barbara Bilge (Philadelphia: Temple University Press, 1996), 19–40; Donna Gabacia, *From the Other Side: Women, Gender, and Immigrant Life in the U.S., 1820–1990* (Bloomington: Indiana University Press, 1994); and Judy Young, *Unbound Feet: A Social History of Chinese Women in San Francisco* (Berkeley: University of California Press, 1995).

12. Betty Friedan, *The Feminine Mystique* (New York: Norton, 1963).

13. Cisneros, *House*, 83–84.

14. Cisneros, *House*, 82.

15. Zavella, *Women's Work*; Hochschild, *The Second*; Maxine Baca Zinn, "Chicanas: Power and Control in the Domestic Sphere," *De Colores* 2 (1975): 19–31; Maxine Baca Zinn, "Political Familism: Toward Sex Role Equality in Chicano Families," *Aztlan* 6 (Spring 1975): 13–26.

16. Maxine Molyneux, "Mobilization Without Emancipation? Women's Interests, the State, and Revolution," *Feminist Studies* 11 (1985): 227–54.

17. Lynn Stephen, *Women and Social Movements in Latin America* (Austin: University of Texas Press, 1997), 6.

18. For an early study of Mexican women and the effect of their participation in the paid labor force on family dynamics, see Lourdes Beneria and Martha Rol-

dan, *The Crossroads of Class and Gender: Industrial Homework, Subcontracting, and Household Dynamics in Mexico City* (Chicago: University of Chicago Press, 1987); Sylvia Chant, *Women and Survival in Mexican Cities: Perspectives on Gender, Labour Markets, and Low-Income Households* (Manchester: Manchester University Press, 1991); Ina R. Dinnerman, "Patterns of Adaptation among Households of U.S. Bound Migrants from Michoacán, Mexico," *International Migration Review* 12 (1978): 485–501; Hondagneu-Sotelo, "Overcoming"; and Hondagneu-Sotelo, *Gendered*.

19. Rafael Alarcón, "El Proceso de 'Nortenizacion': Impacto de la Migracion International en Chavida, Michoacán," in *Movimientos de Poblacion en el Occidente de Mexico*, ed. Thomas Calvo and Gustavo Lópes (Mexico: El Colegio de Michoacán, 1988), 337–53.

20. For a general review of relevant works, see Silvia Pedraza, "Women and Migration: The Social Consequences of Gender," *Annual Review of Sociololgy* 17 (1991): 303–25.

21. Kibria, "Power, Patriarchy"; Nazli Kibria, *Family Tightrope: The Changing Lives of Vietnamese Americans* (Princeton: Princeton University Press, 1993).

22. For a series of essays on the changing gender roles of immigrant women, see Rita James Simon and Caroline B. Brettel, eds., *International Migration: The Female Experience* (Totowa, N.J.: Rowman and Allenheld, 1986).

23. Hondagneu-Sotelo, *Gendered*, 15.

24. Zavella, *Women's Work*, 142–48.

25. Adler, *Mothering*, 38–39.

26. Frances Esquibel Tywoniak with Mario T. García, *Migrant Daughter: Coming of Age as a Mexican American Woman* (Berkeley: University of California Press, 2000), 113–14.

27. Barth, "Introduction"; and Nagel, "Constructing Ethnicity," 156–60.

28. Tuan, *Forever Foreigners*, 119–20.

29. Tuan, *Forever Foreigner*, 120; see also Dana Y. Takagi, *The Retreat from Race: Asian-American Admissions and Racial Prejudice* (New Brunswick, N.J.: Rutgers University Press, 1992).

30. Kibria, "College," 205.

31. García, "The Development"; and Chow, "The Development," 285–93.

32. Tuan, *Forever Foreigners*, 34–36, 49.

33. Nathan Glazer and Daniel Moynihan, *Beyond the Melting Pot: The Negroes, Puerto Ricans, Jews, Italians, and Irish of New York City* (Cambridge, Mass.: MIT Press, 1970).

34. Gloria Steinem, *Outrageous Acts and Everyday Rebellions* (New York: East Toledo Productions, 1983).

35. Judith Teresa González, *Dilemmas of the High Achieving Chicana: The Double Blind Factor in Male/Female Relationships* (Tucson: Mexican American Studies & Research Center, University of Arizona, 1987).

36. G. Napper, *Blacker Than Thou: The Struggle for Campus Unity* (Grand Rapids, Mich.: William B. Erdmann, 1973), 65.

37. Gordon La Vern Berry and Joy Keiko Asamen, *Black Students: Psychosocial Issues and Academic Achievement* (Newbury Park, Calif.: Sage Publications, 1989).

38. Jiménez, "Negotiating," 5–8, 36–42.

39. Espiritu, *Asian-American*; and L. H. Shinagawa and G. Y. Pang, "Asian-American Panethnicity and Intermarriage," *Amerasia Journal* 22 (1996): 127–32.

40. Pérez, "Sexuality," 62–63.

41. García, *Chicana Feminist*, 1–13.

42. García, "The Development," 230–38.

43. García, "The Development"; and Bonnie Thornton Dill, "Race, Class, and Gender."

Chapter 5

1. Chacón, "Chicanas"; and Gándara, "Passing Through," 167–70.

2. López and Stanton-Salazar, "Mexican," 78–79.

3. Pat Mora, *Chants* (Houston, Tex.: Arte Publico Press, 1984).

4. Lucy Guerrero, "The Educated One," in *Palabras Chicanas*, ed. Lisa Hernández and Tina Benitéz (Berkeley, Calif.: Mujeres en Marcha Press, 1988), 7–10.

5. Guerrero, "The Educated," 7 and 10.

6. Chacón, "Chicanas," 91–99. See also Teresa McKenna and Flora Ida Ortíz, eds., *The Broken Web: The Educational Experience of Hispanic American Women* (Claremont, Calif.: Tomás Rivera Center, 1988).

7. Gándara, "Passing Through"; and Gándara, *Over the Ivy*, 36–39.

8. Gándara, *Over the Ivy*, 37.

9. Ruth E. Zambrana, Claudia Dorrington, and Sally Alonzo Bell, "Mexican American Women in Higher Education: A Comparative Study," *Race, Gender, & Class* 4.2 (1997): 127–49. For more findings regarding the role of Mexican American parental support for higher education, see Segura, "Slipping"; S. Anchor and A. Morales, "Chicanas Holding Doctoral Degrees: Social Reproduction and Cultural Ecological Approaches," *Anthropology and Education Quarterly* 21 (1990): 269–87; Michael Olivas, ed., *Latino College Students* (New York: Teachers College Press, Columbia University, 1986); and Solórzano, "A Study."

10. Bettinger-López, *Cuban-Jewish*.

11. Lorene Cary, *Black Ice* (New York: Knopf, 1991).

12. Cary, *Black Ice*, 16.

13. López and Stanton-Salazar, "Mexican," 80.

14. Gándara, *Over the Ivy*, 112.

15. Higginbotham, *Too Much*, 12–13.

16. Ruth Sidel, *Battling Bias: The Struggle for Identity and Community on College Campuses* (New York: Viking, 1994); and Wendy Glasgow Winters, *African American Mothers and Urban Schools* (New York: Lexington Books, 1993).

17. Shaw, *What a Woman*, 14.

18. Winters, *African*; and Collins, *Black Feminist*, 123–37.

19. Higginbotham, *Too Much*, xi–xii.

20. Alder, *Mothering*, 108–9.

21. Cisneros, *House*, 56.

22. Nagel, "Constructing Ethnicity," 152.

23. Barth, "Introduction," 25.

24. Gans, "Symbolic Ethnicity"; and Waters, *Black Identities*, 44–49.

25. Alba, *Italian Americans*; Alba, *Ethnic Identity*; and Lieberson and Waters, *From Many Strands*.

26. Hung Cam Thai, "Formation of Ethnic Identity Among Second-Generation Vietnamese Americans," in *The Second Generation: Ethnic Identity Among Asian Americans*, ed. Pyong Gap Min (Walnut Creek, Calif.: Altamira Press, 2002), 53–83.

27. Anzaldúa, *Borderlands*, 78.

28. Anzaldúa, *Borderlands*, 79.

29. Pat Mora, *Nepantla* (Albuquerque: University of New Mexico Press, 1993), 5–6.

30. Michael T. Nettles, A. Robert Thoeny, and Erica J. Gosman, "Comparative and Predictive Analyses of Black and White Students' College Achievement and Experiences," *Journal of Higher Education* 57 (May/June 1986): 289–317; Chalsa M. Loo and Garry Rolison, "Alienation of Ethnic Minority Students at a Predominantly White University," *Journal of Higher Education* 57 (January/February 1986): 58–77.

31. Higginbotham, *Too Much*; and Joe R. Feagin, Hernan Vera, and Nikitah Imani, *The Agony of Education: Black Students at White Colleges and Universities* (New York: Routledge, 1996).

32. For one of the earliest studies, see Melba Vásquez, "Confronting Barriers to the Participation of Mexican American Women in Higher Education," *Hispanic Journal of Behavioral Sciences* 4.2 (1982): 167–79. See also V. Washington and J. Newman, "Setting our Own Agenda: Exploring the Meaning of Gender

Disparities among Blacks in Higher Education," *Journal of Negro Education* 60.1 (1992): 19–35; Lynne Brodie Welch, ed., *Perspectives on Minority Women in Higher Education* (New York: Praeger, 1992); and S. Nieves-Squires, "Hispanic Women Making Their Own Presence on Campus Less Tenuous" (Washington, D.C.: Project on the Status and Education of Women, Association of American Colleges, 1991).

33. Lisa E. Wolf-Wendel, "Models of Excellence: The Baccalaureate Origins of Successful European American Women, African American Women, and Latinas," *The Journal of Higher Education* 69 (March/April 1998): 141–86.

34. Daniel Gilbert Solórzano, "The Baccalaureate Origins of Chicana and Chicano Doctorates in the Social Sciences," *Hispanic Journal of Behavioral Sciences* 17 (1995): 3–32.

35. Felix M. Padilla, *The Struggle of Latino/a University Students* (New York: Routledge, 1997), 12.

36. David López and Yen Espiritu, "Panethnicity in the United States: A Theoretical Framework," *Ethnic and Racial Studies* 13 (1990): 198–222.

37. Anderson, *Imagined Communities*, 6–7.

38. Eric Hobsbawm, "Introduction: Inventing Traditions," in *The Invention of Tradition*, ed. Eric Hobsbawm and Terence Ranger (Cambridge, U.K.: Cambridge University Press, 1983), 1–14; and Hugh Trevor-Roper, "The Invention of Tradition: The Highland Tradition of Scotland," in *The Invention of Tradition*, ed. Eric Hobsbawm and Terence Ranger (Cambridge: Cambridge University Press, 1983), 15–41.

39. Henry A. Giroux, *Teachers as Intellectuals: Toward a Critical Pedagogy of Learning* (New York: Bergin & Garvey, 1988), 162.

40. Heidi Lasley Barajas and Jennifer L. Pierce, "The Significance of Race and Gender in School Success among Latinas and Latinos in College," *Gender & Society* 15 (December 2001): 859–878, esp. 864.

41. Pepi Leistyna, "Racenicity: The Relationship between Racism and Ethnicity," in *Critical Ethncity: Countering the Waves of Identity Politics*, ed. Robert H. Thai and Mary L. Kenyatta (Lanham, Md.: Rowman & Littlefield Publishers, 1999): 133–71. Leistyna'a article on "racenicity" provided me with the references to these concepts. For a discussion of "fictive kinship," see Signithia Fordham, "Racelessness as a Factor in Black Students' School Success: Pragmatic Strategy or Pyrrhic Victory?" *The Harvard Educational Review* 58 (1988): 54–84. For a discussion of "survival strategies," see John Ogbu, "Variability in Minority Responses to Schooling: Nonimmigrant vs. Immigrant," in *Interpretive Ethnography of Education*, ed. George Spindler and Louise Spindler (Hillsdale, N.J.: Lawrence Erlbaum Associates, 1987), 129–39. For a discussion of "ethnic con-

solidation," see George DeVos, *Japan's Invisible Race: Caste in Culture and Personality* (Berkeley: University of California Press, 1967). For a discussion of "politicized roots culture," see Paul Gilroy, *There Ain't No Black in the Union Jack: The Cultural Politics of Race and Nation* (Chicago: University of Chicago Press, 1987).

42. Leistyna, "Racenicity," 154.

43. For a comparison and contrast of oppositional identity among the second and later generatons, see Pérez, *Growing*; López and Stanton-Salazar, "Mexican Americans."

44. Lowe, *Immigrant Acts*.

45. Wolf–Wendel, "Models," 142–47.

46. Tuan, *Forever Foreigners*, 156.

47. Leif Jensen and Yoshimi Chitose, "Today's Second Generation: Evidence from the 1990 U.S. Census." *International Migration Review* 38.4 (1997): 714–35; Gil and Vega, "The Different"; Alba and Nee, "Rethinking"; Rumbaut, "The Crucible"; and Zhou, "Growing Up."

48. Alejandro Portes and Robert L. Bach, *Latin Journey: Cuban and Mexican Immigrants in the United States* (Berkeley: University of California Press, 1985).

49. Jensen, "The Demographic," 35.

50. C. Wright Mills, *The Sociological Imagination* (New York: Oxford University Press, 1959).

51. Espiritu, "The Intersection," 36–37.

52. Tuan, *Forever Foreigners*, 148.

53. Barth, "Introduction," 18.

54. Nagel, "Constructing Ethnicity," 163.

55. Laura Nichols, *Entering the Ivory Tower: The Life Histories and Experiences of First Generation College Students at Santa Clara University* (Santa Clara, Calif.: Center for Multicultural Learning, 2002). Nichols's research led me to the following source: Patrick T. Terenzini, Leonard Springer, Patricia McYear, Ernest T. Pascarella, and Amaury Nora, eds., "First Generation College Students: Characteristics, Experiences, and Cognitive Developments," *Research in Higher Education* 37 (1996): 1–22.

56. Nagel, "Constructing Ethnicity," 169.

57. Michael Hechter, *Principles of Group Solidarity* (Berkeley: University of California Press, 1987).

58. Charles H. Cooley, *On Self and Social Organization*, ed. Hans-Joachim Schubert (Chicago: University of Chicago Press, 1998).

59. Georg Simmel, *The Sociology of Georg Simmel* (Glencoe, Ill.: The Free Press, 1950).

60. Waters, *Black Identities*, 46.

61. Alejandro Portes and Dag MacLeod, "What Shall I Call Myself? Hispanic Identity Formation in the Second Generation," *Ethnic and Racial Studies* 19 (1996): 527, quoted here from Waters, *Black Identities*, 47.

62. Min and Kim, "Formation," 177.

63. Yancey, Ericksen, and Juliani, "Emergent Ethncity," 399.

64. Nagel, "Constructing Ethnicity," 154.

Chapter 6

1. Oscar Handlin, *The Uprooted: The Epic Story of the Great Migrations that Made the American People* (Boston: Little Brown, 1951), 1.

2. Nagel, "Constructing Ethnicity," 154.

3. Espiritu, "The Intersection," 25.

4. Portes and Rumbaut, *Legacies*, 17–44.

5. Gándara, *Over the Ivy*, 111–25; Vasquez, "Confronting Barriers," 167–70; Michael Olivas, *Latino College Students*, chapters 1–5; Padilla, *The Struggle*, 217–36. For an excellent anthology, see Antonia Darder, Rodolfo D. Torres, and Henry Gutiérrez, eds., *Latinos and Education: A Critical Reader* (New York: Routledge, 1997), 331–486.

REFERENCES

Adler, Susan Matoba. *Mothering, Education, and Ethnicity: The Transformation of Japanese American Culture.* New York: Garland Publishing, 1998.

Alarcón, Norma. "Chicana Feminist Literature: A Re-Vision Through Malintzin: Putting the Flesh Back on the Object." Pp. 182–190 in *This Bridge Called My Back: Radical Writings by Women of Color*, ed. Cherríe Moraga and Gloria Anzaldúa. New York: Kitchen Table-Women of Color Press, 1983.

Alarcón, Norma, Ana Castillo, and Cherrie Moraga, eds. "The Sexuality of Latinas." *Third Woman* (Special Issue) 4 (1989): 169–78.

Alarcón, Rafael. "El Proceso de 'Nortenizacion': Impacto de la Migracion International en Chavida, Michoacán." Pp. 337–53 in *Movimientos de Poblacion en el Occidente de Mexico*, ed. Thomas Calvo and Gustavo Lópes. Mexico: El Colegio de Michoacán, 1988.

Alba, Richard. "The Twilight of Ethnicity among Americans of European Ancestry: The Case of Italians." Pp. 134–58 in *Ethnicity and Race in the USA: Toward the Twenty-first Century*, ed. Richard Alba. London: Routledge and Kegan Paul, 1985.

———. *Italian Americans: Into the Twilight of Ethnicity.* Englewood Cliffs, N.J.: Prentice-Hall, 1985.

———. "Cohorts and the Dynamics of Ethnic Change." Pp. 211–28 in *Social Structure and Human Lives*, ed. Matilda White Riley, Bettina J. Huber, and Beth B. Hess. Beverly Hills, Calif.: Sage Publications, 1988.

———. *Ethnic Identity. The Transformation of White America.* New Haven: Yale University Press, 1990.

Alba, Richard, and M. B. Chamblin. "A Preliminary Examination of Ethnic Identification among Whites." *American Sociological Review* 48 (1983): 240–47.

Alba, Richard, and Victor Nee. "Rethinking Assimilation: Theory for a New Era of Immigration," *International Migration Review* 31.4 (1997): 826–74.

Anchor, S., and A. Morales. "Chicanas Holding Doctoral Degrees: Social Reproduction and Cultural Ecological Approaches." *Anthropology and Education Quarterly* 21 (1990): 269–87.

Anderson, Benedict. *Imagined Communities: Reflection on the Origin and Spread of Nationalism.* New York: Verso, 1983.

REFERENCES

Anzaldúa, Gloria E. *Borderlands/La Frontera: The New Mestiza.* San Francisco: Spinsters/Aunt Lute, 1987.

———. "Writing A Way of Life." Pp. 235–49 in *Interviews Entrevistas,* ed. Ana Louise Keating. New York: Routledge, 2000.

Baca Zinn, Maxine. "Chicanas: Power and Control in the Domestic Sphere." *De Colores* 2 (1975): 19–31.

———. "Political Familism: Toward Sex Role Equality in Chicano Families." *Aztlan* 6 (Spring 1975): 13–26.

———. "Field Research in Minority Communities: Ethical, Methodological, and Political Observations by an Insider." *Social Problems* 27.2 (1997): 209–19.

Baca Zinn, Maxine, and Bonnie Thornton Dill. "Difference and Domination." Pp. 3–12 in *Women of Color In U.S. Society,* ed. Maxine Baca Zinn and Bonnie Thornton Dill. Philadelphia: Temple University Press, 1997.

Baca Zinn, Maxine, Pierrette Hodagneu-Sotelo, and Michael A. Messner, eds. *Through the Prism of Difference: Readings on Sex and Gender.* Trenton, N.J.: Prentice Hall, 1997.

Bacon, Jean. *Life Lines: Community, Family, and Assimilation among Asian Indian Immigrants.* New York: Oxford University Press, 1996.

———. "Constructing Collective Ethnic Identities: The Case of Second-Generation Asian Indians." *Qualitative Sociology* 22.2 (1999): 141–60.

Barajas, Heidi Lasley, and Jennifer L. Pierce. "The Significance of Race and Gender in School Success among Latinas and Latinos in College." *Gender & Society* 15 (December 2001): 859–78.

Barth, Fredrik. "Introduction." Pp. 9–38 in *Ethnic Groups and Boundaries: The Social Organization of Culture Difference,* ed. Fredrik Barth. Boston: Little, Brown and Company, 1969.

Benería, Lourdes, and Martha Roldán. *The Crossroads of Class and Gender: Industrial Homework, Subcontracting, and Household Dynamics in Mexico City.* Chicago: University of Chicago Press, 1987.

Benmayor, Rima. "Testimony, Action Research, and Empowerment: Puerto Rican Women and Popular Education." Pp. 159–74 in *Women's Words: The Feminist Practice of Oral History,* ed. Sherna Berger Gluck and Daphne Patai. New York: Routledge, 1991.

Berry, Gordon La Vern, and Joy Keiko Asamen. *Black Students: Psychosocial Issues and Academic Achievement.* Newbury Park, Calif.: Sage Publications, 1989.

Bettinger-López, Caroline. *Cuban-Jewish Journey: Searchings for Identity, Home, and History in Miami.* Knoxville: University of Tennessee Press, 2000.

Billson, Janet Mancini. *Keepers of the Culture: The Power of Tradition in Women's Lives.* New York: Lexington, 1995.

Blauner, Robert. *Racial Oppression in America*. New York: Harper and Row, 1972.

Borland, Katherine. "'That's Not What I Said': Interpretive Conflict in Oral Narrative Research." Pp. 63–75 in *Women's Words: The Feminist Practice of Oral History*, ed. Sherna Berger Gluck and Daphne Patai. New York: Routledge, 1991.

Bowles, Samuel, and Herbert Gintes. *Schooling in Capitalist America*. New York: Basic Books, 1976.

Butler, Judith. *Gender Trouble: Feminism and the Subversion of Identity*. New York: Routledge, 1990.

Candelaria, Cordelia. "La Malinche, Feminist Prototype." *Frontiers* 5 (1980): 1–16.

Cary, Lorene. *Black Ice*. New York: Knopf, 1991.

Castañeda, Antonia. "Sexual Violence in the Politics and Policies of Conquest." Pp. 15–33 in *Building with Our Hands: New Directions in Chicana Studies*. ed. Adela de la Torre and Beatriz Pesquera. Berkeley: University of California Press, 1993.

Castañeda, María. "Mexican Immigrant Cannery Women Workers: Work, Family, and Culture." Unpublished Senior Sociology Thesis, Santa Clara University, 1998.

Castillo, Ana. "La Macha: Toward a Beautiful Whole Self." Pp. 24–49 in *Chicana Lesbians: The Girls Our Mothers Warned Us About*, ed. Carla Trujillo. Berkeley: Third Woman Press; 1991.

Cerulo, Karen A. "Identity Construction: New Issues, New Directions." *Annual Review of Sociology* 23 (1997): 385–409.

Chacón, María, Elizabeth G. Cohen, Margaret Camarena, Judith González, and Sharon Strover. *Chicanas in Postsecondary Education*. Stanford, Calif.: Center for Research on Women, Stanford University, 1982.

Chant, Sylvia. *Women and Survival in Mexican Cities: Perspectives on Gender, Labour Markets, and Low-Income Households*. Manchester: Manchester University Press, 1991.

Chow, Esther Ngan-Ling. "The Development of Feminist Consciousness Among Asian American Women." *Gender & Society*, 1 (1987): 248–99.

Cisneros, Sandra. *The House on Mango Street*. New York: Vintage, 1989.

———. *Caramelo*. New York: Alfred A. Knopf, 2002.

Collins, Patricia Hill. *Black Feminist Thought: Knowledge, Consciousness, and the Politics of Empowerment*. Boston: Unwin Hyman Press, 1990.

Cook, J. A., and M. M. Fonow. "Knowledge and Women's Interests: Issues of Epistemology and Methodology in Feminist Sociological Research." *Sociological Inquiry* 56 (1986): 2–29.

Cooley, Charles H. *On Self and Social Organization*, ed. and intro. by Hans-Joachim Schubert. Chicago: University of Chicago Press, 1998.

Cornell, Stephen. "That's the Story of Our Life." Pp. 41–53 in *Narrative and Multiplicity in Constructing Ethnic Identity*, ed. Paul Spickard and W. Jeffrey Burroghs. Philadelphia: Temple University Press, 2000.

Cornell, Stephen, and Douglas Hartmann. *Ethnicity and Race: Making Identities in a Changing World*. Thousand Oaks, Calif.: Pine Forge Press, 1998.

Coser, Lewis. *The Functions of Social Conflict*. New York: The Free Press of Glencoe, 1956.

Curry-Rodriguez, Julia. "Reconceptualizing Undocumented Labor Immigration: The Causes, Impact, and Consequences in Mexican Women's Lives." Ph.D. Diss., University of Texas at Austin, 1988.

de Beauvoir, Simone. *The Second Sex*, trans. and ed. by H. M. Parshley. New York: Modern Library, 1952.

———. *Memoirs of a Dutiful Daughter*, trans. James Kirkup. Cleveland: World Publishing Co., 1959.

Darder, Antonia, Rodolfo D. Torres, and Henry Gutiérrez, eds. *Latinos and Education: A Critical Reader*. New York: Routledge, 1997.

Day Hulbert, Kathleen, and Dianne Tickton Schuster, eds. *Women's Lives Through Time: Educated American Women of the Twentieth Century*. San Francisco: Jossey-Bass Publishers, 1993.

de la Garza, Rodolfo O., et al. *Latino Voices: Mexican, Puerto Rican, and Cuban Perspectives on American Politics*. Boulder: Westview Press, 1992.

DeVos, George. *Japan's Invisible Race: Caste in Culture and Personality*. Berkeley: University of California Press, 1967.

Delucia, R. C., and J. Balkin. "Ethnic Identification among Second- and Third-Generation Italian-American Police Officers: Its Presences and Significance." *Ethnic Groups* 7 (1989): 283–96.

Dill, Bonnie Thornton. "Race, Class, and Gender: Prospects for an All-Inclusive Sisterhood." *Feminist Studies* 9 (1983): 131–50.

DiMaggio, Paul. "Culture Capital and School Success." *American Sociological Review* 47.1 (1982): 189–201.

Dinnerman, Ina R. "Patterns of Adaptation among Households of U.S. Bound Migrants from Michoacán, Mexico." *International Migration Review* 12 (1978): 485–501.

Espinosa, Paul, prod. *The Lemon Grove Incident*. Espinosa Productions, 1985. Videocassette.

Espiritu, Yen Le. *Asian American Pan-Ethnicity: Bridging Institutions and Identities*. Philadelphia: Temple University Press, 1992.

———. "'We Don't Sleep Around Like White Girls Do': Family, Culture, and Gender in Filipina American Lives." *Signs* 26 (Winter 2001): 415–40.

———. "The Intersection of Race, Ethnicity, and Class: The Multiple Identities of Second-Generation Filipinos." Pp. 19–52 in *The Second Generation: Ethnic Identity Among Asian Americans*, ed. Pyong Gap Min. Walnut Creek, Calif.: Altamira Press, 2002.

Espiritu, Yen Le, and Diane L. Wolf. "The Paradox of Assimilation: Children of Filipino Immigrants in San Diego." Pp. 157–86 in *Ethnicities of Children of Immigrants in America*, ed. Rubén G. Rumbaut and Alejandro Portes. Berkeley: University of California Press, 2001.

Etter-Lewis, Gwendolyn. "Black Women's Life Stories: Reclaiming Self in Narrative Texts." Pp. 43–58 in *Women's Words: The Feminist Practice of Oral History*, ed. Sherna Berger Gluck and Daphne Patai. New York: Routledge, 1991.

Feagin, Joe R., Hernan Vera, and Nikitah Imani. *The Agony of Education: Black Students at White Colleges and Universities.* New York: Routledge, 1996.

Fordham, Signithia. "Racelessness as a Factor in Black Students' School Success: Pragmatic Strategy or Pyrrhic Victory?" *The Harvard Educational Review* 58 (1988): 54–84.

Flax, Jane. "Postmodernism and Gender Relations in Feminist Theory." Pp. 39–62 in *Feminism and Postmodernism*, ed. Linda J. Nicholson. New York: Routledge, 1990.

Freeman, James M. *Changing Identities: Vietnamese Americans, 1975–1995.* Boston: Allyn and Bacon, 1995.

Friedan, Betty. *The Feminine Mystique.* New York: Norton, 1963.

Gabacia, Donna. *From the Other Side: Women, Gender, and Immigrant Life in the U.S., 1820–1990.* Bloomington: Indiana University Press, 1994.

Gándara, Patricia. "Passing through the Eye of the Needle: High Achieving Chicanas." *Hispanic Journal of Behavioral Sciences* 4.2 (1982): 167–79.

———. *Over the Ivy Walls: The Educational Mobility of Low-Income Chicanos.* Albany: State University of New York, 1995.

Gans, Herbert. "Symbolic Ethnicity: The Future of Ethnic Groups and Cultures in America." *Ethnic and Racial Studies* 26 (January 1979): 1–20.

Gans, Herbert J. "Second-Generation Decline: Scenarios for the Economic and Ethnic Futures of the Post-1965 American Immigrants." *Ethnic Racial Studies* 15.20 (1992): 173–92.

García, Alma M. "The Development of Chicana Feminist Discourse, 1979–1980." *Gender & Society* 1 (1989): 217–38.

———. "'I Work for My Daughter's Future': Entrepreneurship and Mexican American Women." *California History* (Fall 1995): 262–79.

REFERENCES

————. *Chicana Feminist Thought: The Basic Historical Writings*. New York: Routledge, 1997.

————. *The Mexican Americans*. Westport, Conn.: Greenwood Press, 2002.

García, Cristina. *Dreaming in Cuban*. New York: Knopf, 1992.

García, Mario T. *Desert Immigrants: The Mexicans of El Paso, 1880–1920*. New Haven, Conn.: Yale University Press, 1981.

————. "*La Frontera*: The Border as Symbol and Reality in Mexican American Thought." Pp. 89–117 in *Between Two Worlds: Mexican Immigrants in the United States*, ed. David G. Gutiérrez. Wilmington, Del.: Scholarly Resources, 1996.

————. "Introduction." Pp. xi–xxx in *Migrant Daughter: Coming of Age of a Mexican American Woman*. Berkeley: University of California Press, 2000.

García, Richard A. *The Making of the Mexican-American Mind, San Antonio, Texas, 1929–1941: A Social and Intellectual History of an Ethnic Community*. San Antonio, Tex.: Texas A&M University Press, 1991.

————. "Turning Points: Mexican Americans in California History." *California History* 14 (Fall 1995): 221–29.

————. "Towards a Theory of Latina Rebirth 'Renacimiento de la Tierra Madre': The Feminism of Gloria Anzaldúa." *Race, Gender, and Class* 6.3 (1999): 29–45.

Geertz, Clifford. *The Interpretation of Culture: Selected Essays*. New York, Basic Books, 1973.

Giddings, Paula. *In Search of Sisterhood: Delta Sigma Theta and the Challenge of the Black Sorority Movement*. New York: Quill, 1988.

Gil, Andres G., and William A Vega. "The Different Worlds: Acculturation, Stress, and Adaptation Among Cuban and Nicaraguan Families." *Journal of Social and Personal Relationships* 13 (1996): 435–56.

Gilroy, Paul. *There Ain't No Black in the Union Jack: The Cultural Politics of Race and Nation*. Chicago: University of Chicago Press, 1987.

Giroux, Henry A. *Teachers as Intellectuals: Toward a Critical Pedagogy of Learning*. New York: Bergin & Garvey, 1988.

Glazer, Nathan, and Daniel Moynihan. *Beyond the Melting Pot: The Negroes, Puerto Ricans, Jews, Italians, and Irish of New York City*. Cambridge, Mass.: MIT Press, 1970.

Gluck, Sherna Berger, and Daphne Patai, eds. *Women's Words: The Feminist Practice of Oral History*. New York: Routledge, 1991.

Gonzales, Manuel G. *Mexicanos: A History of Mexicans in the United States*. Bloomington: Indiana University Press, 1999.

González, Deena J. "Masquerades: Viewing the New Chicana Lesbian Anthologies." *Outlook* (Winter 1992): 80–83.

González, Judith Teresa. *Dilemmas of the High Achieving Chicana: The Double Blind Factor in Male/Female Relationships.* Tucson: Mexican American Studies & Research Center, University of Arizona, 1987.

Gonzalves, Theodore S. "The Day the Dancers Stayed: On Pilipino Cultural Nights." Pp. 163–82 in *Filipino Americans: Transformation and Identity,* ed. María P. P. Root. Thousand Oaks, Calif.: Sage Publications, 1997.

Gordon, Milton. *Assimilation in American Life: The Role of Race, Religion, and National Origin.* New York: Oxford University Press, 1964.

Guerrero, Lucy. "The Educated One." Pp. 7–10 in *Palabras Chicanas,* ed. Lisa Hernández and Tina Benitéz. Berkeley, Calif.: Mujeres en Marcha Press, 1988.

Haddad, Yvonne Y., and Jane I. Smith. "Islamic Values among American Muslims." Pp. 19–40 in *Family and Gender among American Muslims: Issues Facing Middle Eastern Immigrants and Their Descendents,* ed. Barbara C. Aswad and Barbara Bilge. Philadelphia: Temple University Press, 1996.

Handlin, Oscar. *The Uprooted: The Epic Story of the Great Migrations that Made the American People.* Boston: Little, Brown, 1951.

Hechter, Michael. *Principles of Group Solidarity.* Berkeley: University of California Press, 1987.

Hernández, Inés. "To Other Women Who Were Ugly Once." Pp. 93–94 in *Infinite Divisions: An Anthology of Chicana Literature,* ed. Tey Diana Rebolledo and Eliana S. Rivero. Tucson: The University of Arizona Press, 1993.

Higginbotham, Elizabeth. *Too Much to Ask: Black Women in the Era of Integration.* Chapel Hill, N.C.: The University of North Carolina Press, 2001.

Hill, K. A., and D. Moreno. "Second-Generation Cubans." *Hispanic Journal of Behavioral Sciences* 18 (1996): 175–93.

Hobsbawm, Eric. "Introduction: Inventing Traditions." Pp. 1–14 in *The Invention of Tradition,* ed. Eric Hobsbawm and Terence Ranger. Cambridge: Cambridge University Press, 1983.

Hochschild, Arlie, with Anne Machung. *The Second Shift: Working Parents and the Revolution at Home.* New York: Viking, 1989.

Hondagneu-Sotelo, Pierrette. "Overcoming Patriarchal Constraints: The Reconstruction of Gender Relations among Mexican Immigrant Women and Men." *Gender & Society* 6 (1992): 393–415.

———. *Gendered Transitions: Mexican Experiences of Immigration.* Berkeley: University of California Press, 1994.

Howe, Irving. *The World of our Fathers.* New York: Harcourt Brace Jovanovich, 1976.

Hull, Gloria, Patricia Bell Scott, and Barbara Smith, eds. *All the Women are White, All the Blacks are Men, but Some of Us Are Brave: Black Women's Studies.* Old Westbury, N.Y.: The Feminist Press, 1982.

Ikas, Karin Rosa. *Chicana Ways: Conversations with Ten Chicana Writers.* Reno: University of Nevada Press, 2002.

Jensen, Leif. "The Demographic Diversity of Immigrants and Their Children." Pp. 21–56 in *Ethnicities: The Children of Immigrants,* ed. Rubén G. Rumbaut and Alejandro Portes. Berkeley: University of California Press, 2001.

Jensen, Leif, and Yoshimi Chitose. "Today's Second Generation: Evidence from the 1990 U.S. Census." *International Migration Review* 38.4 (1997): 714–35.

Jiménez, Tomás. "Negotiating Ethnic Boundaries: Multiethnic Mexican Americans and Ethnic Identity in the United States." John F. Kennedy School of Government, Harvard University, Working Paper Series, January 2001.

Keefe, Susan E., and Amado M. Padilla. *Chicano Ethnicity.* Albuquerque: University of New Mexico Press, 1987.

Kibria, Nazli. "Power, Patriarchy, and Gender Conflict in the Vietnamese Immigrant Community." *Gender and Society* 4 (March 1990): 9–24.

———. *Family Tightrope: The Changing Lives of Vietnamese Americans.* Princeton: Princeton University Press, 1993.

———. "Migration and Vietnamese American Women: Remaking Ethnicity." Pp. 247–61 in *Women of Color In U.S. Society,* ed. Maxine Baca Zinn and Bonnie Thornton Dill. Philadelphia: Temple University Press, 1994.

———. "College and Notions of 'Asian Americans': Second-Generation Chinese Americans and Korean Americans." Pp. 183–207 in *The Second Generation: Ethnic Identity Among Asian Americans,* ed. Pyong Gap Min. Walnut Creek, Calif.: Altamira Press, 2002.

Kim, Elaine H. "Beyond Railroads and Internment: Comment on the Past and Future of Asian American Studies." *Association for Asian American Studies Newsletter* 10.4 (1993): 3–7.

Leistyna, Pepi. "Racenicity: The Relationship between Racism and Ethnicity." Pp. 133–71 in *Critical Ethnicity: Countering the Waves of Identity Politics,* ed. Robert H. Thai and Mary L. Kenyatta. Lanham, Md.: Rowman & Littlefield Publishers, 1999.

Lieberson, Stanley, and Mary Waters. *From Many Strands: Ethnic and Racial Groups in Contemporary America.* New York: Russell Sage Foundation, 1988.

Light, Ivan. *Ethnic Enterprise in America: Business and Welfare among Chinese, Japanese, and Blacks.* Berkeley: University of California Press, 1972.

Lipset, Seymour Martin. *The First New Nation: The United States in Historical and Comparative Perspective.* Garden City, N.Y.: Doubleday, 1963.

Loo, Chalsa M., and Garry Rolison. "Alienation of Ethnic Minority Students at a Predominantly White University." *Journal of Higher Education* 57 (January/February 1986): 58–77.

López, David, and Yen Espiritu. "Panethnicity in the United States: A Theoretical Framework." *Ethnic and Racial Studies* 13 (1990): 198–220.

López, David E., and Ricardo D. Stanton-Salazar. "Mexican Americans: A Second Generation at Risk." Pp. 57–90 in *Ethnicities: Children of Immigrants in America*, ed. Rubén G. Rumbaut and Alejandro Portes. Berkeley: University of California, 2001.

Lowe, Lisa. "Heterogeneity, Hybridity, Multiplicity: Marking Asian American Difference." *Diaspora* 1 (Spring 1991): 24–44.

———. *Immigrant Acts*. Durham, N.C.: Duke University Press, 1996.

Marín, Christine. "The Power of Language: From the Back of the Bus to the Ivory Tower." Pp. 85–89 in *Speaking Chicana: Voice, Power, and Identity*, ed. D. Letticia Galindo and María Dolores Gonzales. Tucson: The University of Arizona Press, 1999.

Martínez, Theresa A. "Storytelling as Oppositional Culture: Race, Class, and Gender in the Borderlands." *Race, Gender, and Class* 6.3 (1999): 33–51.

McKenna, Teresa, and Flora Ida Ortiz, eds. *The Broken Web: The Educational Experience of Hispanic American Women*. Claremont, Calif.: Tomás Rivera Center, 1988.

Melville, Margarita, ed. *Mexicanas at Work in the United States*. Houston: Mexican American Studies Monograph No. 5, 1988.

Mills, C. Wright. *The Sociological Imagination*. New York: Oxford University Press, 1959.

Min, Pyong Gap. *Second Generation: Ethnic Identity among Asian Americans*. Walnut Creek, Calif.: Altamira Press, 2002.

Min, Pyong Gap, and Joann Hong. "Ethnic Attachments Among Second-Generation Korean Americans." Pp. 113–27 in *The Second Generation: Ethnic Identity among Asian Americans*, ed. Pyong Gap Min. Walnut Creek, Calif.: Altamira Press, 2002.

Min, Pyong Gap, and Rose Kim. "Formation of Ethnic and Racial Identities: Narratives by Asian American Professionals." Pp. 153–81 in *The Second Generation: Ethnic Identity Among Asian Americans*, ed. Pyong Gap Min. Walnut Creek, Calif.: Altamira Press, 2002.

Molyneux, Maxine. "Mobilization Without Emancipation? Women's Interests, the State, and Revolution." *Feminist Studies* 11 (1985): 227–54.

Moore, Deborah Dash. *At Home in America: Second Generation New York Jews*. New York: Columbia University, 1981.

REFERENCES

————. *To the Golden Cities: Pursuing the American Jewish Dream in Miami and L.A.* New York: Free Press, 1999.

Mora, Pat. *Chants.* Houston, Tex.: Arte Público Press, 1984.

————. *Nepantla.* Albuquerque: University of New Mexico Press, 1993.

————. *House of Houses.* Boston: Beacon Press, 1997.

Moraga, Cherríe. "La Guera." Pp. 27–34 in *This Bridge Called My Back: Radical Writings by Women of Color,* ed. Cherrie Moraga and Gloria Anzaldúa. New York: Kitchen Table Press, 1983.

Morrison, Toni. *The Bluest Eye.* New York: Plume Books, 1993.

Moya, Paula M. L. "Introduction: Reclaiming Identity." Pp. 1–26 in *Reclaiming Identity: Realist Theory and the Predicament of Postmodernism,* ed. Paula M. L. Moya and Michael R. Hames-García. Berkeley: University of California Press, 2000.

Nagel, Joane. "Constructing Ethnicity: Creating and Recreating Ethnic Identity and Culture." *Social Problems* 41 (1994): 152–76.

Napper, G. *Blacker Than Thou: The Struggle for Campus Unity.* Grand Rapids, Mich.: William B. Erdmann, 1973.

Nettles, Michael T., A. Robert Thoeny, and Erica J. Gosman. "Comparative and Predictive Analyses of Black and White Students' College Achievement and Experiences." *The Journal of Higher Education,* 57 (May/June 1986): 289–317.

Nichols, Laura. *Entering the Ivory Tower: The Life Histories and Experiences of First Generation College Students at Santa Clara University.* Santa Clara, Calif.: Center for Multicultural Learning, 2002.

Nieves-Squires, S. "Hispanic Women Making Their Own Presence on Campus Less Tenuous." Washington, D.C.: Project on the Status and Education of Women, Association of American Colleges, 1991.

Nishi, S. M. "Perceptions and Deceptions: Contemporary Views of Asian-Americans." Pp. 3–10 in *A Look Beyond the Model Minority Image: Critical Issues in Asian America,* ed. Grace Yun. New York: Minority Rights Group, 1989.

O'Brien, David J., and Stephen Fugita. *The Japanese American Experience.* Bloomington: University of Indiana Press, 1991.

Ogbu, John. "Variability in Minority Responses to Schooling: Nonimmigrant vs. Immigrant." Pp. 129–39 in *Interpretive Ethnography of Education,* ed. George Spindler and Louise Spindler. Hillsdale, N.J.: Lawrence Erlbaum Associates, 1987.

Olivas, Michael, ed. *Latino College Students.* New York: Teachers College Press, Columbia University, 1986.

REFERENCES

Omosupe, Ekuo. "In Magazines (I Found Specimens of the Beautiful)." Pp. 169–70 in *Making Face, Making Soul/Haciendo Caras: Creative and Critical Perspectives by Feminists of Color*, ed. Gloria Anzaldúa. San Francisco: Aunt Lute Books, 1990.

Orozco, Cynthia. "Sexism in Chicano Studies and the Community." Pp. 11–18 in *Chicana Voices: Intersections of Class, Race, and Gender*, ed. Teresa Córdova et al. Austin: University of Texas Center for Mexican American Studies, 1986.

Orsi, Robert Anthony. *The Madonna of 115th Street: Faith and Community in Italian Harlem, 1880–1950*. New Haven, Conn.: Yale University Press, 1985.

Padilla, Felix. *Latino Ethnic Consciousness: The Case of Mexican Americans and Puerto Ricans in Chicago*. Notre Dame: University of Notre Dame Press, 1985.

Padilla, Felix M. *The Struggle of Latino/a University Students*. New York: Routledge, 1997.

Park, Robert E., and Ernest W. Burgess. *Introduction to the Science of Sociology*. Chicago: University of Chicago Press, 1924.

Pardo, Mary S. *Mexican American Women Activists: Identity and Resistance in Two Los Angeles Communities*. Philadelphia: Temple University Press, 1998.

Pedraza, Sylvia. "Women and Migration: The Social Consequences of Gender." *Annual Review of Sociololgy* 17 (1991): 303–25.

Pérez, Emma. "Sexuality and Discourse: Notes from a Chicana Survivor." Pp. 45–69 in *Chicana Critical Issues*, ed. Norma Alarcón et al. Berkeley: Third Woman Press, 1993.

———. *The Decolonial Imaginary: Writing Chicanas into History*. Bloomington: Indiana University Press, 1999.

Pérez, Lisandro. "The Household Structure of Second-Generation Children: An Exploratory Study of Extended Family Arrangements." *International Migration Review* 38.4 (1997): 736–47.

———. "Growing up in Cuban Miami: Immigration, the Enclave, and New Generations." Pp. 91–125 in *Ethnicities: Children of Immigrants in America*, ed. Rubén G. Rumbaut and Alejandro Portes. Berkeley: University of California, 2001.

Perlmann, Joel, and Roger Waldinger. "Second Generational Decline? Children of Immigrants, Past and Present—A Reconsideration." *International Migration Review* 31.4 (1997): 893–922.

Pesquera, Beatriz M. 1993. "'In the Beginning He Wouldn't Even Lift a Spoon'": The Division of Household Labor." Pp. 181–195 in *Building with*

Our Hands: New Directions in Chicana Studies, ed. Adela de la Torre and Beatriz Pesquera. Berkeley: University of California Press, 1993.

Pido, Antonio J. A. "Macro/Micro Dimensions of Pilipino Immigration to the United States." Pp. 21–38 in *Filipino Americans: Transformation and Identity*, ed. María P. P. Root. Thousands Oaks, Calif.: Sage Publications, 1997.

Ponce, Mary Helen. *Hoyt Street: An Autobiography*. Albuquerque: University of New Mexico Press, 1993.

Portes, Alejandro, and Robert L. Bach. *Latin Journey: Cuban and Mexican Immigrants in the United States*. Berkeley: University of California Press, 1985.

Portes, Alejandro, and Dag MacLeod. "What Shall I call Myself? Hispanic Identity Formation in the Second Generation." *Ethnic and Racial Studies* 19 (1996): 527.

Portes, Alejandro, and Rubén G. Rumbaut. *Legacies: The Story of the Immigrant Second Generation*. Berkeley: University of California, 2001.

Portes, Alejandro, and Alex Stepick. *City on the Edge: The Transformation of Miami*. Berkeley: University of California Press, 1993.

Portes, Alejandro, and Min Zhou. "The New Second Generation: Segmented Assimilation and Its Variants among Post-1965 Immigrant Youth." *Annals of the American Academy of Political and Social Science* 530 (November 1993): 74–96.

Radhakrishnan, R. "Ethnic Identity and Post-Structuralist Difference." *Cultural Critique* 6 (1987): 199–220.

Rebolledo, Tey Diana, and Eliana S. Rivero. *Infinite Divisions: Anthology of Chicana Literature*. Tucson: University of Arizona Press, 1993.

Revilla, Linda A. "Filipino American Identity: Transcending the Crisis." Pp. 95–111 in *Filipino Americans: Transformation and Identity*, ed. María P. P. Root. Thousand Oaks, Calif.: Sage Publications, 1997.

Richman, J. A., et al. "The Process of Acculturation: Theoretical Perspectives and an Empirical Investigation in Peru." *Social Science and Medicine* 25 (1987): 839–47.

Romero, Mary. *Maid in the USA*. New York: Routledge, 1992.

Romo, Harriet D. "The Mexican Origin Population's Differing Perceptions of their Children's Schooling." *Social Science Quarterly* 65 (1984): 635–50.

Romo, Harriet D., and Toni Falbo. *Latino High School Graduation: Defying the Odds*. Austin: University of Texas Press, 1996.

Root, María P. P., ed. *The Multiracial Experience: Racial Borders as the New Frontier*. Thousand Oaks, Calif.: Sage Publications, 1996.

Rosaldo, Renato. *Culture & Truth: The Remaking of Social Analysis*. Boston: Beacon Press, 1989.

Rouse, Roger. "Mexican Migration and the Social Space of Postmodernism." Pp. 247–63 in *Between Two Worlds: Mexican Immigrants in the United States*, ed. David G. Gutiérrez. Wilmington, Del.: Scholarly Resources, 1996.

Rumbaut, Rubén G. "The Crucible Within: Ethnic Identity, Self-Esteem, and Segmented Assimilation among Children of Immigrants." *International Migration Review* 31.4 (1997): 748–93.

Rumbaut, Rubén G., and Alejandro Portes, eds. *Ethnicities of Children of Immigrants in America*. Berkeley: University of California Press, 2001.

Ruiz, Vicki L. "'Star Struck': Acculturation, Adolescence, and the Mexican American Women, 1920–1950." Pp. 109–29 in *Building With Our Hands: New Directions in Chicana Studies*, ed. Adela de la Torre and Beatriz Pesquera. Berkeley: University of California Press, 1993.

———. *From out of the Shadows: Mexican American Women in Twentieth Century America*. New York: Oxford University Press, 1998.

Sánchez, George J. *Becoming Mexican American: Ethnicity, Culture, and Identity in Chicano Los Angeles, 1900–1945*. New York: Oxford University Press, 1993.

Saldívar, Jose David. *Border Matters: Remapping American Cultural Studies*. Berkeley: University of California Press, 1997.

Saldívar-Hull, Sonia. *Feminism on the Border: Chicana Gender Politics and Literature*. Berkeley: University of California Press, 2000.

Sandoval, Chela. "U.S. Third World Feminism: The Theory and Method of Oppositional Consciousness in the Postmodern World." *Gender* 10 (Spring 1991): 1–24.

Segura, Denise. "Chicanas and Triple Oppression." Pp. 47–65 in *Chicana Voices: Intersections of Class, Race, and Gender*, ed. Teresa Córdova et al. Austin: Center for Mexican American Studies, 1988.

———. "Slipping through the Cracks: Dilemmas in Chicana Education." Pp. 199–216 in *The Division of Household Labor, in Building with our Hands: New Directions in Chicana Studies*, ed. Adela de la Torre and Beatriz Pesquera. Berkeley: University of California Press, 1993.

Sennet, Richard, and Jonathan Cobb. *The Hidden Injuries of Class*. New York: Vintage Books, 1972.

Seton-Watson, Hugh. *Nations and States: An Enquiry into the Origins of Nations and the Politics of Nationalism*. Boulder, Colo.: Westview Press, 1977.

Shaw, Stephanie. *What a Woman Ought to Be and to Do: Black Professional Women Workers during the Jim Crow Era*. Chicago: University of Chicago Press, 1960.

Shinagawa, L. H., and G. Y. Pang. "Asian-American Panethnicity and Intermarriage." *Amerasia Journal* 22 (1996): 127–32.

Sidel, Ruth. *Battling Bias: The Struggle for Identity and Community on College Campuses.* New York: Viking Press, 1994.

Simmel, Georg. *The Sociology of Georg Simmel.* Glencoe, Ill.: The Free Press, 1950.

Simon, Rita James, and Caroline B. Brettel, eds. *International Migration: The Female Experience.* Totowa, N.J.: Rowman and Allenheld, 1986.

Steinem, Gloria. *Outrageous Acts and Everyday Rebellions.* New York: East Toledo Productions, 1983.

Stephen, Lynn. *Women and Social Movements in Latin America.* Austin: University of Texas Press, 1997.

Solórzano, Daniel Gilbert. "A Study of Social Mobility Values: The Determinants of Chicano Parents' Occupational Expectations for their Children." Ph.D. Dissertation, Claremont Graduate School, 1986.

———. "The Baccalaureate Origins of Chicana and Chicano Doctorates in the Social Sciences." *Hispanic Journal of Behavioral Sciences* 17 (1995): 3–32.

Takagi, Dana Y. *The Retreat from Race: Asian-American Admissions and Racial Prejudice.* New Brunswick, N.J.: Rutgers University Press, 1992.

Takaki, Ronald. *From Different Shores: Perspectives on Race and Ethnicity in America.* New York: Oxford University Press, 1987.

———. *A Different Mirror: A History of Multicultural America.* Boston: Little, Brown and Company, 1993.

Terenzini, Patrick T., Leonard Springer, Patricia McYear, Ernest T. Pascarella, and Amaury Nora, eds. "First Generation College Students: Characteristics, Experiences, and Cognitive Developments." *Research in Higher Education* 37 (1996): 1–22.

Thai, Hung Cam. "Formation of Ethnic Identity Among Second-Generation Vietnamese Americans." Pp. 53–83 in *The Second Generation: Ethnic Identity Among Asian Americans,* ed. Pyong Gap Min. Walnut Creek, Calif.: Altamira Press, 2002.

Thomas W. I., and Florian Znaniecki. *The Polish Peasant in Europe and America.* New York: Knopf, 1927.

Tickton Schuster, Diane. "Studying Women's Lives Through Time." Pp. 3–31 in *Women's Lives Through Time: Educated American Women of the Twentieth Century,* ed. Kathleen Day Hubert and Diane Tickton. San Francisco: Jossey-Bass Publishers, 1993.

Torres, María de los Ángeles. "Transnational Political and Cultural Identities: Crossing Theoretical Borders." Pp. 370–85 in *Latino/a Thought: Culture, Politics and Society,* ed. Francisco H. Vásquez and Rodolfo D. Torres. Lanham, Md.: Rowman & Littlefield Publishers, 2003.

Trevor-Roper, Hugh. "The Invention of Tradition: The Highland Tradition of Scotland." Pp. 15–41 in *The Invention of Tradition*, ed. Eric Hobsbawm and Terence Ranger. Cambridge, U.K.: Cambridge University Press, 1983.

Tuan, Mia. *Forever Foreigners or Honorary Whites? The Asian Ethnic Experience Today*. New Brunswick, N.J.: Rutgers University Press, 1998.

Tywoniak, Frances Esquibel, with Mario T. García. *Migrant Daughter: Coming of Age as a Mexican American Woman*. Berkeley: University of California Press, 2000.

United States Census Bureau. *Statistical Abstract of the United States*. Washington, D.C.: U.S. Government Printing Office, 1999.

———. *Statistical Abstract of the United States*. Washington, D.C.: U.S. Government Printing Office, 2000.

Vásquez, Melba. "Confronting Barriers to the Participation of Mexican American Women in Higher Education." *Hispanic Journal of Behavioral Sciences* 4.2 (1982): 167–79.

Warner, W. Lloyd, and Leo Srole. *The Social Systems of American Ethnic Groups*. New Haven, Conn.: Yale University Press, 1945.

Washington V., and J. Newman. "Setting our Own Agenda: Exploring the Meaning of Gender Disparities among Blacks in Higher Education." *Journal of Negro Education* 60.1 (1992): 19–35.

Waters, Mary C. *Ethnic Options: Choosing Identities in America*. Berkeley: University of California Press, 1990.

———. *Black Identities: West Indian Immigrant Dreams and American Realities*. New York: Russell Sage Foundation, 1999.

Wei, W. *The Asian American Movement*. Philadelphia: Temple University Press, 1993.

Welch, Lynne Brodie, ed. *Perspectives on Minority Women in Higher Education*. New York: Praeger, 1992.

Winters, Wendy Glasgow. *African American Mothers and Urban Schools*. New York: Lexington Books, 1993.

Wirth, Louis. *The Ghetto*. Chicago: University of Chicago Press, 1928.

Wolf, Naomi. *The Beauty Myth*. New York: W. Morrow, 1991.

Wolf-Wendel, Lisa E. "Models of Excellence: The Baccalaureate Origins of Successful European American Women, African American Women, and Latinas." *The Journal of Higher Education* 69.2 (1998): 141–86.

Yancey, William L., Eugene P. Ericksen, and Richard N. Juliani. "Emergent Ethnicity: A Review and Reformulation." *American Sociological Review* 41 (June 1976): 391–403.

Young, Judy. *Unbound Feet: A Social History of Chinese Women in San Francisco*. Berkeley: University of California Press, 1995.

REFERENCES

Zambrana, Ruth E., Claudia Dorrington, and Sally Alonzo Bell. "Mexican American Women in Higher Education: A Comparative Study." *Race, Gender, & Class* 4.2 (1997): 127–49.

Zavella, Patricia. *Women's Work & Chicano Families: Cannery Workers of the Santa Clara Valley*. Ithaca, N.Y.: Cornell University Press, 1987.

———. "Feminist Insider Dilemmas: Constructing Identity with 'Chicana' Informants." Pp. 138–69 in *Feminist Dilemmas in Fieldwork*, ed. Diane L. Wolf. Boulder, Colo.: Westview, 1996.

Zhou, Min. "Growing up American: The Challenge Confronting Immigrant Children and Children of Immigrants." *Annual Review of Sociology* 23 (1997): 63–75.

———. "Segmented Assimilation: Issues, Controversies, and Recent Research on the New Second Generation." *International Migration Review* 38.4 (1997): 975–1008.

Zhou, Min, and Carl L. Bankston III. "Social Capital and the Adaptation of the Second Generation: The Case of Vietnamese Youth in New Orleans." *International Migration Review* 28 (1994): 821–45.

INDEX

Numbers in italics refer to tables.

ABOUT THE AUTHOR

Alma M. García is a professor of sociology at Santa Clara University. She received her bachelor's degree in sociology from the University of Texas at El Paso and her doctorate from Harvard University. She has been a faculty member at Santa Clara University since 1982 and has served as the director of the Women's Studies Program and the Ethnic Studies Program. She has held numerous positions, including national treasurer, secretary, and chair of the National Association of Chicano/a Studies (NACS) and past president of Mujeres Activas en Letras y Camboios Sociales (MALCS). Professor García's article, "The Development of Chicana Feminist Discourse, 1960–1980," was originally published in *Gender & Society* in 1987 and has since been republished in fourteen anthologies.

Professor García specializes in race, class, and gender studies, Latin American gender relations and social change, and Mexican American studies. She has published in such journals as *Gender & Society*, *Latin American Research Review*, *Journal of American Ethnic History*, and *Journal of Latino Politics*. She is the editor of a volume of primary documents written by Chicana feminists, *Chicana Feminist Thought* (Routledge Press, 1997). She is co-editor of *Race & Ethnicity* (Greenhaven Press, 2001) and author of *The Mexican Americans* (Greenwood Press, 2002). She is co-authoring the monograph *Crusaders for Dignity*, a political and intellectual biography of Congressmen Edward Roybal (California) and Henry B. Gonzales (Texas). She is co-editing an oral history of collected interviews with Mexican American community activists who lived in San Jose, California, from the 1970s through the 1980s. She is also co-authoring a two-volume reference book, *Handbook of Hispanic Businesses* (Greenwood Press).

Professor García was born and raised in El Paso, Texas. Her maternal grandmother came to the United States during the Mexican Revolution. Her mother was born in the United States and her father was a Mexican immigrant.